Online Risk to Children

D1581822

THE NSPCC/WILEY SERIES
in
SAFEGUARDING CHILDREN
The multi-professional approach

Series Editors: Christopher Cloke,
NSPCC, 42 Curtain Road,
London EC2A 3NX

Jan Horwath,
Department of Sociological Studies,
University of Sheffield,
Sheffield S10 2TU

Peter Sidebotham,
Warwick Medical School,
University of Warwick,
Coventry CV4 7AL

This NSPCC/Wiley series explores current issues relating to the prevention of child abuse and the protection of children. The series aims to publish titles that focus on professional practice and policy, and the practical application of research. The books are leading edge and innovative and reflect a multidisciplinary and inter-agency approach to the prevention of child abuse and the protection of children.

All books have a policy or practice orientation with referenced information from theory and research. The series is essential reading for all professionals and researchers concerned with the prevention of child abuse and the protection of children.

Online Risk to Children

Impact, Protection and Prevention

FIRST EDITION

Edited by
JON BROWN

WILEY Blackwell

NSPCC

Registered Offices
John Wiley & Sons, Inc., 111 River Street, Hoboken, NJ 07030, USA
John Wiley & Sons Ltd, The Atrium, Southern Gate, Chichester, West Sussex, PO19 8SQ, UK

Editorial Office
The Atrium, Southern Gate, Chichester, West Sussex, PO19 8SQ, UK

For details of our global editorial offices, customer services, and more information about Wiley products visit us at www.wiley.com.

Wiley also publishes its books in a variety of electronic formats and by print-on-demand. Some content that appears in standard print versions of this book may not be available in other formats.

Library of Congress Cataloging-in-Publication Data is Available
9781118977583 (Hardback)
9781118977576 (Paperback)
9781118977569 (ePDF)
9781118977552 (epub)

Cover image: © Donald Iain Smith / Gettyimages
Cover design by Wiley

Set in 10/12pt Times Ten by SPi Global, Chennai, India
Printed and bound in Malaysia by Vivar Printing Sdn Bhd

10 9 8 7 6 5 4 3 2 1

To Lindy, for your love, support, insight, encouragement, wisdom and honest words

Contents

Foreword

Few of us could have predicted just how much the Internet has become an integral part of our everyday lives. As a force for good, it has changed the way we interact with the world and brings almost endless possibilities for learning and sharing information. For older generations it has been a gradual adjustment, something which has perhaps brought a certain caution along with it. For today's children though, using apps, social media and online tools comes as second nature. They are digital natives who live in a the digital world. Indeed, 12-15 year olds now spend over 20 hours a week online - over half their leisure time.

As with all of us, children's 'digital' time is only likely to increase as the lines between our online and offline lives continue to blur But it's clear from the evidence of my research, and through listening and talking to young people, that while most children have developed the skills to use modern technology from an early age, many do not possess the necessary skills they need to navigate safely through the digital world. Many are unsure about their online rights and their responsibilities, or the potential pitfalls that sit alongside the huge benefits of the internet and social media.

Our children are entitled to expect us to provide them with the skills they need. Just as it is second nature for us to teach them how to survive in the 'offline' world, we owe it to our children to help them understand and become resilient to the risks of the 'online' world.

None of us really know how our online lives will change and develop in the years to come. But we can be sure that they will be shaped in no small part by the interventions we make today. So making sure the right safeguards are in place is absolutely crucial.

The digital world opens up so many avenues for children to learn, to engage in culture, to meet new people and to live fulfilled lives. But we do need to turn the balance of power in their favour. When it was designed 25 years ago, the Internet was created with adults, not children, in mind. It is a space with limited regulation, controlled by a small number of powerful organisations. We have a duty to make sure children are protected in it by equipping them with the information, the power, and the resilience they need to make the most of the amazing opportunities the online world brings.

Anne Longfield, OBE

About the Contributors

John Carr, OBE, writes and consults about internet safety and security. He is one of the world's leading authorities on children's and young people's use of the Internet and associated new technologies. Based in London he works extensively across the UK and in many parts of the world. More recently he has also been working on issues of digital inclusion, particularly concerning older people's use of technology.

Mr Carr is or has been a Senior Expert Adviser to the United Nations (International Telecommunication Union) and an Expert Adviser to the European Union and the European Network and Information Security Agency.

Dr Catherine Hamilton-Giachritsis is a forensic and clinical psychologist with twenty years' experience in child protection and family violence. She worked as a Psychologist in Birmingham Social Services undertaking family risk assessments and later as the Assistant Director of the Centre for Forensic and Criminological Psychology at the University of Birmingham. Recently, her work has focused on victims of online sexual abuse and offenders who use technology to initiate, maintain or escalate their abuse. She is currently Reader in Clinical Psychology at the University of Bath and co-editor of the Wiley book "What Works in Child Maltreatment: An Evidence Based Approach to Assessment and Intervention in Child Protection" (2017).

Dr Elly Hanson is a clinical psychologist with experience and expertise in working with children and young people who have experienced abuse and trauma online and offline. Dr Hanson has developed interventions for children and young people with harmful sexual behaviour and currently works with the National Crime Agency CEOP Command with a particular focus on victim impact.

Dido Harding, Baroness Harding of Winscombe, joined the management consultancy McKinsey after her graduation. She left McKinsey to become marketing director at Thomas Cook Group, and was later appointed commercial director at Woolworths Group. She then joined Tesco within Sir Terry Leahy's office as international support director, before being appointed commercial director of added-value foods in 2001.

Resigning her position in October 2007, she joined the board of directors at Sainsbury's as convenience director. She was named CEO of TalkTalk in 2010, during the period when the group split its Carphone Warehouse retail operation from the group telecoms operation. She was appointed as a non-executive director on The Court of The Bank of England in July 2014. She has also served on the boards of British Land and Cheltenham Racecourse.

Dr Zoe Hilton is the Head of Safeguarding at the CEOP Command of the NCA and has worked for CEOP since 2009. She manages the specialist child protection teams within the centre and oversees the work on complex child abuse inquiries. She also leads the centre's 'Thinkuknow' Education programme, and a range of other services including the UK Missing Persons Bureau and Missing Children's Teams. Prior to this Dr Hilton worked for the NSPCC and was their lead on policy for child sexual abuse, child trafficking and online safety. She has a PhD in criminology and has published a number of articles about issues facing children and young people and practice responses.

Dr Sandy Jung joined MacEwan University in 2007 and is an Associate Professor in the Department of Psychology. She regularly teaches abnormal psychology, forensic psychology, and senior courses in clinical and forensic psychology topics. She actively provides supervision of honours and advanced research students at MacEwan.

Prior to her current academic position, Dr Jung was a forensic psychologist at Forensic Assessment and Community Services in Edmonton. At MacEwan, she maintains an active research programme and has numerous peer-reviewed publications in the field of forensic psychology. She often co-authors papers with her students and collaborators from forensic mental health, law enforcement and other academic institutions. Her research focusses on the prevention of sexual, intimate partner and general violence.

Claire Lilley is Head of Child Safety Online at the NSPCC, where she is responsible for all policy and the charity's related programme of work in relation to child safety online. This includes issues such as child abuse images, online bullying, children's access to adult content online and sexting. Claire is responsible for working with a range of stakeholders to develop innovative ideas that have the potential to make a difference to increasing child safety online. Before joining the NSPCC Claire worked at the consumer charity Which? and prior to that was a secondary school teacher in east London, teaching English and media literacy.

Sonia Livingstone, OBE, is a Professor of Social Psychology at the London School of Economics and Political Science and has dedicated much of her research to children, media and the Internet. She is the author of 18 books and many academic articles and chapters. She has been visiting professor at the universities of Bergen, Copenhagen, Harvard, Illinois, Milan, Paris 11 and Stockholm and is on the editorial board of several leading journals. She was awarded the title of OBE in 2014 for services to children and child internet safety.

Andy Phippen is Professor of Social Responsibility in IT at the University of Plymouth. He is a Fellow of the British Computer Society and a member of the BCS Accreditation Committee. He is currently researching issues in the use of technology in relationships and ethical and professional practices in the IT sector. Professor Phippen's recent publications include 'Impacting Methodological Innovation in a Local Government Context' and 'Preventative Actions for Enhancing Online Protection and Privacy.'

Stephen Smallbone is a Psychologist and Professor in the School of Criminology and Criminal Justice, Director of Griffith Youth Forensic Service, and an Australian Research Council 'Future' Fellow. His research focusses on understanding and preventing sexual violence and abuse online and offline. His publications include the books *Situational Prevention of Child Sexual Abuse* (Wortley & Smallbone, 2006) and *Preventing Child Sexual Abuse: Evidence, Policy and Practice* (Smallbone, Marshall, & Wortley, 2008). He is Editor-in-Chief of *Journal of Sexual Aggression* (since 2014) and a member of the editorial board of *Sexual Abuse: A Journal of Research and Treatment.*

Martin Waller is a full-time classroom teacher with an interest in creative learning and multiliteracies. He believes in learning through doing and advocates this approach through research and practice. He has shared his approaches and research findings at a range of events and conferences around the world. He has also authored book chapters about the use of social media and digital technologies in the classroom.

Martin is first and foremost a classroom teacher who has worked with classes from the early years to upper primary level. He currently works in a large primary school in the northeast of England and is part of the school's Senior Leadership and Management Team with the specific role as strategic Curriculum Leader for E-Learning and Computing as well as being the Key Stage 2 Phase Leader.

Dr Helen C. Whittle has a PhD in Forensic Psychology from the University of Birmingham. She worked at the Child Exploitation and Online Protection centre (CEOP) from 2006 to 2014. Originally involved in the creation and delivery of Thinkuknow education resources, Helen then worked operationally in the

Behavioural Analysis Unit (BAU), regularly supporting police forces across the UK during child sexual abuse investigations. Helen was also heavily involved in research, conducting debriefs with child sex offenders in prisons and interviewing young people who have been victimised. Currently, Helen is working therapeutically with young people exhibiting sexually harmful behaviour, as well as conducting research into the impact technology has on victims of child sexual abuse. Helen is a guest lecturer at a number of UK universities and the lead author on several peer reviewed articles.

Richard Wortley has a PhD in psychology and worked as a prison psychologist for 10 years before moving to academia. He was Head of the School of Criminology and Criminal Justice at Griffith University (Australia) for nine years and is a past national Chair of the Australian Psychological Society's College of Forensic Psychologists. His research interests centre on environmental criminology and situational crime prevention. In recent years his research has been particularly concerned with the role that immediate environments play in facilitating child sexual abuse. He has been a Chief Investigator on eight national competitive grants in Australia with total finding of around AU$2 million.

Acknowledgements

Colleagues at the NSPCC have been as ever helpful and supportive in the provision of advice and information. I am also indebted to the contributing authors for their patience and understanding in the lengthy gestation of this project.

Introduction

Jon Brown

The Internet and its rapid development since the 1990s has fundamentally changed the way we communicate and live our lives. Internet-enabled devices are an indispensable part of the daily lives of many children and young people, who tell us that the first thing they interact with in the morning and the last thing they look at before going to sleep is their smartphone. For many adults this is also increasingly the case. The world for most young people and gradually children is no longer a distinction between online and offline.

This edited collection of chapters draws together contributions from a range of leading thinkers, researchers and practitioners in the field of online child abuse, protection and prevention. The book presents the current state of knowledge regarding practice, policy and research in relation to what must be the fastest developing and changing child protection challenge of our time. As John Carr observes in Chapter 1 the pace of change and the development of risks to children online since the mid- to late-1990s has been exponential and something that few predicted.

It is an often-quoted phrase but one that more than bears frequent repetition that the Internet has in many ways been a huge force for good for many many millions of people across the globe, including children and young people, as an educator, enabler and connector. It has fundamentally affected our lives and is doing so increasingly as we move to 10 years of children who have known nothing other than a permanently switched on and connected life, particularly within industrialised and post-industrial societies.

And yet as with every significant technological development or revolution there come risks as well as opportunities, and this is highlighted in many ways with the development of the Internet. As Stephen Fry (2009) has observed, the Internet can be understood as an (ever-expanding) city comprising places of great wonder as well as dark backstreets where danger lurks and the rule of law is weak or non-existent and where the vulnerable can be exploited and abused.

Online Risk to Children: Impact, Protection and Prevention, First Edition.
Edited by Jon Brown.
© 2017 John Wiley & Sons, Ltd. Published 2017 by John Wiley & Sons, Ltd.

So whilst presenting and indeed delivering on many opportunities for children, the online environment also hosts a range of new risks and potential for harm to children. These include risks from adults, such as the demand for child abuse images and sexual grooming, and it also includes risks from peers, including bullying and peer-to-peer sexual abuse. And the scale of these risks should not be underestimated. The National Crime Agency (2014) estimates that there are 100,000 people (primarily men) in the UK viewing child abuse images; this estimate was made two years ago, and it would be a reasonable assumption that this figure is increasing. Senior police officers are recognising that we cannot arrest our way out of this global child infringement, and there is a growing consensus that to effectively make inroads into dealing with this challenge there needs to be international will and consensus built on three key foundations – deterrence, treatment of victims and offenders – and much more evaluated primary prevention activity as outlined by Stephen Smallbone and Richard Wortley in Chapter 8. All this needs to be driven by a focus on what works and by coordinated action by governments, industry and Non Governmental Organization (NGOs).

We are beginning to witness some of this taking shape, and it is encouraging to see the UK take a lead role in identifying the scale of the challenge and importantly how it can be addressed and prevented. These chapters examine where we are in understanding the scale and nature of the challenge of protecting children online, what we can do to treat its impacts and what we can do to disrupt and prevent it.

Chapter 1 opens with John Carr providing an historic sweep of developments in the field since the 1990s in the UK and internationally.

Drawing on her EU Kids Online work Sonia Livingstone reviews in Chapter 2 recent findings from Europe and offers an evidence-rich insight into children's lives online and the implications of this for their wellbeing and protection. Of particular note is the similarity of children and young people's experiences and concerns across Europe; there are some specific and distinctive national and cultural differences, but the globalised nature of the Internet and its development since the mid-1990s has undoubtedly had some homogenising effects.

In Chapter 3 Andy Phippen examines the risk to children and young people from other children and young people, the phenomenon of peer-to-peer abuse. Phippen makes the point that when we think of risk to and the protection of children we tend to think of the young person as victim and the adult as the perpetrator; in the chapter he challenges us to consider some of the complexities and potential contradictions of the risk that children and young people may or may not pose to each other.

In Chapter 4 Helen C. Whittle and Catherine E. Hamilton-Giachritsis discuss what we know about the source of the challenge, online offender's behaviour, and in Chapter 5 Sandy Jung from Canada then gives an overview of interventions with those who have offended online.

In Chapters 6 and 7 Elly Hanson discusses the impact of online abuse on children and promising treatment approaches for victims and survivors of this form of abuse.

Prevention is of course better than cure, and in Chapter 8 Stephen Smallbone and Richard Wortley offer an analysis of how prevention approaches can be applied to abuse online. In Chapter 9, the book then turns to law enforcement with a contribution from Zoe Hilton from the UK National Crime Agency CEOP Command.

Industry has a key role to play in preventing and responding to the abuse of children online, and in Chapter 10, Dido Harding, CEO of TalkTalk, discusses the responsibilities of industry as innovator and protector.

In Chapter 11, Claire Lilley from the NSPCC discusses UK policy responses and rightly highlights the leading role that the UK has played in responding to this challenge. In Chapter 12, Martin Waller examines how schools can play a creative and critical role in the safety and wellbeing of children online. I end the collection with my epilogues of thoughts about a road map for the future of an online world in which children and young people can thrive in an environment that encourages curiosity and enables enjoyment, learning and promotes a sense of wonder, and where risks and dangers can be understood, monitored and when possible eliminated.

REFERENCES

Fry, S. (2009). *Stephen Fry: The internet and me.* Retrieved from http://news.bbc.co. uk/2/hi/7926509.stm

National Crime Agency (NCA). (2014). *National strategic assessment of serious and organised crime 2014.* London, UK: National Crime Agency.

1 A Brief History of Child Safety Online: Child Abuse Images on the Internet

John Carr

Foreign holidays used to be a rare treat enjoyed by better-off families, but otherwise, until the Internet arrived, the great majority of the world's children and young people spent pretty much their entire day-to-day lives exposed to and governed by the mores, sights, sounds and laws of one country, usually the one where they were born and lived. The opportunities open to children and young people, as well as any threats or dangers they might encounter on their pathway to adulthood, were generally well understood by their parents and their communities, because more or less everyone had lived through similar situations themselves. The Internet[1] changed that. A great many parents and the social institutions charged with safeguarding children were overtaken by events, and it is still by no means clear when or even if a new equilibrium will be established.

UNINTENDED, UNFORESEEN AND UNWANTED CONSEQUENCES

None of the scientists and technologists involved in the early development of the Internet had any idea it would turn out the way it did. Thus in many ways what the world is now having to grapple with in relation to online child abuse images as well as several other areas of crime is an example of the doctrine of unintended, unforeseen and definitely unwanted consequences being played out on an epic scale.

Without computers there could be no Internet. It is therefore tempting to begin a discussion of the history of the Internet by looking first at the history of computing and tracing the journey from there. However, according to the

Online Risk to Children: Impact, Protection and Prevention, First Edition.
Edited by Jon Brown.
© 2017 John Wiley & Sons, Ltd. Published 2017 by John Wiley & Sons, Ltd.

Internet Society[2] the real Internet story does not begin until the 1960s with the development of packet switching and later the ARPANET.

In February 2013, in a famous TED Talk,[3] Internet pioneer Danny Hillis describes the Internet as it was in 1982: '... it was a very small community. We didn't all know each other but we all kinda trusted each other . . .'

For many years, almost by definition, every Internet user was a highly educated adult. There was a great deal of reciprocity involved in running the network – everybody had a more or less equal stake in its continuing success. Users would behave responsibly within a framework of commonly accepted if typically unstated norms.

During his TED Talk Hillis brandishes in his hands a slender volume that contained the names, email addresses and telephone numbers of everyone who had an Internet account in 1982. He suggested that today a similar volume, if it could be constructed at all, would be about 25 miles high.

In short the early developers of the Internet, although they had a good idea about its potential to do good in the world by facilitating rapid communications between researchers and later businesses, they had no idea that what they were building would end up being exploited on a large scale by criminals to make or distribute child abuse images or to engage in any other type of felonious activity. If they had there seems little doubt they would have built in more security protocols to inhibit such antisocial behaviour.

SEXUAL IMAGES OF CHILDREN

Today child abuse images are very heavily identified with the Internet, but nobody would ever seriously argue the Internet is truly a *cause* of children being abused or of images of that abuse being made and distributed. The Internet has certainly opened up pathways that, for practical purposes, never previously existed, but that is a different point albeit one of some importance.

The development of photography and printing techniques in the 19th century first allowed for the larger-scale production and distribution of pornography of every type, including some depicting child sex abuse. However, as far as we can tell, since time immemorial there seems always to have been a small but still numerous minority of people,[4] mainly but by no means exclusively men, who have had an interest in children as objects of sexual desire or in depictions of children engaged in sexual acts.

In the UK in 1986, before the mass Internet emerged, one of the world's top paediatric specialists, Professor Oliver Brooke, was sent to prison after admitting dealing in and collecting child pornography. When police searched his office at St George's Hospital in London, they found more than 300 photographs of children in explicit sexual poses, 22 albums of cuttings from child pornography magazines and a dozen Danish magazines specialising in child pornography. Professor Brooke, who was later barred by the British General

Medical Council from ever practising again as a doctor, was at the time considered to be one of the five top specialists in the world in his field.

Also in 1986 a British local government surveyor, Charles Norris, was sent to prison for sexually abusing young boys and making indecent images of children. Police discovered 5,500 colour slides, 3,500 photographs, 29 photograph albums, 100 videos and 200 books and magazines – mainly featuring young boys – at his home in Kent. Again, Brooke had no connection to the Internet.

Nevertheless, with a limited number of exceptions[5] in modern times any sort of sexual interest in children and depictions of it have been the subject of severe societal disapproval based on an appreciation of the harm done to children by early sexual encounters with adults or by other forms of premature involvement with sex.

The law has intervened to underpin, reinforce and reflect these societal values. For example in all major jurisdictions around the world the possession, production and distribution of images of children engaged in sexual acts is now a criminal offence[6] and the age at which it becomes lawful for someone to be depicted in a published sexual image is not necessarily the same as the age of consent to sex.[7]

In 1995, on the eve of the Internet explosion in the UK, the police in Greater Manchester recorded the seizure of only 12 child abuse images in the entire year. In 1995 UK police as a whole were said to have known of the existence of only 7,000 unique child abuse images. INTERPOL then had records of only 4,000 known unique images.

In 'People Like Us,' commissioned in 1996 and published in 1997, Sir William Utting described the production and distribution of child abuse images as being a 'cottage industry.' That was probably about the last moment a statement like that could have been made.

What Sir William meant was that, traditionally, people who wanted to get hold of child abuse materials had to find or know a person who already had some. Alternatively they would need to take considerable personal risks to locate a stranger who could and would oblige or risk asking someone to send them material through the post. With the Internet, a few mouse clicks could put them in touch with a supplier who could deliver in an instant and on a completely unprecedented scale.

THE WORLD WIDE WEB EXPLOSION

At the end of 1980s and at the beginning of the 1990s the Internet was still nothing like it is today. The World Wide Web and the web browsers that would provide easy access to it were just around the corner.

Web browsers did for the Internet what Windows has done for personal computing: made it accessible to the non-technical masses. As with Windows, browsers deployed a 'graphical user interface,' using *intuitive* icons. These enabled people who did not have a degree in computer science or perhaps a great deal of patience to carry out what would otherwise be quite complex operations potentially involving dozens of obscure, hard-to-remember key-strokes. All they had to do now was click on a little picture.

The first web browser famously was developed at CERN in Switzerland by Tim Berners Lee in 1989–1990. In 1993 the first publicly available web browser arrived. It was called 'Mosaic,' followed in 1994 by 'Netscape,' then in 1995 came Microsoft's 'Internet Explorer.' This was given away free and would go on to capture, at its height, over 95% of the entire web browser market.

Louis XV of France died in 1785, but not before uttering the immortal words 'Apres moi le deluge' (After me, the deluge). Four years later the French Revolution began. The arrival of the web browser was a revolutionary moment of a different kind. Web browsers opened up the Internet to the rough, rude and larger world that hitherto had been excluded from its gentle cloisters.

AFFORDABILITY, ACCESSIBILITY AND ANONYMITY – *THE THREE As* – PROVIDE THE SPUR

The arrival of the web coincided with a fall in hardware prices, a fall in tele-communications costs and an increase in connection speeds. Affordability and accessibility were here. The belief in anonymity would come soon and complete the circle.

As noted, Sir William Utting had observed that prior to the arrival of the Internet the production and dissemination of child abuse images were essentially local and small scale. If there were larger numbers of people who were interested in child abuse images they seemed to be unwilling to take the risks associated with obtaining them or were disinclined to go to the trouble. The Internet was cheap, easy to use from the comfort of one's own home and it was being widely reported in the press that it could be used anonymously. It opened doors many were to go through who very likely would not have done so otherwise, and it is clear many did because they thought they would be anonymous.

However, the anonymity proffered or suggested in those early days was a false promise, which can largely be laid at the door of inaccurate reporting in the mass media. It was to cost a number of men their lives.[8] When they were eventually caught and arrested for child abuse image offences, a number of downloaders chose to commit suicide rather than face the humiliation of a public trial. For that reason today in the UK anyone arrested for this type of offence is usually put on 'suicide watch' or given some other form of support.

In the beginning it appears people would log on to different parts of the Internet or use their credit card to buy illicit items seemingly believing they had been rendered invisible. Even today some of the individuals who still go online look-ing for child abuse images apparently believe they are protected by anonymity, but such has been the publicity about so many cases that only the naïve, the foolish or the reckless can now labour under this kind of misapprehension.

The truth is it is almost impossible to go online without leaving some sort of footprint. The only question that matters therefore is whether or not your case will become one that the police choose to investigate. Such are the volumes in many countries there might have to be something exceptional or unusual about you or your case for it to rise to the top of the pile, and the worry is many criminals now know this.

More shocking still, perhaps, the world discovered that the Internet was also enabling like-minded people to find each other in ways that were simply impossible or impractical before. People with a sexual interest in children or an interest in child abuse images started to form groups, sometimes quite large with hundreds of members, dedicated solely to the production, distribution or exchange of child abuse images.

Groups were forming online in which participants would swap advice and give each other tips about how to find children to abuse and how to do it with minimal risk of being caught or successfully prosecuted. Some of this abuse would result in new images being made and distributed; some of it would not. By and large, though, the people in these groups would never have met in real life and probably never could have done so because they were scattered all over the planet.

Worse, these groups in effect became communities. They would reinforce and 'normalise' the behaviour of everyone in the group. Someone who had probably always thought of himself as being a bit of an oddball, who knew he had to keep quiet about his sexual preferences or interests and watch his behaviour generally, was now in touch with people just like himself. Maybe he started thinking he wasn't so strange after all. Maybe his tastes weren't that peculiar. When everyone else was being so censorious about the sort of sexual images he was interested in he could convince himself they had just got it wrong or hadn't yet realised what they were missing.

A *Panorama* programme broadcast by the BBC[9] in 2001 showed an interview with a man (David Hines) who, during Operation Cathedral, was arrested for possessing child abuse images that he had downloaded from the Internet or had been sent to him by people with whom he was in touch. In the TV interview Hines said, 'Thanks to the Internet, for the first time in my life I had friends. I had friends all over the world.'

THE NUMBER OF ARRESTS AND POLICE
OPERATIONS START TO CLIMB

In 1988 the total number of people found guilty in Magistrates' Courts for child abuse image–related offences in England and Wales was 33. By 1992 it had grown to 72 and by 1995, arguably the Internet's year 0 in the UK, it had increased to 91.[10] The trajectory was moving in only one direction. It rose to 340 in 2001 and, when Operation Ore later got underway, the yearly numbers exceeded or were about 1,700. They settled back to a 'normal' level in excess of 1,000 before rising again to about 3,000.

The other feature of this growth in the number of arrests was the numbers of images being seized by police. As previously noted, during pre-Internet times, typically an arrest might lead to the confiscation of a handful or a few hundred pictures, or as in cases such as Brooks and Norris, thousands. In the digital world a great many seizures would be counted in the tens if not hundreds of thousands and, not infrequently, in millions, although here there would be vast number of repeats of the same images. Following a Freedom of Information request made by the NSPCC it emerged that in England and Wales, within a two-year period ended in March 2012, five local forces had seized a total of 26 million images. If extrapolated to the whole of England and Wales, this suggests that in excess of 300 million images may have been in circulation during the same two-year period. Moreover it emerged that the police had identified between 50,000 and 60,000 individuals across the UK as a whole who had engaged with illegal child abuse images online, and in 2016 this number was revised upwards to 100,000.[11] When set against the police's historic record of arrests for these types of crime (see the previous paragraph) a very depressing picture emerges that underlines how unlikely it is that this type of crime will ever be satisfactorily addressed via traditional or conventional law enforcement methods. And the key point to grasp here is that although these numbers are very obviously derived from a single country, the UK, there is absolutely no reason at all to believe that the situation will be significantly different in any other jurisdiction where similar levels of Internet access and access speeds exist.

By the mid-1990s it was clear that 'something had to be done' about this 'new-fangled' and still uncertain technology called *the Internet* and the evil that seemed to be arriving in its wake. But what? There were no textbooks to guide anybody. One of the solutions that people eventually came up with was Internet hotlines. These were places where members of the public, employees of Internet service providers or indeed anyone, could report any child abuse images they had seen online, in anticipation of them being investigated and removed as soon as possible. At that time there was a widespread consensus that the scale of the problem was such that finding ways of involving the public in the fight against these images was an essential component.

The UK, Norway and Holland were the first in the field. In each country the pressures were the same but the organisational arrangements turned out differently. Here we look in a little more detail at how the UK's hotline emerged.

THE EMERGENCE OF HOTLINES

In the early 1990s a steady stream of stories of arrests for child pornography offences started to reach the UK media. They received huge coverage in the press. Partly this was a reflection of the fascination by journalists and their readers, viewers and listeners with an awesome new technology. Partly it was a reflection of a natural if somewhat ghoulish curiosity in something so viscerally awful. Elements of the Internet industry complained loudly about how unfairly they were being treated by the media, but in a democracy where a free press is highly valued, the sort of coverage the stories were given was 100% predictable and 100% inevitable. It was no use crying 'foul.'

Although there was a lot of development going on in the background, from the public's point of view the UK's Internet industry then consisted principally of a small number of Internet service providers (ISPs) who were delivering Internet connectivity to people's homes. The largest of these was BT.

Perhaps the real problem was that the fledgling industry was unable to promote or establish in the public's mind an alternative explanation, a better or more convincing, reassuring narrative that would put into perspective or explain how it was that their new systems were suddenly facilitating such appalling behaviour.

Eventually, in 1995, an industry trade association would form – Internet Services Providers' Association (ISPA) – to act as an intermediary and spokes-person for the industry, but they still found themselves overwhelmed and drowned out by the noise and anger that child abuse images seemed to create whenever the issue was discussed in public.

Some newspapers and TV or radio stations undoubtedly did occasionally overstate or sensationalise aspects of police operations in this space. This cer-tainly increased the pressure on the police and politicians to be seen to act. But none of the media outlets was making it all up. There was a lot of smoke, but there was plenty of fire creating it.

Opinion polls started showing high levels of anxiety among parents about the threat to children that the Internet seemed to represent, much of it trig-gered by stories about child abuse images, although this was added to consider-ably when stories about the easy accessibility of legal adult pornography and other materials not suitable for children started to appear.

MPs were hearing about these issues on the doorstep, in letters from con-stituents and at their surgeries. Politicians were becoming convinced that they had to act but there was no clear idea about what they should do. Lead respon-sibility for this area of policy within government lay with the (then) Depart-ment of Trade Industry (DTI) who, broadly speaking, saw their job as helping the Internet in the UK to grow as quickly as possible. They did not see them-selves as being in the business of promoting any kind of restrictions for fear this might kill off the goose that everyone hoped was going to lay the golden egg of new kinds of economic growth.

But who was responsible and for what exactly? There seemed to be little technical understanding of how the Internet operated among the UK's police forces and even less among the crime correspondents of the major media outlets.

Despite some wild assertions to the contrary that surfaced from time to time nobody seriously believed the owners or employees of any of the UK's ISPs were intentionally or knowingly causing or allowing illegal images to be stored or distributed through their systems. Thus the element of intentionality, essential for almost every major crime, was simply not there. Absent such intentionality, how far was it reasonable to go to expect the people who were developing the exciting new Internet industry in Britain to step in and deal with the problem, and just what did 'dealing with the problem' mean in practical terms?

Media stories were starting to reach the UK from overseas, in particular from France and Hong Kong. The police there were being very muscular and direct in their dealings with their local ISPs. They were reported simply to have walked on to the ISPs' premises, unplugged the servers and took them away, arresting and detaining for questioning any directors or senior employees they could find. They did not sit about and engage in philosophical debates about culpability, causation and intentionality. Their simple view was the images were coming off or being distributed from their machines so they must be responsible. The British media noted this with approval. They wanted some of it here. Pressure was mounting.

Events began to move rapidly in the summer of 1996.

THE BIRTH OF THE INTERNET WATCH FOUNDATION

The Internet Watch Foundation (IWF) owes its immediate existence principally to three far-sighted men. One was Chief Inspector Stephen French of the Metropolitan Police's Clubs and Vice Unit. The second was Ian Taylor, MP, Minister for Technology at the DTI, in John Major's Conservative Government. The third was Peter Dawe, founder of Pipex, one of the UK's first commercial ISPs. Dawe sold Pipex for a very large sum of money and became extremely rich. This meant he could do things that others could not. Dawe did not have to convince a committee or anyone else to put up money for this or that idea. He decided for himself.

First step forward Chief Inspector Stephen French. In August 1996 he sent his famous open letter to ISPA and to several of the larger ISPs. He said the police had identified more than 130 Usenet Newsgroups[12] that they believed contained illegal material and that the police's view, in essence, was that the ISPs were in effect the publishers of it. The police wanted the named groups to be banned.

The key part of his letter said

'This list is not exhaustive and we are looking to you to monitor your newsgroups identifying and taking necessary action against those others found to contain such material. As you will be aware the publication of obscene articles is an offence. This list is only the starting point and we hope, with the co-operation and assistance of the industry and your trade organisations, to be moving quickly towards the eradication of this type of newsgroup from the Internet . . . We are very anxious that all service providers should be taking positive action now, whether or not they are members of a trade association. We trust that with your co-operation and self-regulation it will not be necessary for us to move to an enforcement policy.'

This was not a very thinly veiled threat, although in truth the police and the Crown Prosecution Service were not at all sure what the basis for any arrests might be. Here is where the government came in through Ian Taylor. Taylor made it clear that if the industry did not sort things out via a self-regulatory initiative of some sort there would be legislation to create arrestable offences.

There had already been something of precedent for self-regulation in the Internet space in Britain. In May 1996 it had been agreed that Nominet would be established as a self-regulatory body to take over the complex task of administering the .uk domain space.

The Observer ran a major story that honed in on the distribution of child abuse images by British ISPs.[13] It became crystal clear to the Internet industry that this issue was not going to go away any time soon. In September 1996 Dawe got enough people from the industry around the table to sign up to a new body that initially was to be called the 'Safety Net Foundation' but would finally become the IWF. Its role was to receive reports of child abuse images that were found on the Internet and to secure their removal as rapidly as possible by issuing a notice to the hosting company that, in practice (though not in theory), required them to remove the image forthwith.

However, there was never any serious suggestion that the businessmen and - women who had formed the UK's first ISPs knew or could know who was posting illegal material to their servers or where it was being kept. What was being expressed by the media and politicians was a *cri de coeur* (cry of the heart). What the police and others were looking for was help to deal with some of the nastier consequences of the rollout of the technology from which the ISP shareholders hoped to profit. The police and government wanted industry to show it felt some sense of responsibility, of ownership.

Fortunately, wise counsels prevailed. Big companies such as BT and several others saw that what Peter Dawe was saying was right anyway, whether or not it got them a get-out-of-jail card. They didn't want those sorts of images circulating on their networks. They did not want to be thought of as 'child porn merchants.' They recognised the need to create new machinery to help them identify the illegal pictures and inform them of their whereabouts, so they could remove them as rapidly as possible.

The fact that BT came out in this way was highly significant. It was also a harbinger. The plain truth is that as more and more bigger businesses started to get involved in the Internet attitudes started to change, or to put it more bluntly, a division opened up which more or less corresponded with the size of the firm. The bigger the company the more it was accustomed to working in the consumer space. Larger firms were already on the High Street, metaphorically and in some cases also literally. These firms had no difficulty grasping the importance of being seen to deal vigorously with an issue such as child abuse images.

Admittedly these larger companies were likely to be more highly capitalised than their smaller rivals and therefore were better able to cope with changing or new demands, all of which cost money and could consume valuable engineering time with perhaps little to show for it on the bottom line in the short run.

Internet self-regulation as an official policy in the UK for dealing with child abuse images therefore grew out of necessity and the exigencies of the moment. It started with a letter from a policeman. Self-regulation was not a carefully selected option picked from a range of possible choices. Civil servants in the Home Office or elsewhere with any sort of background in how the Internet worked were somewhere between thin on the ground and non-existent. Presumably there were people in the security services who were on the case but they weren't much in evidence near Westminster and Whitehall at the time.

Aside from Chief Inspector French and a small number of his colleagues in the Metropolitan Police, almost nobody in mainstream law enforcement then knew anything about the Internet. The National Criminal Intelligence Service was taking a leadership role but, at the operational end, the National Hi Tech Crime Unit would not be established until 2001. The police and the government were just relieved that the IWF came along to take the strain.

One of the major and continuing unsung benefits of the IWF and other hotlines around the world is how much it saves in police time and hence taxpayer money. About two-thirds of all the reports the IWF receives concern images or things that are not illegal but the person reporting them thought they should be. The IWF in effect acts as a filter.

As already noted for many years the lead department for anything and everything to do with the Internet was the DTI, thus emphasising the focus of government policy back then. Even the Internet Crime Forum was run under the DTI's umbrella. The first written communication between the UK's children's charities and the UK government on anything to do with the Internet was in March 2000, and it was in the form of a letter to Patricia Hewitt, MP at the time Minister for Small Business and E-Commerce. It would be a while before the Home Office and what would become the Ministry of Justice became fully engaged.

What was happening in the UK was also happening everywhere else in the developed world. A paper discussing the role that hotlines could play in a campaign to eradicate online child abuse images was presented to the 1st World Congress Against Commercial Sexual Exploitation of Children, held in Stockholm in August 1996. The paper had been written and presented by Save the Children Norway and the Norwegian Children's Ombudsman, but the Norwegian hotline did not actually begin operations until January 1997. To begin with and for several years, Save the Children, Norway, managed the hotline, working closely with the Norwegian police.

As a percentage of the total population of Internet users worldwide and in absolute numbers, in the beginning the largest concentration of Internet account holders was in the United States, home of the Internet. Even so the United States did not establish a hotline until 1998 when the National Center for Missing and Exploited Children created their Cyber Tip Line.

In Holland the prime movers seemed to be the Internet industry. In Norway it was a children's organisation. As we have seen in the UK it was the police and the government that encouraged the industry to act, and the IWF, an NGO, was the result. Similar coalitions started to be formed in many parts of the developed world although in some, for example, Australia, it was the state that directly initiated the hotline.

INHOPE, a global association of hotlines, was established in 1999 and today has 54 member hotlines in 45 countries. That means there are more than 150 countries in membership of the United Nations that do not have a hotline, although some of these are very small and have not featured as major hosts of child abuse materials, at least not yet. Alternatively members of the public have to report via the police.

INHOPE has recently established a charitable foundation with the express aim of helping countries in the developing world to create operational hotlines. The IWF has also developed a package that is thought to be particularly suitable for smaller countries where hosting illegal images is not an issue but where, nonetheless, the public still want to be able to report illegal content to a site that is locally based and in their own language.

More worryingly there are still a substantial number of countries around the world that still do not have an adequate legal framework to deal with online child abuse images. Published in 2016, the eighth edition of the International Centre for Missing & Exploited Children's global review[14] indicated that there were still 50 mainly smaller countries in the world where simple possession of child abuse images is still not illegal.

NOT A VERY PROMISING START

At the beginning of the IWF's operations the main focus was Usenet Newsgroups. Chief Inspector French's letter referred only to Newsgroups. The rule established early on was that the IWF staff members had no power or authority to go looking for child abuse material on the Internet. They had to wait for a report to come in, and then they had to deal with each report individually.

This idea of only reacting to reports received is still very common in the Internet space but, at root, it is in many ways a rather curious proposition. If someone goes online looking for material they are interested in and they find it they are hardly going to report it if that might lead to it being removed from the Internet altogether. This is even more the case when the material in question is itself illegal, and it is also a crime to seek it out intentionally.

The IWF used to have several people who regularly reported material to them and staff members were obliged to point out that, however noble their intentions might be, if they were deliberately seeking out child abuse images they would in fact be breaking the law. The worry was such individuals might be trying to establish an alibi or a plea in mitigation when in truth they were simply collecting child abuse images for their own consumption. Thus the whole basis on which the IWF was established relied on people reporting material they had found accidentally or that had arrived in their in-box unsolicited.

Thus, under the originally agreed processes within the IWF if someone posted a photograph with a caption that informed the viewer it was a 'picture of a baby being raped' in a Newsgroup that might be called 'Pictures of Babies Being Raped' all the IWF staff members could do was confirm that the image was illegal and issue a notice the effect of which would be to get that specific posting taken down. It could be back up again within minutes, in exactly the same Newsgroup, yet the staff members were powerless to act until a further complaint was received. Similar procedures were in place in other hotlines in other countries.

The system was seen by some in the UK as being absurd; moreover, a little legal research led to the discovery that the Protection of Children Act 1978, specifically s.1 (1) (d), says it is an offence for a person

> 'to publish or cause to be published any advertisement likely to be understood as conveying that the advertiser distributes or shows . . . indecent photographs or pseudo-photographs of children or intends to do so.'

Was a Newsgroup name an advertisement? The question was not definitively answered until July 2002 when barrister Anthony Hudson replied in the affirmative. Meanwhile what about those Newsgroups that, whatever their name, regularly had child abuse images posted to them?

In early 2001 it was suggested the IWF embark on a new policy of banning entire groups that appeared to advertise the availability of child abuse images and groups that regularly contained such images irrespective of its individual name. Eventually this policy was agreed on, even though it was anathema to the then-traditions of the internet.

The monumental nature of this decision cannot be overstated. If the decision on Newsgroups had gone the other way, it is inconceivable that the IWF and BT would later have felt there was any point in co-operating in the experiment that lead to the announcement of *Cleanfeed* in June 2004[15] (see more in the next section), a world first that is now emulated across the planet.

THE TERRAIN SHIFTS AND URL BLOCKING EMERGES

In the early part of the 21st century, child abuse images started popping up on websites with greater frequency. The web was a completely different environment from Newsgroups. The problem was that, overwhelmingly, the images being reported were hosted outside of the UK. It could sometimes take weeks, months, even years for them to be removed.

The unconscionable delays in take-down times were very effectively exposed in a study published by Richard Clayton and Tyler Moore of Cambridge University.[16] They contrasted the average speed with which phishing sites could be removed – hours – with the length of time it took child abuse images to be removed. Their explanation was simple and devastating. Phishing sites could cost the banks money. The banks were on the case. There was no comparable system of incentives that worked in relation to child abuse images.

The delays in pictures being taken down meant two things. First was the implication that the image was being ignored or not dealt with promptly by the local police in whatever country it had ended up. This meant no one could have any confidence that serious efforts were being made to locate the children and rescue them from whatever catastrophic situation they must be in for the events shown in the images to be possible in the first place.

Second, for as long as the images stayed up on the website they remained visible within the UK. For that reason their continuing publication further violated the rights of the child or children depicted in them and could put them in danger of being abused again; to the extent that their continued visibility and availability for download encouraged or sustained paedophile activity within the UK, they represented a continuing threat to children living in the UK.

Following the decision on Newsgroups the UK government became convinced that a similar approach might be tried in relation to the web. Nonetheless this time around, when thinking about how to deal with the web, in 2003 the Home Office decided to convene a working group of ISPs to discuss the technical feasibility of blocking web addresses.

There was considerable opposition from most of the ISPs on the working group to the idea of attempting to block web addresses. To their eternal credit BT said they were willing to try to build and test a URL-blocking system if the IWF would agree to give them a list of URLs. The IWF did. Officers of the Metropolitan Police were also on the working group. They indicated that they had no objection to such an experiment being carried out but, unlike their earlier intervention in Newsgroups in 1996, they were not the prime movers on this occasion.

Out of this BT developed *Cleanfeed*, which, as noted, came blinking into the world in June 2004. Once it became established in the public domain that blocking was technically feasible and was in fact happening, the need for the Home Office working group disappeared. It never met again.

Today almost 100% of domestic broadband users in the UK now belong to ISPs that deploy the IWF list. Every mobile phone network deploys it, and all of the major WiFi providers in the UK also use it on their networks. It is also used by all the major search engines. There is no question that this BT-IWF initiative was hugely important, and now very many countries around the world are emulating it. In Italy URL blocking is required by law. Blocking even found its way into an EU Directive on Child Protection in 2011.

TECHNOLOGY COMES TO THE RESCUE OF A PROBLEM TECHNOLOGY HELPED TO CREATE

As we have seen, law enforcement agencies no longer have the resources to investigate every case in which someone is suspected of being engaged in the distribution or downloading of child abuse images.

The first attempts to use technological solutions to reduce or eliminate the traffic in images started to be deployed with the emergence of hotlines that arranged for the images to be removed from the Internet, then largely within Usenet Newsgroups. Later this evolved in the UK and a growing number of countries into the use of blocking lists of URLs known to contain illegal images or to restricting access to certain Usenet Newsgroups. Yet the volumes continued to grow. The emergence of social media sites and file locker services[17] also presented a vastly increased number of opportunities to persons with an interest in these images to store and distribute them. New solutions were needed.

Although for some time a number of smaller companies had been working on technical solutions that would enable known illegal images to be identified, no major technology players were known to be engaging with the challenge. Many saw this as a law enforcement problem not a business opportunity. Microsoft was the first big player to step forward. In 2009 the company announced that it had been working with technologists at Dartmouth College to develop PhotoDNA. Microsoft describe PhotoDNA as 'an image-matching technology . . . It creates a unique signature for a digital image, something like a fingerprint, which can be compared with the signatures of other images to find copies of that image. NCMEC and online service providers such as Microsoft and Facebook currently use PhotoDNA to help find, report and eliminate some of the worst known images of child pornography online, helping identify thousands of these horrific images that would previously have gone undetected.'

These unique fingerprints are more commonly referred to as 'hashes,' and law enforcement agencies and companies around the world are pooling their hashes and allowing them to be assembled into large databases that can then be used to identify matching images. This can help save an enormous amount of time and effort of the part of the police, who will no longer find they are investigating an image that has already been dealt with by a police force in another country. Google, Twitter and many other companies are now using PhotoDNA, and the hope must be that every company that operates online will do so.

The main drawback with PhotoDNA is that it works only with still images. It does not work with video footage of which there is now a huge quantity online. Google has stepped into the breach to try to solve this problem with a programme that works with video clips in a similar way to PhotoDNA and stills. In late 2016 the Canadian hotline started using a hash database with very impressive results.[18]

THE ROLE OF SEARCH ENGINES

In the aftermath of the trials for the murders of April Jones and Tia Sharp in 2012 a great deal of attention fell on the role of search engines in helping paedophiles to locate child abuse material on the Internet. This was to have global consequences. Google and Microsoft said they were going to make changes to the way in which their search engines operated, making it harder for anyone to locate paedophilic content. They also indicated their intention to introduce *splash pages*. Thus in future if people used either search engine to attempt to find paedophilic material a message would appear on the search page warning them that they were likely committing a criminal offence and also pointing them towards potential sources of help if they were worried about their behaviour. Both companies said they were going to roll out this new approach in every language and territory in which they operate. Precise information on the progress being made in delivering on these promises and on the impact of these measures has yet to be made publicly available by either company.

THE UNANSWERED QUESTIONS ABOUT
TECHNICAL SOLUTIONS

In some quarters there is undoubtedly a degree of ambivalence about the idea of looking to technology to solve the problems presented by the extremely large quantities of child abuse images being circulated on the Internet. Undoubtedly some would rather we simply increased the number of police officers employed in this work so that anyone who engaged with the images might, as a result, reasonably fear that sooner rather than later there would be a knock on their door following which they would be arrested then later convicted.

It is sometimes pointed out that a significant proportion of those who *are* picked up following an online investigation into child abuse images have not previously been known to the police or other authorities; consequently, the Internet is presenting an unprecedented opportunity to uncover potential or actual child abusers in ways that otherwise do not exist. In the end this argument is circular and self-serving. It is a bit like arguing law enforcement should tolerate the continued distribution of drugs in order to follow the trail to discover who the drug addicts are. Implicit in this line of thinking is also the suggestion that the right to privacy and human dignity of the victims depicted in the images counts for a great deal less than it should. Moreover it is important to remember it is not just the numbers of trained police officers that count here. With an increased number of arrests for image-related offences would also come an increase in the demand for forensic examinations of seized equipment, an increase in the demand for staff members capable of carrying out psychological or other assessments of those arrested, an increase in probation and prison staff members, possibly also an expansion in the number of prison places, not to mention an increase in the number of court rooms, judges, lawyers and associated staff members to make all this work. It is doubtful, in the midst of a global recession and times of austerity, whether it is realistic to expect countries even in the richer parts of the world to be able to contemplate the sorts of expansion in public expenditure such an approach suggests, and it is surely completely unrealistic to expect less prosperous parts of the globe to be able to do likewise.

Naturally everybody would much rather find effective ways to prevent any kind of child abuse from happening in the first place but, absent that, dealing with images of it, without more resources, is a vitally important policy goal in its own right. Dealing with illegal images of children with the current level of resources should never be considered secondary to or of less importance than other important policy objectives in this space. There is no hierarchy of need or importance. Each aspect requires specific approaches. Neither should they be seen as being in competition with each other.

NOTES

1 There are now a wide range of devices that can connect to the Internet, many of them highly portable and used by children and young people on a large scale, for example, smartphones, tablets and games consoles. All references to the Internet encompass the use of any and all of these, although the degree of risk associated with any particular method of connecting can vary by degrees.
2 Leiner, B. M., Cerf, V. G., Clark, D. D., Kahn, R. E., Kleinrock, L., Lynch, D. C., Postel, J., Roberts, L. G., & Wolff, S. (2016). *A brief history of the internet*. Internet Society. Retrieved February 14, 2017, from www.internetsociety.org/internet/what-internet/history-internet/brief-history-internet
3 Danny Hillis: The internet could crash. We need a plan b. *TED Talk*. Retrieved February 14, 2017, from www.bing.com/videos/search?q=Danny+Hillis+TEDTALK &view=detail&mid=6E28E5B88111C9A59CF46E28E5B88111C9A59CF4 &FORM=VIRE
4 Stephenson, W. (July 30, 2004). How many men are paedophiles? *BBC News*. Retrieved February 14, 2017, from www.bbc.co.uk/news/magazine-28526106; see for a summary of Michael Seto's views.

5 In some Scandinavian countries for a brief period in the 1960s child pornography and sexual acts between adults and children were not illegal.

6 International Centre for Missing & Exploited Children. (2016). *Child pornography: Model legislation & global review* (8th ed.). Retrieved February 14, 2017, from www.icmec.org/wp-content/uploads/2016/02/Child-Pornography-Model-Law-8th-Ed-Final-linked.pdf. But note (page 10) 50 countries still do not outlaw simple possession.

7 Child Exploitation and Online Protection Centre. (June 2012). *A picture of abuse: A thematic assessment of the risk of contact child sexual abuse posed by those who possess indecent images of children* [Executive summary] (p. 4). Retrieved February 14, 2017, from www.ceop.police.uk/Documents/ceopdocs/CEOP%20IIOCTA%20Executive%20Summary.pdf

8 Tendler, S., & Searle, D. (January 11, 2005). Operation Ore link in suicide of navy chief. *The Times*. Retrieved February 14, 2017, from www.thetimes.co.uk/tto/news/uk/article1921242.ece

9 Wonderland Club paedophile ring (Operation Cathedral). *BBC News*. Retrieved February 14, 2017, from www.youtube.com/watch?v=iHAgCQdvw94

10 Offending and Criminal Justice Group (RDS), Home Office Ref: IOS 503–03.

11 Gallagher, P. (October 13, 2016). Number of people accessing child abuse images feared to have doubled in three years. *News: The Essential Daily Briefing*. Retrieved February 14, 2017, from https://inews.co.uk/essentials/news/health/thousands-seek-help-child-abuse-images-online/

12 McKay, N. (August 22, 1996). British police list 133 obscene newsgroups. *Computerworld*. Retrieved from www.computerworld.co.nz/article/519610/british_police_list_133_obscene_newsgroups/

13 Connett, D., & Henley, J. (August 25, 1996). These men are not paedophiles: They are the internet abusers. *The Observer*.

14 International Centre for Missing & Exploited Children. (2016).

15 Blight, M. (June 6, 2004). BT puts block on child porn sites. *The Guardian*. Retrieved February 14, 2017, from www.theguardian.com/technology/2004/jun/06/childrensservices.childprotection

16 Moore, T., & Clayton, R. The impact of incentives on notice and take-down. *Seventh Workshop on the Economics of Information Security* (WEIS 2008), June 25–28, 2008. Retrieved February 14, 2017, from www.cl.cam.ac.uk/-rnc1/takedown.pdf

17 Cyberlocker. *Techopedia*. Retrieved February 14, 2017, from www.techopedia.com/definition/27694/cyberlocker

18 A game changer? (January 26, 2017). *Desiderata*. Retrieved February 14, 2017, from https://johnc1912.wordpress.com/2017/01/26/a-game-changer/

2 Children's and Young People's Lives Online

Sonia Livingstone[1]

The line between online and offline is getting harder to draw, as society becomes ever more reliant on internet-enabled activities and infrastructures. But this doesn't mean children no longer care about the difference; on the contrary, they are very interested in the different communication opportunities available to them—and spend a lot of time working out which are more or less private, more or less easy to share, more or less naughty or risky, or more or less visible to parents. In trying to make meaningful choices, much depends on children's digital and social media literacy, and how education and experience can guide them. The design of online sites and services is also important—are they intelligible, child-friendly, informed by best practice, or exploitative, deceptive, or serving interests other than those of their users (Livingstone, Ólafsson, O'Neill, & Donoso, 2012)?

The line between online opportunities and online risks is also getting harder to draw, with children seeing this line differently from adults (Livingstone, Kirwil, Ponte, & Staksrud, 2014). And the balance between opportunities and risks is different for children who are more resilient and those who are more vulnerable (Livingstone, Palmer, et al., 2012). Online, both children and adults sometimes struggle to work out what's real, what's honest, what's going to happen when they click on something, and how to deal with the consequences (Livingstone, 2014a). New sites and services springing up everywhere capitalize on or exploit the exciting ambiguities of "risky opportunities" that attract young teenagers especially (Livingstone, 2008), thus situations can get rapidly out of hand, problems escalate, and just walking away gets ever harder.

To grasp the implications of the fast-changing digital environment for children, research is vital. Interestingly, however, as the body of available research grows,[2] it doesn't always confirm expectations, tending to confound the most panicky predictions promulgated in the popular media

Online Risk to Children: Impact, Protection and Prevention, First Edition.
Edited by Jon Brown.
© 2017 John Wiley & Sons, Ltd. Published 2017 by John Wiley & Sons, Ltd.

(Mascheroni, Ponte, Garmedia, Garitaonandia, Murray 2010). In this chapter, I first review some of the unfolding trends in children's internet use, and then consider the implications for policy and practice, in the hope of a future internet that advances children's online opportunities and minimizes the associated risk of harm.

TRENDS IN CHILDREN'S INTERNET USE

Contrary to popular belief, new technology doesn't always mean more technology. While the tablet is proving a hugely popular device in the UK, mobile phone ownership, especially among younger children, along with television sets in children's bedrooms, is tailing off (Ofcom, 2016). What does this mean? In interviews with parents, our research finds that as parents become more familiar with digital media, some are establishing a "no screen in the bedroom" rule to protect homework and sleep, thereby preferring the more manageable tablet to the TV set. Meanwhile, for younger children the tablet offers entertainment without the problems associated with mobile phone communication (Blum-Ross & Livingstone, 2016). Relatedly, recent years have seen increased public talk of the benefits of a "digital detox" as families begin to redress the balance between digital and other activities and priorities in their lives.

Second, more technology doesn't always mean more time on technology. It may be that overall screen time is leveling out—with more time online/on mobile devices but less time watching television or reading (Childwise, 2016). Perhaps a human limit is being reached, although engaging with multiple screens at once, and watching short videos rather than concentrating on long films or texts mark significant shifts in literacy practices, partly in response to increased efforts on the part of the content industry to grab and hold children's attention. This makes it all the more important for parents to consider the nature of screen time in terms of content, context, and social connections rather than simply counting hours (Blum-Ross & Livingstone, 2016).

Third, younger and younger children are using technology. A recent report reveals that 25% of 0- to 2-year-olds in Britain now own their own tablet, as do 36% of 3- to 5-year-olds—and they use their tablets for over an hour each day (Marsh, Plowman, Yamade-Rice, Bishop, Lahmar, Scott, et al. 2015). This is unsurprising when one realizes that preschool children—who cannot read or write—do not find the computer keyboard an intuitive interface compared with the touch screen, and they struggle to manage the distance between mouse and screen on a computer or laptop. The result is that today's child must master a new repertoire of digital skills and practices—not only to open and close apps, but also to swipe, drag, tap, click, pinch, find, and create content at will. Knowing how long it takes children to learn to read a book, hold a pencil, or write their name, this new-found ability to manage content well before the age of five suggests a startling change in children's capacity to engage with media content.

Fourth, more technology means less sharing. The more devices and services family members can access, and the more these become tailored and targeted to specific groups (mums or dads, toddlers or teens, girls or boys), the less there may be that families share. While not becoming unduly nostalgic about shared media experiences that never really happened very often in practice, it is noteworthy that as people engage ever more with their personal screens, it is not only harder for parents to look over their children's shoulder or casually discuss what they're watching but, more important, it is harder to find content enjoyed across gender and generational divisions (Ofcom, 2016).

Last, more technology also means different technology. There is growing interest in and concern over various kinds of smart technologies, many of them still regarded as "in the future" by parents even though they are already entering the children's marketplace—these include smart watches, activity trackers, virtual reality headsets, wearables, and the "Internet of Toys" (Croll, 2016). At this stage, the hype tends to outweigh any practical assessment of either benefits or risks. What we might anticipate from the adoption of previous technologies, however, is that these will become commonly used before society has developed robust policy to manage the risks or—perhaps more surprisingly—formulated a clear vision of the benefits either.

PARENTAL RESPONSES AND RESPONSIBILITIES

What could be hoped for from children's Internet use? Internet Matters' (2015) survey is the latest in a long line to find a discrepancy between children and parents' Internet experiences, with children using the Internet more than parents, and parents underestimating children's usage. Of the various findings reported, perhaps the most striking is that "most parents and children don't think the Internet is a safe place for children to be"—striking given the scale of use among both parents and children. In the US, too, a recent survey found that parents are more concerned about their children's online privacy than their school performance, relationships, or health (FOSI, 2015). Yet the same report shows that US parents remain optimistic about the benefits of digital activities for their children. Ofcom's qualitative *Children's media lives* (2015) study helps us understand why UK families use the Internet despite their concerns: It offers a new outlet for children's creativity, it inspires new forms of learning, it invites emotional investment (especially in gaming worlds), it engages children's identity commitments and motivations, and, of course, it fills the time that parents are too busy to occupy. No wonder that ambivalence is one of parents' strongest reactions to the Internet. And no wonder that still, when parents want to show how they are "good parents," they talk about shared non-digital activities (going to the park, sports, or craft activities at home), all of these firmly established in the culture of parenting (even though, in practice, families may enjoy a television program or film together on the sofa; see Blum-Ross & Livingstone, 2016).

Even though they bought the digital goods at home, conversations with parents quickly falter when asked what they see as really beneficial about digital media. For sure, these devices serve as useful ways to occupy children when parents are busy or tired, as parents will ruefully admit. And for sure, children welcome such moments, especially as it means they get to do what they really like on their digital media "under the radar." But is the time children spend with media just a kind of parental failure, more babysitting than quality time, to be confessed rather than supported? After a very general mention of the benefits of "learning" and "information" or "staying in touch with granny," parents often have little more to say. They struggle to recall a range of good sites for their children. They spend a lot of time stopping them doing certain activities but much less time encouraging others. Despite all the hype about a digital future, just what children could really learn, what information can benefit them, or who they might communicate with online remains confused and confusing, mixed up with anxieties about risk, and lacking trusted signposts to quality resources or recognized criteria for judging the benefits of using different sites or apps. Parents say they would love to know of more imaginative sites that stretch and stimulate their child. They wish their child's school would do this, and some do—though many don't. For traditional media—think of children's books or films   parents could turn to librarians or children's bookshops or other trusted intermediaries to advise them, but in relation to the Internet, such intermediaries are lacking, or are driven by commercial interests (Livingstone, 2014b). As a result, children tend to visit a rather narrow range of sites that are either highly commercialized or made for people much older than they are (Ofcom, 2016).

Still, in some families, parents seek to "scaffold' or structure their child's learning. In some families, too, parents are themselves skilled and diverse users, far from the "digital immigrants" of the early days of the Internet, and so their children can learn just by being around them (Blum-Ross & Livingstone, 2016). But in some homes, parents are nervous of new technologies, using digital technologies as an occasion for reward or punishment rather than learning or creativity, and tending to impose restrictions on use rather than guiding children towards really beneficial or diversified activities. Many, too, tend to keep their own uses as separate from their children's, and so their children have little opportunity to pick up skills from them. Yet more and more, parents are getting the message from policy-makers that they should not simply impose rules but instead, find ways to share online experiences with their children, being supportive rather than anxious in the face of the problems that will inevitably occur. The differences across families could be regarded as a matter of personal choice, but concerns arise when systematic factors appear to structure these choices—with more educated or digitally skilled parents more likely to support their children's online opportunities and less privileged families tending to restrict more than enable their children's Internet use (Mascheroni, Livingstone, Dreier, & Chaudron, 2016).

For a small minority of children, parents pose a risk—both directly (for "at risk" children) and insofar as forms of family deprivation or vulnerability offline tend to increase children's vulnerability online. For these children, targeted strategies to strengthen protective factors or ameliorate risk factors are needed, and it is a particular problem that children's services have not always grasped the ways in which the Internet may compound risk for these children. For a further group of children, parents limit their Internet use as a result of lack of digital literacy, awareness of youthful needs, or fear of online risks. This is particularly evident in relation to the management of teenagers' sexual interests, for instance, when they turn to the Internet (and often, problematically, find online pornography), when in search of information regarding sexual identity and sexual advice that they cannot obtain elsewhere (Horvath, Alys, Massey, Pina, Scally, & Adler, 2013; Livingstone & Mason, 2015).

DIGITAL SKILLS AS MEDIATORS—WHY IS IT HARD TO GET THIS RIGHT?

For both children and parents, digital skills are crucial to maximizing online opportunities and minimizing risks, as well as to parental mediation of children's online activities (Livingstone, Ólafsson, Helsper, Lupiáñez-Villanueva, Veltri, & Folkvord, 2017). However, digital skills are not generally acquired easily or automatically—skills worth having require effort to learn, and there are gradations in skill from novice to expert (van Dijk & van Deursen, 2014). The pedagogic process of learning critical digital skills means that short-run interventions will rarely be sufficient, while embedding digital literacy more thoroughly in the school curriculum is a persistent challenge to policy and practice, and reaching parents, once they have finished education, is yet more challenging.

Indeed, many children are not yet gaining many of the benefits of the digital age because parents don't know how best to guide or direct them or because society doesn't yet provide enough varied, imaginative, yet child-friendly resources for them. Further, as research on the "ladder of opportunities" illustrates (Livingstone & Helsper, 2007; Ofcom, 2016), only a few children have the motivation and digital skills to create their own content or become the expressive creators, critics, or civic participants that advocates of children's rights and youth voice have hoped for in the digital age (Ito, Gutiérrez, Livingstone, Penuel, Rhodes, Salen, Schor, Sefton-Green, & Watkins, 2013), and those that do tend to be from more privileged backgrounds. After all, societal and educational resources available to motivate and support people to gain digital skills—as for other skills—are generally unequally distributed, and heavily dependent on prior educational achievements. The risk is that generic population programs will result in the rich getting richer, so targeting interventions to the "hard-to-reach" (themselves a highly heterogeneous group, so labeled for good reason) is vital if demanding.

Then, people can only learn what is learn-able. More like reading a book than riding a bike, digital literacy depends on legibility—and this is significantly a matter for industry provision, responsibility, and design. People will continue to struggle to locate what they need online, evaluate search results, decide what to trust, create their own content, or collaborate with others online so long as the technological interface is "hard to read" or "hard to use." Absence of quality markers, lack of user-friendliness, presence of financial scams and other abuses of trust, opaque and inflexible terms and conditions, difficulty of obtaining just-in-time advice, and a context of constant change—all these pose problems for what children and parents can actually learn. They also limit the transferability of skills learned in one domain to another.

Increasingly the digital environment not only affords the means of acting as an agent but is also the means by which others will do things to and for us, whether or not we are online and aware of their actions. Many children now have a digital footprint even if they post nothing about themselves. Nearly everyone is included in a digital database that has consequences for how the state and economy will treat them, whether or not they realize it. Figuring out how to fix things when they go wrong is becoming a highly skilled job, and the skills burden will increasingly be demanding of parents and children.

THE EMERGING BALANCE OF OPPORTUNITIES AND RISKS

EU Kids Online research found that, across seven European countries, fewer than half of children said it is "very true" that "there are lots of things on the Internet that are good for children of my age." Most important, fewer said this in 2014 than in 2010, especially in non-English speaking countries, and among girls and younger children (Livingstone, Mascheroni, Ólafsson, & Haddon, 2014). So if we are to inspire today's children to make wider and deeper use of the Internet, providers of online content and services will need to do more. In this respect, the UK is doing rather well, but could still do better. Half (56%) of UK children said it is "very true" and 40% say it is "a bit true" that there are lots of good things for them to do online; only 4% say the statement is "not true" (Livingstone, Haddon, Vincent, Mascheroni, & Ólafsson, 2014). Ofcom (2016) figures give us some hints as to why. Top sites visited by UK 6- to 14-year-olds in May 2016 include Google (ranked first, giving UK children access to many more language-compatible sites than are available for children from minority or small language communities across Europe) and BBC sites (providing excellent content for children that is the envy of many across Europe; see Steemers, 2016).

In terms of the risks, EU Kids Online found, across Europe from 2010 to 2014, that 9- to 16-year-olds' exposure to potentially negative forms of user-generated content (such as hate, pro-anorexic, or self-harm content) online became more common, and the percentage of children aged 11–16 who reported receiving nasty or hurtful ("cyberbullying") messages rose from 8% to 12% (Livingstone, Mascheroni, et al., 2014). Relatedly, the UK Safer Internet Centre (2016) reported that the prevalence of exposure to online hate has been building over recent years. By "hate," they refer to hostility or bullying messages that focus less on individuals and rather on a group (defined in terms of ethnicity, religion, sexuality, etc.). Their survey shows that, among 13- to 18-year-olds, 82% say they have witnessed online hate of some kind, and 24% have themselves been the target. At its worst, hate messages may indicate online extremism, and this is a new challenge for parents and schools—leading UK schools to now monitor students' online activities, and stimulating, in turn, a new market in developing software for tracking and checking that may, in turn, risk students' privacy and freedom of expression (Tucker & Vance, 2016). In their more everyday—but still potentially painful—incarnation, hate messages can be part of the taunting or cyberbullying that characterizes many children's school days, leading policy-makers to seek ways to help build children's digital resilience (Przybylski, Mishkin, Shotbolt, & Linington, 2014), since we can hardly wrap them in cotton wool, and nor can we turn the Internet off easily.

Putting these two stories together, EU Kids Online compared the balance of risks and opportunities online reported by children in Europe. It was striking to discover that in Denmark, Italy, and Romania (and less in Ireland), it is still the case that more opportunities are accompanied by more risk. But in Belgium, Portugal, and the UK, children are now benefiting from more online activities without an equivalent increase in risk (and, if anything, risk in these countries has declined). It is not, therefore, inevitable that increasing opportunities means increasing risk, so this seems a timely moment to call for more efforts to support and enhance children's online opportunities—to match the considerable (and in many ways successful) efforts already invested in reducing the risk of harm.

These points are all illustrated in Figure 2.1, which shows the positive correlation for children in seven European countries between online opportunities and risks in 2010 and the same correlation a few years later. While the overall picture remains similar, we might ask ourselves how some countries (e.g., UK and Italy) have managed to increase children's online opportunities without substantially adding to their risks, while other countries have increased children's opportunities only at the cost of also increasing their risks. How will societies reach this balance, in different countries and for different children, in the future? Some preliminary answers can be found in O'Neill (2014) and O'Neill, Staksrud and McLaughlin (2013).

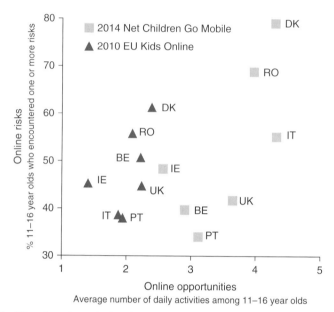

Figure 2.1   The changing relation between children's online risks and opportunities, by country
Note: Belgium (BE), Denmark (DK), Ireland (IE), Portugal (PT), Romania (RO), United Kingdom (UK). Source: Livingstone, Mascheroni, Ólafsson, & Haddon (2014).

EVIDENCE-BASED IMPLICATIONS FOR POLICY AND PRACTICE

Let me distil some of the main evidence regarding children's online risks and opportunities into six key points that policy-makers, parents, and practitioners would do well to remember.

THE IDEA OF INTERNET ACCESS AS A RIGHT

As children go online for longer, ever younger, and in more countries across the globe, the nature of Internet use is changing—more mobile and personalized, more embedded in everyday life, harder to supervise by parents yet ever more tracked by companies. As children see it, Internet access is now a right, and so, too, is digital literacy (Third, Bellerose, Dawkins, Keltie, & Pihl, 2014). They claim these as rights out of both enthusiasm and necessity—not so much because they value engaging with the Internet in its own right, but because they engage with the world *through* the Internet. And this they see as their route to wellbeing now and to better life chances in the future. However, not all online opportunities are automatically translated into demonstrable benefits for children, as more have gained access to hardware than to the knowledge of how to use it effectively or, indeed, to offline or online spaces where their voices can be heard.

ADDRESSING THE PARTICIPATION GAP

Children's enthusiasm alone is not enough. Even in the world's wealthier countries, most tend to use the Internet primarily as a medium of mass communication, and mainly receive (view, stream, download) content produced by others, most of it commercial. It is only the minority of children—more of them older and relatively privileged—who are genuinely creative or participatory in their online contributions. Many therefore fail to gain the benefits of the Internet, and don't have the chance to see their own experiences and culture reflected in the digital environment. This raises two challenges: (i) to media literacy educators, and the Ministries of Education that support them, to facilitate creative, embedded, ambitious uses of digital media, and (ii) to the creative industries, to build more imaginative and ambitious pathways for children to explore online and fewer walled gardens, sticky sites, and standardized content.

BEYOND DIGITAL NATIVES AND DIGITAL IMMIGRANTS

In the early days of the Internet, parents and teachers tended to feel disempowered as their children knew more about the Internet than they did. But as the Internet has become a familiar part of everyday life, the reverse generation gap (in which children's digital skills outweigh those of their parents') has tended to reduce, with parents and teachers increasingly able to share in and guide children's Internet use. Evidence shows that if parents are knowledgeable and confident in using the Internet themselves, they offer the kinds of guidance that children themselves accept as useful (and you can tell if that's the case by reflecting on whether your child spontaneously shows you, or asks for help with, what they're doing online). This means more authoritative guidance—sharing, discussing, setting some limits – and fewer top-down restrictions or bans that children are likely to evade. So efforts to build parents' digital literacy will help parents, children, and teachers in using the Internet wisely (and that, in turn, might help regulators who prefer not to intervene).

GETTING ONLINE RISK IN PERSPECTIVE

Society has become used to media headlines panicking about media risks online, and clinical and law enforcement sources do show that these are real and potentially deeply problematic for a small minority of children. But for the vast majority of children, the online world is no more risky—and perhaps even less risky—than the offline world. Reliable evidence suggests that the incidence of risk of harm for most internet-using children is relatively low—in Europe and the US, for instance, between 5% and 25% of adolescents have encountered online bullying, pornography, sexting, or self-harm sites.

RISK IS (ONLY) THE PROBABILITY OF HARM

Research also shows that online (and offline) risks are generally positively correlated—for example, children who encounter online bullying are more likely to see online pornography or meet new online contacts offline, and vice versa (Livingstone, 2013). Moreover, offline risk seems to extend (and sometimes get amplified) online, while online risk of harm is often felt (and made manifest) in offline settings. However, not all risk results in actual harm. Indeed, some evidence suggests that exposure to some degree of risk is, for many children, associated with the development of digital skills and coping strategies, as children build up resilience through their online experiences. Children are no more homogeneous than the adult population, so a host of factors as diverse as gender norms, family resources, and regulatory context all make a difference in the distribution of risk and harm, vulnerability, and resilience.

RISKS AND OPPORTUNITIES GO HAND IN HAND

The more often children use the Internet, the more digital skills and literacies they generally gain, the more online opportunities they enjoy and—the tricky part for policy-makers—the more risks they encounter. In short, the more, the more: So Internet use, skills, opportunities, and risks are all positively correlated. This means that policy efforts to promote use, skills, and opportunities are also likely to engender more risk. It also means that efforts to reduce risk (by policy-makers, parents, and other stakeholders) are likely to constrain children's Internet use, skills, and opportunities. This poses a conundrum that demands recognition and careful thought. How much risk is society ready to tolerate to support children's digital opportunities? And, most important, can governments and industry take action to redesign children's online experience so as to enhance their wellbeing and rights?

CONCLUSION

More and more children are using the media in more and more ways, including for work, shopping, education, and political participation. Media literacy is no longer a matter of simply engaging with the media but of engaging with society through the media. The more that the media mediate everything in society, the more vital it is that children—and their parents and teachers—are informed about and critically engaged with digital media, so that all are able to judge how digital media can be most effectively accessed, what's useful or misleading, how they are regulated, when they can be trusted, or what commercial or political interests are at stake. Such knowledge represents a moving target. At the same time that society becomes more dependent on the media, the media are themselves becoming more complex, fast-changing, commercial, and globalized. Such circumstances can too easily result in widening and unequal knowledge gaps within populations unless counter-measures are instituted in the interests of social justice (Stoilova, Livingstone, & Kardefelt-Winther, 2016). In short, without attention and resources devoted to media and digital literacy, society faces growing inequalities in terms of access, information and skills, more safety and security difficulties and abuses of personal data, and a narrowing of opportunity, understanding and critical judgment.

Who will take this agenda forward? Many organizations concerned with children's wellbeing offline are still taking their first steps to address children's experiences online, important as this is for professionals who work in schools, social work, health practice, and mental health services. Ideally, matters of online empowerment and online risk would be thoroughly embedded in all the regular services that work with children. But often such professionals say the Internet poses new technical challenges, and a pace of change they simply cannot manage, hence the continued need for policy regarding the online environment. Complicating matters, the online environment has, in effect, privatized much of children's lives—where they play, how they talk to their friends, how they research school work, what games they play. All this and more used to be in the public domain but now takes place on privately owned services where the terms of service, customer care policies, and forms of redress do not always consider the specific needs of children, and to which public bodies have little access or information.

REFERENCES

Blum-Ross, A., & Livingstone, S. (2016). *Families and screen time: Current advice and emerging research*. LSE Media Policy Project, Media Policy Brief 17. London: LSE. Retrieved from http://eprints.lse.ac.uk/66927/

Childwise (2016). *Childwise Monitor 20th anniversary report: Connected kids: How the internet affects children's lives now and into the future*. London: Childwise.

Croll, J. (2016). *Let's play it safe: Children and youths in the digital world*. ICT Coalition. Retrieved from www.ictcoalition.eu/gallery/100/REPORT_WEB.pdf

FOSI (Family Online Safety Institute) (2015). *Parents, privacy and technology use*. Washington, DC: FOSA. Retrieved from www.fosi.org/policy-research/parents-privacy-technology-use/

Horvath, M. A. H., Alys, L., Massey, K., Pina, A., Scally, M., & Adler, J. R. (2013). *"Basically … porn is everywhere": A rapid evidence assessment on the effects that access and exposure to pornography has on children and young people*. London:

Office of the Children's Commissioner for England. Retrieved from www.mdx. ac.uk/__data/assets/pdf_file/0026/48545/BasicallyporniseverywhereReport.pdf

Internet Matters (2015). *Pace of change: Research focused on how parents and children differ in their use of the internet*. London: Internet Matters. Retrieved from www .internetmatters.org/wp-content/uploads/2015/12/Internet_Matters_Pace_of_ Change_report-final_2.pdf

Ito, M., Gutiérrez, K., Livingstone, S., Penuel, B., Rhodes, J., Salen, K., Schor, J., Sefton-Green, J., & Watkins, C. (2013). *Connected learning: An agenda for research and design*. Irvine, CA: Digital Media and Learning Research Hub. Retrieved from http://dmlhub.net/wp-content/uploads/files/Connected_Learning_report.pdf

Livingstone, S. (2008). Taking risky opportunities in youthful content creation: Teenagers' use of social networking sites for intimacy, privacy and self-expression. *New Media & Society, 10*(3), 393–411. Retrieved from http://eprints.lse.ac.uk/27072/

Livingstone, S. (2013). Online risk, harm and vulnerability: Reflections on the evidence base for child internet safety policy. *ZER: Journal of Communication Studies, 18*, 13–28. Retrieved from www.ehu.eus/zer/hemeroteca/pdfs/zer35-01-livingstone.pdf

Livingstone, S. (2014a). Developing social media literacy: How children learn to interpret risky opportunities on social network sites. *Communications. The European Journal of Communication Research, 39*(3), 283–303. Retrieved from http://eprints.lse.ac.uk/62129/

Livingstone, S. (2014b). What does good content look like? Developing great online content for kids. In L. Whitaker (Ed.), *Children's media yearbook 2014* (pp. 66–71). Milton Keynes: The Children's Media Foundation. Retrieved from http://eprints.lse.ac.uk/62223/

Livingstone, S., Haddon, L., Vincent, J., Mascheroni, G., & Ólafsson, K. (2014). *Net children go mobile: The UK report. A comparative report with findings from the UK 2010 survey by EU Kids Online*. Milan, Italy: Net Children Go Mobile. Retrieved from http://eprints.lse.ac.uk/57598/

Livingstone, S., & Helsper, E. J. (2007). Gradations in digital inclusion: Children, young people and the digital divide. *New Media & Society, 9*(4), 671–696. Retrieved from http://eprints.lse.ac.uk/2768/

Livingstone, S., Kirwil, L., Ponte, C., & Staksrud, E. (2014) In their own words: what bothers children online? *European Journal of Communication. 29*(3):271–288. Retrieved from http://eprints.lse.ac.uk/62093/

Livingstone, S., & Mason, J. (2015). *Sexual rights and sexual risks among youth online: A review of existing knowledge regarding children and young people's developing sexuality in relation to new media environments*. Rome: eNACSO (European NGO Alliance for Child Safety Online). Retrieved from http://eprints.lse. ac.uk/64567/

Livingstone, S., Mascheroni, G., Ólafsson, K., & Haddon, L. (2014). *Children's online risks and opportunities: Comparative findings from EU Kids Online and Net Children Go Mobile*. London: EU Kids Online, LSE. Retrieved from http://eprints. lse.ac.uk/60513/

Livingstone, S., Ólafsson, K., O'Neill, B., & Donoso, V. (2012). *Towards a better internet for children: Findings and recommendations from EU Kids Online for the CEO Coalition*. London: EU Kids Online, LSE. Retrieved from http://eprints.lse. ac.uk/44213/

Livingstone, S., Ólafsson, K., Helsper, E. J., Lupiáñez-Villanueva, F., Veltri, G., & Folkvord, F. (2017). Maximizing opportunities and minimizing risks for children online: The role of digital skills in emerging strategies of parental mediation. *Journal of Communication*.

Livingstone, S., Palmer, T., with others (2012). *Identifying vulnerable children online and what strategies can help them*. Report of the seminar arranged by the UKCCIS Evidence Group, March. Retrieved from http://eprints.lse.ac.uk/44222/

Marsh, J., Plowman, L., Yamada-Rice, D., Bishop, J. C., Lahmar, J., Scott, F., Davenport, A., Davis, S., French, K., Piras, M., Thornhill, S., Robinson, P., & Winter, P. (2015). *Exploring play and creativity in pre-schoolers' use of apps: Final project report*. Retrieved from http://techandplay.org/tap-media-pack.pdf

Mascheroni, G., Livingstone, S., Dreier, M., & Chaudron, S. (2016). Learning versus play or learning through play? How parents' imaginaries, discourses and practices around ICTs shape children's (digital) literacy practices. *Media Education: Studies and Research, 7*(2), 261–280.

Mascheroni, G., Ponte, C., Garmendia, M., Garitaonandia, C., & Murray, M. F. (2010). Comparing media coverage of online risks for children in southern European countries: Italy, Portugal and Spain. *International Journal of Media and Cultural Politics, 6*(1), 25–44.

O'Neill, B. (2014). *Policy influences and country clusters. A comparative analysis of internet safety policy implementation*. London: EU Kids Online, LSE. Retrieved from http://eprints.lse.ac.uk/57247/

O'Neill, B., Staksrud, E., & McLaughlin, S. (Eds.) (2013). *Children and internet safety in Europe: Policy debates and challenges*. Göteborg: Nordicom.

Ofcom (2015). *Media lives: Wave 10 (2014) and ten year retrospective*. Retrieved from http://stakeholders.ofcom.org.uk/binaries/research/media-literacy/medialives10-2014/MediaLives10-2014.pdf

Ofcom (2016). *Children and parents: Media use and attitudes report*. London: Ofcom. Retrieved from www.ofcom.org.uk/research-and-data/media-literacy-research/children/children-parents-nov16

Przybylski, A. K., Mishkin, A., Shotbolt, V., & Linington, S. (2014). *A shared responsibility: Building children's online resilience*. London: Parent Zone. Retrieved from http://parentzone.org.uk/sites/default/files/VM%20Resilience%20Report.pdf

Steemers, J. (2016). *Policy solutions and international perspectives on the funding of public service media content for children: A report for stakeholders*. London: University of Westminster. Retrieved from https://camri.ac.uk/wp-content/uploads/2016/06/1.-UoW-final-14-June-1.pdf

Stoilova, M., Livingstone, S., & Kardefelt-Winther, D. (2016). Global Kids Online: Researching children's rights globally in the digital age. *Global Studies of Childhood, 6*(4), 455–466. doi:10.1177/2043610616676035

Third, A., Bellerose, D., Dawkins, U., Keltie, E., & Pihl, K. (2014). *Children's rights in the digital age: A download from children around the world* (2nd edition). Melbourne, VIC: Young and Well Cooperative Research Centre and UNICEF. Retrieved from www.unicef.org/publications/files/Childrens_Rights_in_the_Digital_Age_A_Download_from_Children_Around_the_World_FINAL.pdf

Tucker, J. W., & Vance, A. (2016). *School surveillance: The consequences for equity and privacy*. Alexandria, VA: National Association of State Boards of Education. Retrieved from www.nasbe.org/wp-content/uploads/Tucker_Vance-Surveillance-Final.pdf

UK Safer Internet Centre (2016). *Creating a better internet for all: Young people's experiences of online empowerment and online hate*. London: Safer Internet Centre. Retrieved from http://childnetsic.s3.amazonaws.com/ufiles/SID2016/Creating%20 a%20Better%20Internet%20for%20All.pdf

van Dijk, J. A. G. M., & van Deursen, A. J. A. M. (2014). *Digital skills, unlocking the information society*. Basingstoke: Palgrave Macmillan.

NOTES

1 Thanks to the EU Kids Online network, funded by the European Commission's (EC) Better Internet for Kids program, and the Parenting for a Digital Future project, funded by the MacArthur Foundation's Connected Learning Research Network. This chapter draws on ideas published on the blogs http://blogs.lse.ac.uk/ mediapolicyproject/ and www.parenting.digital and www.weforum.org/agenda/

2 For a continually updated summary of the UK evidence base relating to children's Internet safety, visit www.saferinternet.org.uk/research

3 Cyberbullying and Peer-Oriented Online Abuse

Andy Phippen

I've received Ask.fm questions telling me to drink bleach, hang myself etc…

The digital world presents many opportunities and benefits for our young people. In a single generation technology now provides them with the opportunities to find out anything they like, to interact and play games with people on the other side of the world, to create content and upload it for anyone to see and to connect with friends, family and other 'friends' (the distinction and quotes are deliberate) through social media via PCs, laptops and mobile devices. These interactions happen many, many times per day and I am sure we are all familiar with the sight of young people walking around their neighbourhoods looking not at the world around them but at the digital device they have in their hand. Clearly there are many benefits to this digital world – countless children tell me homework starts and finishes online these days, keeping in touch with friends and family is easier than ever and, certainly in my experience, young people's enthusiasm for technology can be transformed into lucrative careers.

However, for all of the benefits there are clearly risks associated with going online and using connected technologies, and these are being explored in depth throughout this book. When considering child protection and online technology, the focus can often lead to a perception of 'young person as victim, adult as offender'. Although this is clearly important and dealt with extremely well throughout this book, in this chapter I would like to explore a different focus of 'child safety' in the online world – that of peer abuse. With peer abuse we have a more complex child protection proposition – on the one hand there clearly still are offenders and victims, although there are less clear boundaries between who is an offender and who is a victim. From an offender's perspective, we cannot be sure that the person performing the abuse is aware of the

Online Risk to Children: Impact, Protection and Prevention, First Edition.
Edited by Jon Brown.

impact of his or her actions, or even if he or she views his or her actions as abusive in the first place. And from the view of the victim, does this victim know that he or she is experiencing abuse or that the behaviour he or she is being subjected to is unacceptable? In considering these issues, this chapter will present a number of different challenges and also explore the potential for solutions in which we have less of a clear-cut child protection perspective and in which exploration of offender motivations cannot so readily claim responsible action.

In exploring these issues I will draw primarily from my own experience working with young people about how technology affects their lives but I will also consider the wider discussion and observation about this field of 'online child safety.' I spend a lot of working life talking to young people about their use of technology, from Key Stage 1 (the UK education system's definition of education from ages 5–7) up to higher education. Generally speaking this will not be a 'planned' research project where as a researcher I establish a context to address a particular question. Generally these conversations emerge from other activities either in school or other youth settings. For example, in the last year I have carried out assemblies, classes and workshops with more than 2,000 young people across the country. The sorts of activities I have been involved with range from, for example, workshops as part of a 'collapsed timetable,' sex and relationship education days to assemblies on staying safe online to small-group activities talking to primary-aged children about how they use the Internet.

In addition to working with young people I often find that I am asked to work with adults, for example, parent sessions in schools talking about online safety, staff training and presentations and Q&A sessions with practitioners looking at the gulf between adult's perceptions on children safety and the reality of what it is like for young people to grow up in this digital world. As such, this 'ethnography' of young people and digital behaviours allows for an immersive and rich experience and, although it seems facile to say it, one in which I spend more time listening than I do talking. This in turn provides a very detailed 'data set' comprising transcripts, quotes and extensive field notes that illustrate the complexity of relationships in the online world and how interrelated all of these issues are.

Drawing from this work, this chapter will explore the issues concerning online peer abuse. The rationale for this is that this is where the majority of my conversations with young people reside – although we might, on some occasions, talk about predatory behaviour, 'stranger danger' and similar, it is far more likely that an issue about 'people being mean' or 'I was asked by a boy/girl in class to do something I was uncomfortable with' will arise rather than the classic perspective on online child protection.

In exploring the issues concerning peer abuse, I will be drawing extensively on the conversations I have with young people specifically on sexting. Although this might, at first glance, seem to be a very narrow focus, it enables an exploration of wider cultural interaction and shows how technology presents challenges for communication and potentially normalise what we might view as unacceptable if we remove the digital element of the interaction. However, before exploring this phenomenon in depth, I also want to look at approaches to online child protection from the policy perspective and, to start, from the view of a parent.

PERSPECTIVES ON ONLINE CHILD PROTECTION FROM PARENTS

> I am so grateful my girls are sensible and level headed. They don't need to be advised how to be safe on the Internet as they aren't stupid.

This quote is taken from a parent after her children had attended an assembly I had done at a school in the southwest of the UK. I had been asked by the school to do two assemblies, one for years 7 and 8 looking at the basics of social media and the silly things people do on it, along with some slightly more serious topics such as online harassment, and then another for the years 9 and 10 exploring these issues in more depth and also looking at more 'adult' topics such as sexting and adult content. This parent had two girls in year 7, and she was upset that her girls attended an assembly she considered to be inappropriate for children their age. The quote is taken from a much longer complaint that seemed to take issue on a number of levels:

- Her girls were too young to hear about the subject matter in the assembly.
- Her girls didn't use social media and children of that age that did 'deserved everything they got.'
- Her girls might be in some way distressed by hearing about the 'morally wrong' behaviours carried out by people who did use social media.
- The school should focus on academic, not social, education.
- As the comment mentions, her daughters do not need to hear about staying safe online because they are not stupid.

Interestingly, although the comments made by this parent were unusual in that she believed isolation was a sound approach to online child protection, the concerns and beliefs expressed are not unusual in my conversations with adults and illustrate one of the commonly held beliefs by adults – namely that online abuse happens only to those who engage with the online world, and therefore if they keep away they will be fine.

However, an issue I immediately take with this is that it assumes that 'online' is something that can be contained, yet it fails to appreciate the diversity of digital communication and also how we build resilience from an early age rather than dealing with issues in a reactive way. I have also visited many primary schools and the ethos at some is that there is no reason to talk about Facebook and other forms of social media with the pupils because 'they shouldn't be on it'. As a counter to this I would draw on the wisdom of a 14-year-old girl I spoke to about where online safety should be delivered in the curriculum, and her views on her primary school whose leadership thought they didn't have to address online safety education. Her response was simply:

> 'It's like saying we shouldn't have to do sex education until we're actually having sex.'

Returning to the opening quote in this section, my response to the teacher who shared this 'complaint' was twofold. First, how does this parent know her children don't use social media? I have spoken with many young people who say they have signed up to services and platforms and are not telling their parents because they know they will be told off/challenged/have the account removed. Second, and perhaps more important, regardless of what the girls get up to, how can she prevent an unsolicited message or abuse in the same way the parent might wish to prevent abuse in the playground. To extend the playground metaphor, the girls might be very sensible and well behaved but unless they are removed from the playground or placed in a different playground from everybody else, how can the parent ever ensure they will be free from abuse? Surely a better approach is to say, 'OK, I know you won't do this, but some will, so you need to be aware this sort of thing goes on, and I want you to tell me if something happens to you.'

I have spoken to many teenagers about whether they would turn to a parent, or indeed a teacher, if, for example, they were asked to send someone an indecent photograph of themselves or, as is sometimes the case an unsolicited indecent photograph of someone else. Invariably they say there is no way they'd mention this to an adult and the rationale is usually the same (and a recurring theme we will return to in this chapter) and that is 'I don't want to be judged.' Even when we explore this issue further and they realise if they have received such a message with no encouragement on their part, it is not their fault if they receive such a request or content, they still say they wouldn't tell a parent. The fear that telling a parent if this sort of thing happens will result in them getting told off or, in a worst case, have their digital technology (mobile, tablet, etc.) confiscated.

However, this type of concern is certainly not just something perpetuated by parents. A facet of online safety worthwhile of further exploration is the current policy perspectives concerning this topic since April 2012 of the UK government administration as they reinforce the belief that technological problems (or perceived technological problems) should be resolved with the use of technology too and that, with these protection mechanisms in place, we can ensure child safety online.

POLICY RESPONSES AND 'PREVENTION' MECHANISMS

> The fact is that the growth of the Internet as an unregulated space has thrown up two major challenges when it comes to protecting our children.

This comment comes from a speech that David Cameron, the former UK Prime Minister, gave in July 2013 on online child protection. This section explores his speech in the wider context of policy change concerning this area and how this demonstrates a particular attitude towards online child protection. This is not intended to be a critique of the policy direction, more a reflection of responses to social matters that are seen to be facilitated via digital technology and also to further understand where comments such as the one in the previous section by the mother originate.

The current policy position from the UK government has evolved over a number of years, arguably stemming from the *Byron Review* (Byron, 2008), which was the first UK-government commissioned report on child online safety (albeit by the previous, Labour, government). In this report Tanya Byron called for 'better regulation' and a self-regulating industry that would adhere to codes of practise for child online safety by which they could be independently assessed and, if they failed to meet the code, risk reputational and potentially financial damage. However, from 2010 onwards the government policy approach, which was initially looking at self-regulation, seemed to refocus from the broad approaches to online safety detailed in the *Byron Review* towards a specific aspect of protection, one that focussed entirely on content control.

The whole policy drive, supported in part by the media in the UK, has aimed to place pressure on Internet service providers (ISPs) to ensure that young people cannot gain access to 'inappropriate content' – this being such content as pornography, gambling, 'hate' sites, and similar. The policy gained a lot of support from some parts of the UK press, with headlines such as 'Children grow up addicted to online porn sites: Third of 10-year-olds have seen explicit images' (*MailOnline*, 2013) supporting the need for industry to do more to make this happen.

Clearly this is a concern and something that needs to be addressed but these headlines do nothing to help the debate. When picking apart these statistics it becomes apparent that they come from a very small study, and it is unclear by what we mean by 'explicit.' These statistics do not reflect my own experience of talking with many primary-aged children. Although I, of course, do not walk into a school and ask all of the children in a year 6 class to put up their hands if they've seen pornography I do explore what they believe people are concerned about them seeing online and what sort of content has caused upset among their peers. I will return to this further on in the chapter but what I would say now is that very few children of this age have even mentioned pornography (or 'rude pictures') as content they have either come across or voluntarily access.

The pornography debate is a complex one and the research on its influence on children, and adults, is equally difficult. The recent, excellent review of the influence of pornography (Horvath, Alys, Massey, Pina, Scally, & Adler, 2013) for the Office of the Children's Commissioner came to a number of conclusions (for example, that those who commit violent sexual assaults often have viewed violent pornography), but it also quite clearly stated there is a lot we still do not know (for example, whether accessing violent pornography causes consumers to commit violent sexual acts). The other issue with this debate is that from a government perspective it seems you either supported their plans or 'want to let children see pornography.' Again their binary approaches to debate are not helpful. There are very few people in this field who would happily say that they don't believe pornography has any impact whatsoever on young people and they should be free to access it. Certainly from my own conversations with teens many, both girls and boys, are concerned about too much access, desensitisation, issues of disrespect, unrealistic expectations, body image, and so on.

However, to suggest that filtering is a solution to these complex challenges is concerning and relates back to the mother's previous comments about how adults approach prevention and control of content. We are looking to technology to solve these problems because the perception is that technology causes these problems. Yet how much technology can actually do is limited. Indeed, in the *Byron Review* a comment was made that heavily filtered access in schools (schools have struggled with the filtering issue for well over 10 years now) is actually counterproductive. And although they will certainly be effective and prevent some content, they work by either blocking at a web address level (for example, making www.pornhub.com inaccessible) or by keyword, matching site content to make a 'decision' about the sort of content therein. For example, 'gay,' 'cock,' or 'sex' are all words a filter would look for.

The choice of these three words is deliberate because for all of these there is an ambiguity of meaning – without context it is difficult to say for sure whether these words relate to inappropriate content or something such as sexuality, sex and relationship education or even ornithology. Yet these are the choices the filter has to make and on a lot of occasions these decisions will be incorrect and may even be preventing access to useful content (for example sex education sites).

The filtering 'debate' provides further evidence that for some of the adult population *content* is the key issue and *prevention* is the solution. The fact is this was a policy approach looking to technology to solve a social problem. This is not to say that such approaches aren't useful – certainly there is some benefit in placing technical countermeasures in place to prevent younger children from accidentally accessing content. However, issues of overblocking and bypassing controls mean that they do not even provide a solution to the content problems they are trying to address.

As many teens tell me, 'porn sites' are only one route to accessing adult material; there are many others, such as those that show up on social media sites, shared via mobiles, self-generated, and so on. These things are complex and not solved with attempted prevention. However, they also fail to acknowledge that young people are not passive observers in their online lives – although content can present some issues, these are people immersed in the online world as an extension of their social lives. They are not just consuming, there are interacting, and as a result prevention of access to specific content is just the tip of the iceberg in addressing online child protection.

The remainder of this chapter explores this complexity through conversations with young people, focussing on aspects of peer-oriented abuse and how prevention is not a solution. It draws extensively from countless conversations with young people and also initially a data set from the South West Grid for Learning,[1] one of the leading eSafety charities in the UK, that has been running a survey in schools since 2012 over the last three years asking young people basic questions about internet access, use of technology and aspects concerning interaction. In total this survey, recently published (Phippen, 2016), collects the opinions of more than 8,000 young people from the age of 7 to 18 (the majority being between 7 and 13). Although a lot of the results are outside of the scope of this analysis, there is useful supporting evidence from the research to underpin some of the points coming from conversations with young people.

GROWING UP IN THE ONLINE WORLD

> Well I've been sent a rude picture on my tablet, been paedophiled before and received bad comments on a few of my videos and instagram by some idiots but its all ok now and I'm getting nothing bad anymore I'm very wary nowadays.

This comment comes from a 12-year-old boy. It's a lot to take in and provides, within a few words, a great deal of colour to illustrate growing up in the online world. By the age of 12 this young person has been sent inappropriate content, contacted by a predator (who approached him on a gaming site and tried to move him into a private online space, which, thankfully, was declined and reported) and abused by trolls who didn't like the content he had created and posted in public spaces online. The comment very clearly shows the complexity of online life, the potential exposure to harm and also the resilience of someone who can come through such abuse unscathed. He was a very easy-going, relaxed young person who loved being online and gained so many positives from this, he could deal with, and to a certain extent shrug off, the negatives. Nevertheless, he was someone who had developed resilience from having to deal with negativity online.

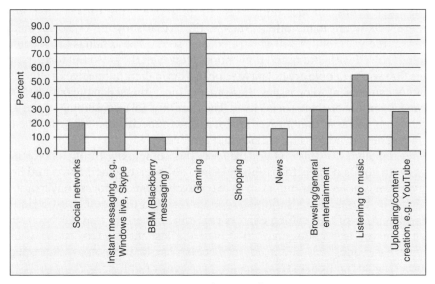

Figure 3.1   KS2 pupils (*n* = 1,500) online activities

But what this comment also shows is that online abuse is complex, can come from multiple channels and cannot be prevented if one is to fully engage with the online world. When looking at the South West Grid for Learning (SWGfL) survey data (Figure 3.1) for Key Stage 2 children aged 8 to 11) more than 80% are *engaged* in online gaming and about 30% are already *engaged* with content creation. It is clear that even at this young age being online is not a passive experience and with this engagement comes the risk of harm or upset.

However, if we initially return to the issue of content, within the survey data we do pose the question, 'Have you ever seen anything online that has upset you?' Although there are many responses to this question (about 25% of KS2 children say they have seen something online that has been upsetting), the following examples show the breadth of content that might cause upset:

- 'Swearing'
- 'People being mean'
- 'Videos where animals get hurt'
- 'Upsetting adverts'

In these four statements we see a range of issues – from people generally just being abusive to the range of content that causes upset. Animal abuse is mentioned a lot in the comments – there are many examples in the survey of young people being upset as a result of seeing animal cruelty, from postings from charities hoping to solicit money to 'gross out' images posted by individual intended to shock through to mainstream media clips from natural history programmes. Again, reflecting on how we use technology to 'prevent' access to this sort of material, what would be the cut-off point in prevention? If we are saying a programme such as David Attenborough's *Life Story* can cause distress to a child, should this be filtered, too?

Interaction on gaming also arises frequently in the comments, generally as a result of abuse from other gamers:

- 'On a game, and then somone said to me "fuck off."'
- 'Someone said on binweevils they would chop my head off.'
- 'Minecraft, some one said I was gay when I love my dad.'
- 'They called me "you f****** quitting p***."'

Another interesting example was a comment that was initially confusing:

- 'A project on the Victorians'

But this was explained in more detail by the responder who was asked to do some homework on Queen Victoria's family and was searching for information on her husband (Prince Albert) and retrieved some images they were not expecting. Although Prince Albert is indeed the name of Queen Victoria's husband, it is also the term for a genital piercing. This is an interesting point because with some sort of technical intervention this could have been prevented – with a 'safe search' option enabled on the search engine the explicit images would not have been retrieved yet clearly in this young person's home this wasn't the case. Which does illustrate that even when technical interventions *can* be put in place, often they are not.

However, two comments stand out because they illustrate distress caused by something no technical intervention could solve:

- 'When my dad told me on Facebook he didn't want to see me anymore.'
- 'A picture of my baby brother Noah who I don't live with.'

These both show upset caused by family conflict – although the delivery of the distressing comment or image was online, these are things that no level of filter or technical intervention could prevent. These are social interactions that have extended into the online world, which is frequently the case now that social discourse is underpinned through social media platforms. Again, if we reflect on a preventative strategy for this, it seems unlikely that a technical solution could stop this sort of thing happening. Indeed it is unlikely that any preventative approach would put a stop to this sort of social discourse.

However, perhaps the clearest illustration of this is when we 'word cloud' all responses from the Key Stage 2 respondents. A word cloud is simply a visual representation of textual data that shows larger-type words the more frequently they appear; Figure 3.2 shows a word cloud from all of the comments (about 1,100 comments in total):

Figure 3.2   Word cloud of comments from KS2 children about what upsets
them online

Interestingly if we compare this with the responses from Key Stage 4 (ages
14 to 16) children, there is not a huge amount of difference with the focus (see
Figure 3.3).

Clearly once again people are a major cause of upset for these young people.
However, it is interesting to see the significance of bullying in Figure 3.2 compared to Figure 3.3. For KS2 children, although there are plenty of examples
given that one might consider to be bullying, the term doesn't really register
with many that age; it is only when they are older it becomes recognised as
such. It is also interesting to note that the content that has caused upset for
KS4 children is as diverse at that from those in KS2.

Figure 3.3   Word cloud of comments from KS4 children about what upsets
them online

When reflecting on my conversations with young people about online abuse, what was interesting was that although 'cyberbullying' was a general term used in a lot of the discussion, the reality was peer abuse manifested in many different forms – aggression and threats of violence, abusive language, sexual discourse and harassment, homophobia, and so on – and across a variety of online social interactions. In the next section this is explored more in context of the online phenomenon of sexting.

THE 'CULTURE' OF SEXTING

Popular girls don't sext.

Sexting – the self-generation and distribution of explicit images to either one or more recipients – is a modern phenomenon that is rarely out of the media (see, for example, *MailOnline*, 2012, 2014a). Although this is not a practise exclusively carried out by teenagers, this seems to be where the majority of the media's attention lies. I am often asked by journalists, 'Why do you think teenagers sext?' And my usual, somewhat facetious response, is, 'Why wouldn't they?'

I find the question strange – why would teens not emulate something clearly practised by celebrities and the wider adult population? They have, at their disposal the technology to take a photograph of themselves and send it to someone of their choosing in a very swift and efficient manner. Has this sort of behaviour not been practised for a long time – the popularity of Polaroid cameras in the 1970s and 1980s were, in part, because of the opportunity to take 'private' images with them without the embarrassment of having to take a film to the developers? However, what was missing from that particular scenario was the easy means to reproduce and distribute such a photograph. This is certainly the case now, and this is what makes sexting such a risky practise. Although, perhaps it would be better to clarify the risk in sexting – not so much the sending of a self-produced image but the unauthorised redistribution of the image either by the recipient or others.

In this section we don't just reflect on the practise of sexting in itself but on how it becomes a means for abuse and how the abuse manifests. Again, this exploration is intended to illustrate the complexities of the connected world young people grow up in and how preventative measures are rarely the solution.

This complexity is brought into focus by the comment at the start of this section – 'Popular girls don't sext.' This was said to me by a 14-year-old boy in a school I visited where we were discussing whether online technologies make society increasingly sexist. In exploring what he meant by this simple, four-word sentence, he elaborated by explaining that why would a popular girl need to do such a thing? People do it because they want a boyfriend or girlfriend and believe the way to achieve this is to send someone they are attracted to such an image. This would not be needed by someone already popular, some-one who is already likely to have a boyfriend or girlfriend and who wouldn't need to promote him- or herself in order to get attention. This is a fundamental issue concerning a lot of my discussions with young people about technology and relationships: A lot of behaviours are merely underpinning a desire to be attractive and to have a relationship with someone.

Sexting is something I have been exploring with young people for a number of years: we conducted some early research into the phenomenon back in 2009 (Phippen, 2009), mainly as a reaction to many school visits in which a senior leader would say he or she had an 'incident' related to sexting and wasn't sure what to do about it. The early work was survey based and reached about 1,000 14- to 16-year-olds in which a number of questions were posed. Although we won't explore these issues in detail in this chapter, one statistic does stand out: When responders were asked whether they know anyone who had 'sexted,' 40% said they had. What is interesting is if I quote this statistic to young people of a similar age now, they are surprised at how low that per-centage is.

Exploring these subsequent conversations (some of which were dissemi-nated in a report for the National Society for the Prevention of Cruelty to Children (NSPCC) [Phippen, 2012]), what is clear is not that the entire teen-aged population is doing this but that many are aware that is goes on and there are a few in each year group usually engaged in such practises. Although descriptions of those engaged in sexting (to the knowledge of others in the year) are generally not complimentary, their behaviours do relate back to the description from the 14-year-old – these are people who are attention seeking, they are trying to be liked and they are trying to be popular. However, the belief is also that perhaps they are not going about it in the correct manner.

One of the more shocking things, from my own perspective of a researcher in his forties with children of his own, I find in my discussions with young peo-ple is how mundane this sort of thing is – yes, people do it, and, yes, these images often get sent far beyond the intended recipient, and sometimes the person in the photograph will receive abuse as a result, but is it really that big a deal? The sense seems to be that an incident 'gets old really quickly,' meaning that any shame, or resultant abuse, will pass quickly. It is interesting, however, to observe that although many teenagers are very aware of Amanda Todd and her treatment, they just can't empathise with it.

Abuse invariably centres on the person in the image and raises an interest-ing observation on how sexting is reflecting wider blame culture, something we will return to further on in this chapter. In the majority of cases, but certainly not all, the victim will be female and subject to abuse from males and females within her peer group. Having discussed this with many young people, the focus of abuse seems to be on the victim being a 'slut' for sending such an image (generally the view of female abusers). When challenged on this, young people will happily acknowledge that they will probably know others who have done such things and, in some cases, abusers will have also engaged in such practises, but the victim's mistake is she got 'caught out.' Sometimes girls tell me they think that the victim will be abused because she is getting attention from boys that the bullies would like themselves, so jealousy is a rationale for conducting abuse. On a number of occasions I have also had young people say they will join in with the abuse because it will detract from the potential for them to be subject to bullying. In joining in with the pack, those who are less popular, or have been subject to abuse themselves, can divert attention from themselves onto another victim.

I have also explored why it is unlikely that the recipient of the image, who is most likely to have passed the image to others, will be subject to abuse, given the lack of respect and breakdown of trust such a resend would demonstrate. This is generally met with some confusion from those I speak with, as though the person who has sent the image further has done nothing wrong, and if the sender didn't want others to see the image, he or she should not have sent it in the first place. It is rare that anyone will acknowledge the fact that further distribution is a betrayal of trust or done for cruel motives. It is also interesting to note that in the majority of cases, given the further distribution is carried out by a male, some reflect that this is 'just the sort of thing' that boys will do, again reinforcing there is nothing wrong with it. In general (although certainly not always) boys who send an image that is then distributed further will receive far less abuse than girls who do the same. The view seems to be that for boys this is just 'banter' and they will shrug off any embarrassment far more quickly than girls. Although it is also acknowledged that a male is far less likely to be subjected to prolonged abuse for similar reasons – the impact of the abuse is less likely to be significant; therefore, it's not worth carrying out.

One other facet of the sexting phenomenon that demonstrates something of a twisted logic concerning this issue is the fact that males are, however, far more likely to ask a girl for an image than the other way around. Therefore in a number of cases it is likely that a girl sends an image in the first place only as a result of being asked to do so. Yet they will receive the abuse if and when the recipient sends it out further. In addition, in exploring the nature of peer abuse and how technology might facilitate this, we have an interesting acceptability of these sorts of requests. I have spoken on many occasions with girls who feel pressure to take and send images and, in some cases, have experienced abuse ('you're frigid,' etc.) as a result of not sending such. However, when we explore this, they also see nothing wrong with being asked to do this sort of thing, which very much does illustrate a change in attitude facilitated by technology. When presented with the concept of someone being asked to send an explicit image in a face-to-face meeting, for example, during a casual chat in a work environment, most young people have said that is unacceptable with some saying anyone who says such a thing should be sacked (generally the view being that this is sexual harassment). However, when challenged on the difference between this scenario and an online one when, for example, someone receives a text message requesting an explicit image, they generally agree that this *should* be unacceptable but for some reason it isn't. In unpicking this understanding we might observe that young people believe sexual harassment is acceptable only if delivered via online technology.

To further illustrate gender differences, there is also a particularly male aspect to one type of sexting, and that is the volunteered image, sent to impress or 'court' a potential partner. Typically a male carries this out and, I am told, although these might be torso or 'six-pack' images, the image might also be a self-generated photograph of the sender's genitals. It seems in a number of discussions I have had with teenaged males that they are aware of peers who do this as part of the courtship ritual – they believe this is an appropriate way to embark on a relationship with someone! A quote I often use, from a young adult working in a male-oriented workplace, further illustrates the gender imbalance about the sexting phenomenon:

> 'I work on refineries and many men cheat on there and due to me being the only under 40 female on site for 800 guys many flirted with me sending pics of cocks.'

The word in this quote I would take most issue with is 'flirting.' Again, this highlights the difference between behaviour conducted online and that done offline or in a face-to-face setting. I am sure that this individual would not be using the term 'flirting' if males were walking up to her in person and exposing themselves, but because it is delivered to her mobile she is, in some way, legitimising the behaviour of her colleagues, even though is it clearly not flirting, but sexual harassment.

A particularly concerning aspect of my discussions is that it is very unlikely a young person subjected to this sort of abuse would turn to an adult for help. As discussed, when asked who they would turn to for help, the vast majority of young people said their peers. The idea that an adult might help, or even understand, was lost on a lot of young people who felt that if they were to mention such abuse to an adult, they would be 'judged' as having done something wrong. This concern was amplified when exploring who to turn to if one was a victim of a sexting image being distributed further – the vast majority of young people I have spoken to have said there would be no way an adult could help with this sort of incident.

A recent case that gained significant media coverage also raised the wider issues concerning legitimised sexual harassment and abuse. In this case (*MailOnline*, 2014b) a drunken student got a friend to film him slapping a girl's face with his genitals, and the video was subsequently shared. Thankfully in this case the victim did recognise this for what it was – sexual assault – and the offender received a prison term. However, in exploring this with my own students, it is interesting to observe that a number view this amusing banter and the accusation of assault an overreaction. It is also interesting to note that there isn't a clear gender split with this view – as many females as males expressed this opinion.

This demonstrates the fact that sexting is not a distinct practise; it is part of a wider shift illustrating how technology normalises unacceptable behaviour and cultural influences legitimise what we might once have felt to be offensive. Sexting is not a secluded phenomenon; it is part of growing up in a connected age in which technology enables lives to be expressed on a public stage and supported through wider influences such as celebrity, and the cult of personality and the resultant abuse also relates to cultural influences wider than just the peer group. The following section explores this in more detail.

WIDER INFLUENCES

She had it coming to her.

I have often used the Steubenville case in the United States – in which a drunken 16-year-old girl passed out at a party and was subsequently stripped and sexually assaulted by two males who were subsequently arrested and jailed – as a discussion topic with older teens to explore attitudes towards gender and respect. We explore the public response to the fact that the two who carried out the assault were charged and imprisoned – where most of the focus is not on their unacceptable behaviour but on how they had made 'a mistake' and it was a shame that they were imprisoned.

On three separate occasions, young females have expressed that 'she had it coming to her.' These views have been made by teenaged girls in different parts of the country and from different social classes. Although this is certainly not the view of the majority of young people I have discussed this with, it is concerning that the same opinion has been expressed a number of times. In unpicking their rationale for saying this, on each occasion girls have said that although the behaviour of the males was unacceptable, the girl should not have gotten into the position that she could have this happen to her. As I was told in one session, 'you shouldn't get that drunk at a party unless you have a friend to look after you; otherwise, you should expect this sort of thing to happen.'

If this is the culture in which our young people are growing up, is it any wonder that they develop strange views on courtship, 'acceptable' harassment and victim blaming. When we explore sexting and similar behaviours in isolation we will always fail to understand the motivations and rationales for engaging in such practise.

In this chapter we have explored the nature of online children protection with a focus on peer abuse, its nature and young peoples' responses to it. In doing so, we have initially put forward the proposal that it is people, not technology, that causes upset online, and that although we can clearly show that growing up in today's online environment makes it likely that young people will see the sorts of language, images and interactions they would have been unlikely to experience so prevalently in the previous, disconnected world, we can also show that technology does not solve these problems.

From exploring sexting, we can see that it is not just those who engage in such practises who might be affected – this is a generation that expects to see at least a few explicit images of peers as they progress through their secondary school years. Although, our immediate reaction might be to try to stop this sort of thing happening, is it not better to acknowledge that it does happen and try to understand why? As we bring this chapter to a conclusion we will explore, again through discussions with young people, what might be good approaches to 'child protection' based on the aspects of abuse we have presented.

ADDRESSING PEER ABUSE

When are you coming back?

Issues related to the abuse we have explored have illustrated that although online environments might be the places where abuse is delivered, the nature of the abuse can vary and really does not show anything particularly novel as a result of the technology involved. Within this chapter we have explored various issues concerning the nature of abuse:

- Self-esteem
- Attention seeking
- Legitimisation
- Normalisation
- Peer validation
- Bullying and victimisation

With all of these things we can see issues of empathy, peer respect and a lack of emotional intelligence playing a part – a lot of the types of abuse we have explored arise from a lack of thought about the impact of actions, and the technological delivery of a lot of the abuse can extend the disconnect between abuser and victim. In these cases, although some technological approaches might provide some level of intervention, such as monitoring to identify potentially abusive communication, the heart of these issues falls far beyond digital intermediations.

This is also something I have spent a lot of time discussing with young people: as mentioned at the start of the chapter, young people see peer abuse as a far more significant concern than access to inappropriate content. The quote at the start of this section is something I hear from a lot of the young people when I visit their schools and is an indication of the frustration they feel in talking about these concerns – essentially this is not something that forms part of their education. I often find that, after an hour or so talking with young people on all manner of online-related topics, they will say 'we never get to talk about this at school.' Which is of course a worry when these are the sorts of things that are very central to growing up in this digital, connected age.

I was recently visiting a school I work with frequently to do a session on technology and sexism. After an hour's enjoyable, amusing and passionate debate among the young people in the session, focussing mainly on how people are braver behind the safety barrier of their mobile or online technology and why victims are abused as a result of things such as sexting, I mentioned to the group that I was visiting the Houses of Parliament the next day. I said I was going there to meet a peer to talk about the sort of things we'd been discussing. I asked them what I should tell the peer so that they might do something to improve the lives of young people. I took one comment from a 15-year-old girl with me:

'Tell them to give us better sex education.'

Effective sex, relationship and social education are clearly where young people see these issues reside and they are very keen to have the opportunity to *discuss* how technology affects their lives, issues such as cyberbullying, sexting and so forth. How is it that young people can see how these online abuse practises have a place in effective and up-to-date sex and relationship education, yet those who define education policy do not? Currently in the UK there is no compulsory requirement to deliver any sexual and relationship education in schools aside from the biology of reproduction, and personal, social and health education (PSHE) has little national coordination. Without this coordination, it is down to schools to decide whether or not to deliver these topics and, in my experience, the education of young people can vary greatly between schools. The sorts of topics in need of discussion should start at an early age – respect and boundaries are not things that cannot be grasped at, for example, Key Stage 1 or 2, and they form the core of many of the issues explored in this chapter.

Although we, the adult population, might see a difference between young peoples' online and offline needs and experiences, this is an artificial distinction for young people themselves. They are not growing up partly in the online world and partly in the offline world – they are growing up in an environment that has both online and offline elements, and put simply, it is just 'life' to them. And although there are clearly many positives to the connected experiences they have, and they are, arguably, the first generation to grow up in a wholly internet age, they have to learn that, rather than being told 'be good and bad things won't happen,' 'you might experience these things, and you don't have to put up with them because they're unacceptable.' From my experiences some of the most surprising things for me is talking to young people who can see nothing wrong with asking someone for an explicit image. This doesn't mean they are bad people or in some way growing up uncontrolled and deviant. It does, however, mean that they are experiencing these situations with their peers and have never had the opportunity to learn about the implications of these actions or the impact that words (or abuse) can have on individuals.

Young people are asking for the opportunity to talk about these issues at school, but we are not providing them with safe, non-judgemental environments in which to do this. Yet we seem to assume they should magically know that such behaviour is unacceptable and wrong and that, if we can control their use of technology, we will ensure they never behave in such a way. We can learn far more about how to address these issues from listening to young people, rather than judging them on their mistakes as they grow up.

REFERENCES

Byron, T. (2008). *Safer children in a digital world: The report of the Byron Review*. London, UK: Dept. for Children, Schools and Families and the Dept. for Culture, Media and Sport.

Cameron, D. (2013). *The internet and pornography: Prime Minister calls for action*. Retrieve January 2015 from https://www.gov.uk/government/speeches/the-internet-and-pornography-prime-minister-calls-for-action

Horvath, M. A. H., Alys, L., Massey, K., Pina, A., Scally, M., & Adler, J. R. (2013). *'Basically ... porn is everywhere': A rapid evidence assessment on the effects that access and exposure to pornography has on children and young people*. London, UK: Office of the Children's Commissioner for England.

MailOnline. (2012). Sex texts epidemic: Experts warn sharing explicit photos is corrupting children. Retrieved January 2015 from http://www.dailymail.co.uk/news/article-2246154/Sex-texts-epidemic-Experts-warn-sharing-explicit-photos-corrupting-children.html#ixzz3RKpm6QJt

MailOnline. (2013). Children grow up addicted to online porn sites: Third of 10-year-olds have seen explicit images. Retrieved January 2015 from http://www.dailymail.co.uk/news/article-2131799/Children-grow-addicted-online-porn-sites-Third-10-year-olds-seen-explicit-images.html

MailOnline. (2014a). Fury as former Tory minister whose naked selfies were made public says HE felt 'mentally raped.' Retrieved January 2015 from http://www.dailymail.co.uk/news/article-2833016/Having-sexting-messages-public-like-mentally-raped-claims-ex-Tory-minister-Brooks-Newmark.html#ixzz3RKqdRVQT

MailOnline. (2014b). Student jailed for slapping a sleeping woman in the face with his penis while a friend filmed it on his phone. Retrieved January 2015 from http://www.dailymail.co.uk/news/article-2803524/Student-jailed-slapping-sleeping-woman-face-penis-friend-filmed-phone.html#ixzz3RKspE0RF

Phippen, A. (2009). *Sharing personal images and videos among young people*. Sowton, Exeter, UK: South West Grid for Learning & University of Plymouth, UK. Retrieved January 2015 from http://www.swgfl.org.uk/ Staying-Safe/Sexting-Survey

Phippen, A. (2012). *Sexting: An exploration of practices, attitudes and influences*. Retrieved January 2015 from http://www.nspcc.org.uk/preventing-abuse/research-and-resources/sexting-focus-groups/

Phippen, A. (2016). *Children's online behaviour and safety: Policy and rights challenges*. London, UK: Palgrave.

NOTE

1   Retrieved January 2015 from http://www.swgfl.org.uk/

4 Offender Behaviour

Helen C. Whittle and Catherine Hamilton-Giachritsis

Since the 1990s, increasing attention has been devoted to the issue of child sexual abuse in society. Although figures suggest that online offending continues to contribute to a relatively small proportion of all child sex offending (Elliott, 2016), online sex offending against children and young people is a substantial global problem; since 2009 more than 1,900 offenders have been identified by Interpol (2013). In addition, the definition of online offending is likely to affect how the rates of offending are calculated. As outlined in more detail in this chapter, online offending can occur in a variety of ways, including grooming with a view to online or offline abuse, the distribution of images and, arguably, the incitement of others to offend.

Through research, policing and policy, professionals in this field hope to increase the effectiveness with which child sexual abuse crimes are understood, responded to and prevented in the future. In parallel, the last 20 years have witnessed immense technological changes through the internet, which have affected countless aspects of human behaviour and interactions. Although the Internet mirrors and extends many positive features of human society, inevitably more sinister aspects of human behaviour also manifest online, and child sex offending is no exception. Many individuals who have a sexual interest in children are known to use the internet for abusive purposes, and it is understood that crimes involving child sexual abuse online have risen substantially over the last few years (Wolak, Finkelhor, & Mitchell, 2009). Although our knowledge of child sex offender behaviour offline has been increasing for considerable time, our comprehension of child sex offender behaviour online is less developed. This chapter seeks to summarise our current understanding of online child sex offending behaviour and identify knowledge gaps for further development.

Online Risk to Children: Impact, Protection and Prevention, First Edition.
Edited by Jon Brown.
© 2017 John Wiley & Sons, Ltd. Published 2017 by John Wiley & Sons, Ltd.

Before addressing this issue, it is important to outline specifically what behaviours are encapsulated by the term 'online child sex offending.' This behaviour can include these actions:

- Viewing child sexual abuse material
- Collecting child sexual abuse material
- Disseminating child sexual abuse material for personal interest or financial gain
- Grooming children with the purpose of inciting them to engage in sexual acts online
- Grooming children with the purpose of meeting offline for contact sexual abuse
- Networking with others who are sexually interested in children
- Participation in live streaming of child sexual abuse online (adapted from Beech & Elliott, 2012; Durkin, 1997; Lanning, 2001)

These behaviours can be directed towards children and young people of any age, from infancy until late in adolescence. Each of these online offending behaviours will be addressed in turn during this chapter, but first the mediating impact of the online environment must be addressed.

THE IMPACT OF THE ONLINE ENVIRONMENT

Although there is an increasingly recognised convergence between online and offline communications (Child Exploitation and Online Protection [CEOP], 2010), it is important to recognise the impact that the online environment can have on human behaviour. A key feature of the online environment is the perception of anonymity (Cooper, 1998; Suler, 2004). As part of the 'Online Disinhibition Effect', Suler (2004) describes anonymity as the sense of being unidentifiable online (e.g., through use of user names rather than real names); thus, individuals can avoid the obligation to 'own' one's behaviour. Furthermore, the feeling of invisibility afforded by the Internet can give a person courage to act in ways from which he or she would usually refrain. Indeed, online child sex offenders have identified perceived anonymity online as contributing to increased confidence when offending (Webster et al., 2012). Suler (2004) also refers to 'dissociative imagination' online, whereby a person can create online characters in his or her imagination, leading to a fictional dimension separating offline 'fact' from 'online fantasy.' Such a process can psychologically distance offenders from their actions, which assists the development and sustainability of cognitive distortions and/or denial. The behaviour of children and young people online is also likely to be affected by perceptions of anonymity and invisibility, and this can be advantageous to child sex offenders (Whittle, Hamilton-Giachritsis, Beech, & Collings, 2013). Once the offender is in contact with a young person, the young person is likely to talk more freely about intimate matters than he or she would offline (Whittle, Hamilton-Giachritsis, & Beech, 2014; Wolak, Finkelhor, Mitchell, & Ybarra, 2008).

In the offline environment, individuals with a sexual interest in children may have to take considerable steps to gain and maintain access to a potential victim, such as joining a profession involving children or choosing a partner who is a parent. If the victim is unknown to the offender he or she may have to endorse some high-risk strategies to facilitate the abuse, for example, committing the offences in a public place. While child sex offenders continue to endorse these behaviours, the Internet provides these individuals with the opportunity to access numerous young people in an environment of perceived anonymity and without their actions necessarily having an immediate impact on their life.

Routine activity theory (Cohen & Felson, 1979) stipulates that predatory criminal behaviour requires a motivated offender, a suitable target and lack of supervision. It is recognised that children and young people are avid users of online technologies (Haddon & Livingstone, 2012), thus the Internet affords offenders access to children and young people like never before. A motivated offender is provided with access to countless children and young people online in a relatively unsupervised environment. It is possible, therefore, that individuals who are motivated to sexually abuse children but have refrained from doing so in the past may become tempted to offend online (Babchishin, Hanson, & Hermann, 2011).

OFFENDING ONLINE

VIEWING CHILD SEXUAL ABUSE MATERIAL

Although child sexual abuse material (CSAM) commonly refers to photographic images of child sexual abuse (stills and videos), there can be an assumption that online child abuse material refers only to such images. However, the term also encapsulates other forms of abusive material, such as visual material (including manipulated photos, computer-generated images, drawings and cartoons); written material (including fictional and real stories of child abuse, shared written fantasies and training guides on how to groom and abuse); and also audio representations of child sexual abuse (Gillespie, 2010). Although much of the current research in this area focusses on child abuse images, rather than other visual, written and audio material, the authors of this chapter feel it is important to highlight the other forms of abusive content.

Perhaps the most widely recognised form of offender engagement with CSAM online is the searching for and viewing of such material. A recent report from Interpol (2013) based on information captured in their global database states that, since 2009, approximately 3,500 unique victims within images have been recorded. There are now expected to be millions of child abuse images circulating the internet (CEOP, 2012). However, the reasons behind this abusive behaviour continue to be debated. Building on previous research (e.g., Krone, 2004; Lanning, 2001; Sullivan & Beech, 2002), Elliott and Beech (2009) suggested there are four broad types of offending individuals who contribute to the sexual abuse of children and young people online:

- *Periodically prurient*: those who access child sexual abuse imagery impulsively or out of a general curiosity. This behaviour may be sporadic and potentially part of a broader interest in pornography, including extreme pornography.
- *Fantasy driven/online-only*: those who access and/or trade child sexual abuse imagery to fuel a sexual interest in children but who have no *known* history of contact sexual offending (e.g., Osborn, Elliott, Middleton, & Beech, 2010; Seto, Hanson, & Babchishin, 2011; Webb, Craisatti, & Keen, 2007).
- *Direct victimisation*: consisting of those who utilise online technologies as part of a wider pattern of contact and non-contact sexual offending, including sexually explicit material involving children and the gaining and subsequently abusing the trust of an individual or children online in order to facilitate the later commission of contact sexual offences (Krone, 2004).
- *Commercial exploitation*: consisting of the criminally minded who produce or trade images to make money (Lanning, 2001).

The authors are wary to typologise individuals, because offending behaviour online can be diverse and complex, unlikely to fit neatly into categories. However, these four typologies may assist in better understanding the behaviours exhibited by online offenders and contextualising the motivations for offending behaviours. Individuals from any of these groups may be involved in viewing CSAM as part of their online offending; therefore, motivations for viewing are likely to be diverse.

It is known that child sex offenders often use cognitive distortions (Salter, 1988) and abuse supportive thinking (Sullivan & Sheehan, 2016) to minimise, rationalise, justify, deny and support their offending, and these psychological techniques are particularly prominent for those who view CSAM. For example, those individuals who have not directly abused or incited the abuse of a child may be able to relinquish responsibility for the abuse more easily than those more directly involved. If an individual has viewed existing material but not stored or shared it, he or she may be able to compartmentalise his or her interest in CSAM as transient and not contributing to victimisation. Given the nature and speed of the online environment, officers conducting digital forensic examinations on suspect technological devices can unfortunately find hundreds or even thousands of CSAM files. This can be retrieved from a suspect's internet search history; however, a significant proportion of offenders also choose to save and store CASM.

COLLECTING CHILD ABUSE MATERIAL

Although collecting abusive images of children has always been a behavioural feature of some child sex offenders, the online environment and the pace of technological change has exacerbated this aspect of offending. Large collections of all forms of CSAM can be relatively easily acquired, exchanged and expanded online in a way that is not possible offline (Cohen-Almagor, 2013). Digital CSAM collections can provide a unique insight into the nature of an offender's arousal, including the young people that they are likely to be fantasising about. Officers have been known to find highly organised and categorised collections of CSAM within offenders' digital devices, often demonstrative of how 'precious' the collection is to the holder. Frequency of access and the value placed on material by the holder can also be implied by knowledge of the collection. For example, material stored on a portable device (such as a smartphone or tablet) may be used more frequently than material stored on an external hard drive that cannot be so readily accessed. This may indicate this material is particularly 'precious' to the offender, or that they perceive it to be less of a risk than some of the other CSAM that they have on their person. It is common for offenders to use encryption software to protect their collections, not only from discovery by law enforcement but also often from discovery by others in their home or those who have access to their hardware. Similar to viewers, those who collect CASM online have a tendency to 'self-distance'; they often downplay accountability and do not acknowledge their contribution to child victimisation (Winder & Gough, 2010). This can be particularly apparent if the offender is collecting CSAM that has been self-generated by the child or young person without coercion from an adult. This includes material that was generated as part of consensual peer interactions and has been made public (consensually or not), for example, 'sexting' (Jonsson & Svedin, 2012).

It is unlikely that collectors would be included in Elliott and Beech's (2009) group of periodically prurient offenders, because the very nature of collecting infers that the behaviour cannot be sporadic. However, the motivations associated with the remaining three categories of offending behaviour could lead an individual to collect CSAM. Some child sex offenders collect CSAM for their own personal use and would not want this shared among others; they may even be quite possessive of their collections. However, for others, collecting is all part of wider picture of sharing and disseminating the abuse material. In addition, some offenders are known to offer (for a price) the pictures or film of a child being abused in the future, in line with 'requests.'

DISSEMINATING CHILD ABUSE MATERIAL

One of the ways in which an offender can access further CSAM and add to his or her collection is to disseminate and trade the material online. It is likely that if an offender wishes to obtain more abusive content, he or she will have to provide some in return. This may be considered a 'fair' exchange or be required to prove their identity (i.e., that they are not law enforcement). For some offenders, the need to exchange may contribute to their motivation to commit contact offences, because with no other means of accessing CSAM, they may seek to create their own. Evidence suggests that being sexually aroused has a strong impact on judgement and decision making; sexually aroused men are found to be more likely to be sexually excited by a wide range of stimuli, be more likely to engage in morally questionable behaviour in order to gain sexual gratification and engage in unsafe sex than men who are not sexually aroused (Ariely & Loewenstein, 2006). Therefore, a sexually aroused offender looking to exchange CSAM may make different decisions about contact sexual abuse than if he were not sexually aroused.

Peer2Peer (P2P) websites and hidden offender communities online enable the trading of CSAM between individuals. What material is considered 'valuable' to an individual is likely to differ between offenders, based on their motivation and the nature of their arousal. Some individuals will trade for personal satisfaction, in line with their sexual arousal, whereas others may trade in images for financial reward. The latter are outlined by the fourth group in Elliott and Beech's (2009) typology as those offending as part of 'commercial exploitation.' To date, it is unclear what percentage of individuals are 'traders' with no sexual interest in children and only financial motivation. However, as with trafficked children, this may be an area of 'commercial' activity that seems to offer good financial rewards to groups of individuals whose focus is monetary gain in any area.

In contrast to those interested only in financial gain, there is evidence to suggest that some individuals go online to avoid negative emotional states. Quayle, Vaughan and Taylor (2006) identify that when sex offenders access CSAM and use this as part of masturbatory fantasy, they are provided not only with reward but also further promotion of emotional avoidance. Sexual fantasy is widely accepted to be a fundamental aspect within child sexual offending and for some individuals it can be considered the 'blueprint' to offending (Quayle & Taylor, 2002). Fantasies provide an insight into the arousal of an individual, may include elements of behaviour with which they would like to be engaged in reality but are not static and can evolve over time to encompass new material. Therefore, online CSAM that is accessed by an offender is likely to become incorporated into their masturbatory fantasy. New material accessed by offenders as part of their dissemination and trade is likely to indicate the evolving nature of their arousal. The 'fantasy-escalation effect' (Sullivan & Sheehan, 2002) refers to the process whereby an offender becomes bored with a particular image or fantasy and will move towards increasingly explicit and extreme fantasy material to satisfy his or her sexual arousal. Trading gives the offender an opportunity to access the more explicit, which may not have been otherwise available. This may be interrelated to indications that indecent images of children online appear to becoming more extreme and graphic in nature, as well as involving younger children and babies (Beech, Elliott, Birgden, & Findlater, 2008; Internet Watch Foundation, 2012).

GROOMING CHILDREN WITH THE PURPOSE OF INCITING THEM TO ENGAGE IN SEXUAL ACTS ONLINE

Child sex offenders are known to use the online environment to groom children and young people in preparation for sexual abuse. Grooming encompasses a wide range of manipulative behaviours that may include rapport building, flattery, blackmail, bribery, force or threats (Craven, Brown, & Gilchrist, 2006; Kloess, Beech, & Harkins, 2014; O'Connell, 2003; Whittle et al., 2014). Social media and communication technology enable offenders to contact their victims via multiple communication platforms persistently and even simultaneously, entrenching themselves within the young person's life (Whittle et al., 2014; Wolak, Finkelhor, &Mitchell, 2004). Briggs, Simon and Simonsen (2011) identified that online offenders appear to be either fantasy driven (i.e., their goal is to obtain child sexual abuse material) or contact driven (i.e., their aim is to meet a young person offline to commit contact sexual offences). Other research has shown that many offenders are interested in committing online-only offending (i.e., via a webcam) with many not even attempting to meet their victims offline (Kloess, Seymour-Smith, Hamilton-Giachritsis, Long, Shipley, & Beech, 2015; Whittle, Hamilton-Giachritsis, & Beech, 2013); the extent to which some offenders then upload this material for others' use is as yet unknown.

An offender who is grooming a child or young person with the purpose of committing online sexual abuse will be seeking to sexualise and incite the victim to engage in sexual acts. This encompasses a range of behaviours including (but not restricted to) sexual chat, sexual posing via photos or webcam, viewing the offender engaging in sexual acts and/or performing sexual acts. Sexual acts can include stripping, sexual touching and/or masturbation, but offenders are also able to groom children and young people into sexual acts that are considerably more extreme, such as those involving the use of objects and even bestiality (Kloess et al., 2015). The offender may be inciting this activity to view, store, share or all of the above. Offenders who exploit children and young people in this way often record the CSAM and use it as a blackmailing tool if the victim threatens to report them or stop engaging in the sexual behaviour. Numerous victims have experienced threats of the offender sharing the content with family members, friends and teachers, or uploading it online, if they

refuse to provide further sexual material. Such offender manipulation techniques further entrench the victim in the abuse. Essentially, the offender is
looking for leverage with which to exert control over the victim's behaviour. If
the leverage cannot be obtained through possession of sexual material of that
particular child or young person (either self-generated or incited), the offender
may use other features of the online environment. For example, the offender
may become a skilled user of an online game that is popular with young people
and offer advice or cheats to those who struggle with the game in return for the
generation of sexual material.

The way in which online child sex offenders approach their victims varies
considerably. This is because of the heterogeneous nature of online offenders,
which is a theme throughout this chapter. More recent research (Kloess, 2014)
suggests that there has been a change in the approaches used by some online
offenders (the *direct victimisation* group in Elliott and Beech, 2009, categorisa-
tion), with a rise in those who employ little (if any) grooming strategies and are
immediately overtly sexualised, even aggressive in their requests of victims.
This is potentially an important new development that needs to be investigated further and reflects, perhaps, the fact that with so many potential victims,
some offenders feel a prolonged grooming period is unnecessary.

However, research has begun to explore the ways in which offenders may
approach victims online. From their sample, The European Online Grooming
Project (Webster et al., 2012) identified three groups of offenders who were
approaching victims online in differing ways. Some offenders were found to be
intimacy seeking and were likely to build a rapport with overtly vulnerable
young people to sexually exploit them. Other offenders were found to be hyper-
sexualised and more likely to approach overtly risk-taking young people
online. This approach may be less targeted than the intimacy-seeking offenders
and relates to the technique often termed as 'scatter gun': making an approach
to numerous young people at random or through sharing contact lists and waiting to see who responds. The final group identified by the European Online
Grooming Project (Webster et al., 2012) was offenders who adapted their
behaviour depending on the situation; these offenders exert intimacy-seeking
or hyper-sexualised behaviours when required, based on the victim they are
seeking to groom and abuse. Online groomers who aim to sexually abuse children and young people online could be represented by either the 'fantasy-
driven' or the 'direct victimisation' group within Elliott and Beech's (2009)
typology. More recent research identifies that offenders may adopt either a
'direct' or 'indirect' approach when communicating with victims (Kloess, 2014).
This study, involving analysis of chat logs between offenders and young victims,
identified that an indirect approach would involve a build in conversation, flattery and gradual rapport (an approach that includes features long associated
with grooming). However, interestingly the direct approach was also widely
used by offenders in this sample and involved immediate sexual approaches to
potential victims, with no attempts at rapport building (Kloess, 2014).

Many online offenders use the internet to access, groom and abuse victims who are previously unknown to them. However, it is a common misconception that this is the case for the vast majority. Family and acquaintance offenders using the Internet have been found to be nearly as numerous as offenders who go online to meet victims previously unknown to them (Mitchell, Finkelhor, & Wolak, 2005). The authors found that these family and acquaintance offenders tend to use the internet to further their crimes by grooming, storing or distributing images of the victim, sharing victim details, communicating with the victims, providing rewards and arranging meetings (Mitchell, Finkelhor, & Wolak, 2003).

GROOMING CHILDREN WITH THE PURPOSE OF MEETING OFFLINE FOR CONTACT SEXUAL ABUSE

The second group identified by Briggs et al. (2011) is offenders who are contact driven. These individuals will use the online environment for the preparatory stages of abuse, but ultimately they seek to meet their victims offline and commit contact sexual offences. The grooming behaviours mirror those described previously and victims of contact sexual abuse may also have been sexually exploited online by their offenders before and after they are abused offline (Whittle, Hamilton-Giachritsis, & Beech, 2015). In fact, the victims within a recent study sample experienced online abuse that was similar in nature, regardless of whether the victims were also being abused offline (Whittle et al., 2014). Offenders who groom children and young people online with the purpose of committing contact sexual offences would fit within the direct victimisation group of Elliott and Beech's (2009) typology. For these offenders, the technology assists the grooming process by facilitating access and enabling grooming, but the online environment may not necessarily feature within the sexual abuse itself. The use of technology will depend on the individual offender and his or her offending goals, the individual characteristics of the victim as well as the unique dynamic between the offender and the victim.

NETWORKING WITH OTHERS WHO ARE SEXUALLY INTERESTED IN CHILDREN

In addition to facilitating access to young people, the internet also affords offenders access to like-minded individuals, and those who make use of the 'darknet' are more difficult to locate by law enforcement agencies. The subculture of paedophiles online has recently begun to be explored and evidence suggests that the values of paedophilic culture support and encourage emotional and sometimes sexual relationships with children, online and offline (Holt, Blevins, & Burkert, 2010). Such offender interactions not only assist individuals in developing the skills to avoid detection but also support distorted attitudes about the sexual abuse of children (Quayle & Taylor, 2003) and are likely to lead to the escalation of fantasies through normalisation. Online, child sex offenders are able to find support and reassurance for their views and behaviour (Cohen-Almagor, 2013). This may be particularly dangerous for those who have the motivation to sexually abuse children but have not yet taken any steps towards offending (perhaps because of feelings of guilt or fear). When confronted with an online community who support and encourage this behaviour, offending will become normalised and cognitive distortions supported; thus, such individuals may become encouraged to offend.

Holt and colleagues (2010) found that four normative orders of (1) marginalisation, (2) sexuality, (3) law, and (4) security shape relationships among child sex offenders in online forums and in wider society. These norms define paedophilic identity and form the boundaries of their subculture. When presented with individuals who share similar values online, offending behaviours are reinforced and remain unchallenged (Quayle & Taylor, 2003). With regard to the typologies put forward by Elliott and Beech (2009), those who network in these ways online are most likely to come from either the fantasy-driven or direct victimisation groups, because networking implies a persistent sexual interest in children and/or young people.

Given society's view of paedophilia, those with a sexual interest in children are often marginalised from the community at large (O'Halloran & Quayle, 2010). However, the Internet affords offenders more opportunities to co-offend and share victims within a wider network, often compiled with individuals they have never met. Online offending groups, such as the Pedophile Information Exchange (PIE) and the North American Man-Boy Love Association (NAMBLA), exemplify how offenders can network online to facilitate abuse in a seemingly organised manner. Associations with forums such as these, particularly those that focus on terms such as 'boy lovers,' can assist those who are sexually interested in children in maintaining a positive self-concept (O'Halloran & Quayle, 2010). The language often used in such communities tends to focus on loving sexual relationships with children, avoiding terminology associated with exploitation and abuse. Associating with others in this way not only reinforces cognitive distortions but also enables offenders to maintain a positive self-concept (O'Halloran & Quayle, 2010). In addition to these groups, networking online also provides offenders with the opportunity to work together in streaming abuse via the Internet.

PARTICIPATION IN LIVE STREAMING OF CHILD SEXUAL ABUSE ONLINE

Live streaming of child sexual abuse is a relatively new form of online child sexual offending, and thus empirical research on this behaviour is limited. Live streaming abuse involves an offender identifying an individual who has access to a child and is willing to sexually abuse this child via webcam for the offender's sexual gratification. There are two offending roles within live abuse streaming:

first that of the offender who has requested the abuse and second that of the offender who is physically committing the abuse. Typically, the individual committing the contact abuse is paid for providing the child and engaging in this behaviour; therefore, this individual may be motivated solely by the financial reward, solely by a sexual interest in children, or by both financial and sexual gratification. Additionally, there may be others who, working purely for financial gain, act as a third party connecting the 'purchaser' with the offender who commits the actual offence.

Through this form of crime, 'inciting' offenders are able to gain access to a child who fits their sexual interest, as well as request abusive behaviours that fit their preferred sexual fantasies. Individuals who enjoy the feeling of power and control over another are also likely to enjoy being able to manipulate the actions of the co-offender(s) and the victim(s). This individual may have extensive involvement in directing the abusive acts actually committed against the child. The offender who commits the contact sexual abuse is likely to have been selected as a result of his or her existing access to vulnerable children; therefore, grooming the child or young person is often minimal or non-existent within this form of abuse. There is practice (but little research) evidence that this type of offending often occurs across international borders, with the subsequent child protection difficulties that incur; for example, a western offender inciting the sexual abuse of a child in a country that has complex economic and political challenges (and hence the financial cost may be relatively low for someone from a more wealthy country). Children in these countries are more likely to be inherently vulnerable and thus accessible to offenders with little or no grooming. For example, the child may be seeking work to support his or her family and be available to hire. Offenders who seek to live-stream abuse are able to locate these vulnerable children, make the small payment for their time and sexually abuse them while another offender watches online. There remains much still to learn about this form of abuse and the psychological processes that underlie the behaviours of offenders within this abusive scenario.

COMPARISON WITH OFFLINE OFFENDERS

There is an increasing body of literature addressing how online offenders may differ from offline offenders or dual offenders (those who sexually offend against children both online and offline). There are inherent difficulties when drawing comparisons between these offending groups, because knowledge of whether an offender is 'online,' 'offline' or 'dual' is often based on conviction data; therefore, the true extent of the offences may be unknown. Furthermore, even when self-report data is used, the analysis depends on the honesty of the offender's disclosure. Therefore, the findings of comparison studies are by no means conclusive, but several pieces of research add valuable contributions to this issue.

As part of a meta-analysis, Babchishin and colleagues (2011) reported several differences between online and offline offenders. Demographically, online offenders were more likely to be Caucasian and slightly younger than offline offenders; they are also more likely to be unemployed than the general population (Babchishin et al., 2011). Recent studies, however, have not found distinct differences between online-only and dual offenders (Kloess, 2014; Whittle et al., 2014). These studies involve small sample sizes, so applicability to wider populations is tentative. Several vulnerabilities are noted as being associated with child sexual offending, and these appear to be similar for online and offline offenders. Offline and online offenders were more likely to have experienced physical and sexual abuse than the general population, as well as demonstrating similarities on measures of loneliness and self-esteem (Babchishin et al., 2011). However, there is evidence to suggest that internet sex offenders were more likely to have been sexually victimised at an older age than offline offenders, and the abuse was more likely to be extra-familial (Howitt & Sheldon, 2007). Furthermore, the authors found that the majority of their sample of internet offenders displayed secure attachment styles, whereas contact and dual offenders were more likely to display fearful or preoccupied attachment styles (Howitt & Sheldon, 2007).

Psychologically some differences have been identified: online offenders were found to have greater victim empathy, greater sexual deviancy and lower impression management than offline offenders (Babchishin et al., 2011; Babchishin, Hanson, & VanZuylen, 2014). Internet offenders were also found to have fewer victim empathy distortions and cognitive distortions than contact offenders, indicating that contact offenders are more likely to have difficulty in identifying the harmful impact of abuse on their victims (Elliott, Beech, Mandeville-Norden, & Hayes, 2008). Similar findings were reported in more recent research that compared internet offenders, contact offenders and offenders who abused in both environments. Contact offenders were found to have less victim empathy, greater impulsivity and an externalised locus of control in comparison to internet and mixed offenders (Elliott, Beech, & Mandeville-Norden, 2013). This research concluded that the key factor distinguishing among the groups was offence-supportive attitudes. Such research suggests that those who engage in internet offending may have less entrenched pro-offending beliefs, which would indicate less likelihood of persistent and escalating offending, as well as greater receptivity to treatment. McCarthy (2010) reported a further difference between online and offline offenders, in that contact offenders were more likely to engage in combination offending activities, such as trading, paying for, concealing and/or organising abusive images, than those who engaged in non-contact offending.

There is also a range of literature seeking to understand the links between online and offline offending, focussing on whether non-contact internet offenders pose a risk of contact offending (e.g., Bourke & Hernandez, 2009; Seto et al., 2011). Results of such studies are largely inconclusive and extend beyond the scope of this chapter. However, although the debate concerning the differences between online and offline offending continues, it should be noted that an individual engaging in either behaviour is likely to have a sexual interest that includes children and/or young people. Therefore, without intervention, individuals with this interest could be considered a risk to children, online and offline.

GAPS IN OUR KNOWLEDGE

Although research, and consequentially our knowledge of child sex offending online, has grown exponentially during the last few years, there remains much more to learn about this issue. The ways in which offenders are using the online environment to abuse children are increasingly understood (Kloess et al., 2015; Whittle et al., 2014), and steps have been taken to apply these behaviours to established theories of child sex offending offline (e.g., Beech & Elliott, 2012; Elliott, 2016). However, the pace of technological change and resulting adaptations in offending behaviour require this understanding to be regularly re-addressed and evaluated. There is much more to learn about how those who offend online may differ and be similar to those who offend offline, because consistent and robust findings across large populations are yet to be reported. In addition, the relationship between online and offline offending (i.e., dual offenders) also requires further exploration to aid the process of risk assessing those who are convicted of online offending. As this chapter demonstrates, many individuals who engage in child sex offending online do not fit neatly into one offending group, and their behaviours may overlap into several categories of offending. This and the difficulty in identifying the true nature of an individual's offending create problems for analysis. However, there is an ever-increasing body of data from which to learn and a substantial momentum of research interest.

CONCLUSION

There are indications that the number of detected online offenders continues to increase. It is possible that the large number of arrests relating to CSAM reflect investigative advances, rather than an increase in the prevalence of this crime type (Wolak, Finkelhor, Mitchell, & Jones, 2011). However, in part, it may also reflect an increase because of increasing ease of access for individuals with an interest. This chapter has identified the wide range of behaviours that are encapsulated by the term 'online sex offending,' which are important to bear in mind. These include viewing child sexual abuse material, collecting child sexual abuse material, disseminating child sexual abuse material for personal interest or financial gain, grooming children with the purpose of inciting them to engage in sexual acts online, grooming children with the purpose of meeting offline for contact sexual abuse, networking with others who are sexually interested in children and participation in live streaming of child sexual abuse online. It should also be noted that online sexual abuse (e.g., via webcam) can be more serious than is sometimes acknowledged (e.g., including bestiality).

Finally, it should be recognised that an overwhelming body of evidence suggests that those who commit sexual offences against children and young people online are a heterogeneous group (McCarthy, 2010; Mitchell, Finkelhor, & Wolak, 2003). Furthermore, the behaviours outlined within this chapter were found often to span multiple categories within Elliott and Beech's (2009) typology. Therefore it is important that professionals in this field 'typologise' the behaviour, rather than the individual. This will help to avoid oversimplifying the issue and missing the subtleties of offending behaviour online. Although gaps have been identified in our knowledge, given the substantial increase in research, practitioners, academics and police have a growing comprehension of child sex offender behaviour online. If knowledge development and exploration in this field can continue with this current momentum, there is reason to believe that our ability to understand, detect and prevent the online sexual abuse of children can be further enabled.

REFERENCES

Ariely, D., & Loewenstein, G. (2006). The heat of the moment: The effect of sexual arousal on sexual decision making. *Journal of Behavioral Decision Making, 19,* 87–98. doi:10.1002/bdm.501

Babchishin, K. M., Hanson, R. K., & Hermann, C. A. (2011). The characteristics of online sex offenders: A meta-analysis. *Sexual Abuse: A Journal of Research and Treatment, 23,* 92–123.

Babchishin, K. M., Hanson, R. K., & VanZuylen, H. (2014). Online child pornography offenders are different: A meta-analysis of the characteristics of online and offline sex offenders against children. *Archives of Sexual Behavior, 44*(1), 45 66. doi:10.1007/s10508-014-0270-x.

Beech, A. R., & Elliott, I. A. (2012). In K. Ribisl & E. Quayle (Eds.), *Internet child pornography: Understanding and preventing on-line child abuse.* Cullompton, Devon, UK: Willan.

Beech, A. R., Elliott, I. A., Birgden, A., & Findlater, D. (2008). The internet and child sex offending: A criminological review. *Aggression and Violent Behavior, 13,* 216–228.

Bourke, M. L., & Hernandez, A. E. (2009). The 'Butner Study' redux: A report of the incidence of hands-on child victimization by child pornography offenders. *Journal of Family Violence, 24,* 183–191.

Briggs, P., Simon, W. T., & Simonsen, S. (2011). An exploratory study of internet-initiated sexual offenses and the chat room sex offender: Has the internet enabled a new typology of sex offender? *Sexual Abuse: A Journal of Research and Treatment, 23,* 72 91.

Child Exploitation and Online Protection Centre (CEOP). (2010). *Strategic overview 2009–2010*. Retrieved from http://ceop.police.uk/Documents/Strategic_Overview_2009-10_%28Unclassified%29.pdf

Child Exploitation and Online Protection Centre (CEOP). (2012). *A picture of abuse: A thematic assessment of the risk of contact child sexual abuse posed by those who possess indecent images of children.* Retrieved from http://ceop.police.uk/Documents/ceopdocs/CEOP%20IIOCTA%20Executive%20Summary.pdf

Cohen, L. E., & Felson, M. (1979). Social change and crime rate trends: A routine activity approach. *American Sociological Review, 44,* 588–608.

Cohen-Almagor, R. (2013). Online child sex offenders: Challenges and countermeasures. *The Howard Journal, 52,* 190–215.

Cooper, A. (1998). Sexuality and the internet: Surfing into the new millennium. *CyberPsychology and Behavior, 1,* 187–193. doi:10.1089/cpb.1998.1.187

Craven, S., Brown, S., & Gilchrist, E. (2006). Sexual grooming of children: Review of literature and theoretical considerations. *Journal of Sexual Aggression, 12,* 287–299. doi:10.1080/13552600601069414

Durkin, K. F. (1997). Misuse of the internet by pedophiles: Implications for law enforcement and probation practice. *Federal Probation, 61,* 14–18.

Elliott, I. A. (2016). Applying sexual offence theory to online sex offenders. In D. P. Boer, A. R. Beech & T. Ward (Eds.), *The Wiley handbook on theories, assessment and treatment of sexual offending* (Vol. 1). Chichester, UK: Wiley.

Elliott, I. A., & Beech, A. R. (2009). Understanding online child pornography use: Applying sexual offender theory to internet offenders. *Aggression and Violent Behavior, 14,* 180–193. doi:10.1016/j.avb.2009.03.002

Elliott, I., Beech, A., & Mandeville-Norden, R. (2013). The psychological profiles of internet, contact, and mixed internet/contact sex offenders. *Sex Abuse Journal of Research and Treatment, 25,* 3–20.

Elliott, I. A., Beech, A. R., Mandeville-Norden, R., & Hayes, E. (2008). Psychological profiles of internet sex offenders: Comparisons with contact sexual offenders. *Sexual Abuse: A Journal of Research and Treatment, 21,* 76–92.

Gillespie, A. (2010). Legal definitions of child pornography. *Journal of Sexual Aggression, 16,* 19–31.

Haddon, L., & Livingstone, S. (2012). *EU kids online: National perspectives.* London, UK: The London School of Economics and Political Science. Retrieve from http://eprints.lse.ac.uk/46878/

Holt, T. J., Blevins, K. R., & Burkert, N (2010). Considering the paedophile subculture online. *Sexual Abuse: A Journal of Research and Treatment, 22,* 3 24.

Howitt, D., & Sheldon, K. (2007). The role of cognitive distortions in paedophilic offending: Internet and contact offenders compared. *Psychology, Crime and Law, 13,* 469–486.

Internet Watch Foundation. (2012). *Internet Watch Foundation annual report and charity report.* Retrieved from https://www.iwf.org.uk/assets/media/annual-reports/FINAL%20web-friendly%20IWF%202012%20Annual%20and%20Charity%20Report.pdf

Interpol. (2013). *Crimes against children: Fact sheet.* Retrieved from http://www.interpol.int/en/News-and-media/Publications/Fact-sheets/Crimes-against-children/

Jonsson, L., & Svedin, C. G. (2012). Children within the images. In E. Quayle & K. M. Ribisl (Eds.), *Understanding and preventing online sexual exploitation of children* (pp. 23–43). New York, NY: Routledge.

Kloess, J. A. (2014). The process of online interactions between offenders and victims. Paper presented to British Psychological Society's Department of Forensic Psychology Conference, Glasgow, UK.

Kloess, J. A., Beech, A. R., & Harkins L. (2014). Online child sexual exploitation: Prevalence, process and offender characteristics. *Trauma, Violence and Abuse, 15*, 126–139.

Kloess, J. A., Seymour-Smith, S., Hamilton-Giachritsis, C.E., Long, M. L., Shipley, D., & Beech, A. R. (2015). A qualitative analysis of offenders modus operandi in sexually exploitative interactions with children online. *Sexual Abuse: A Journal of Research and Treatment*. doi:10.1177/1079063215612442

Krone, T. (2004). A typology of online child pornography offending. *Trends and Issues in Crime and Criminal Justice, 279*, 1–6.

Lanning, K. V. (2001). *Child molesters: A behavioral analysis* (4th ed.). Arlington, VA: National Center for Missing and Exploited Children. Retrieved from http://www.missingkids.com/en_US/publications/NC70.pdf

McCarthy, J. A. (2010). Internet sexual activity: A comparison between contact and non-contact child pornography offenders. *Journal of Sexual Aggression, 16*, 181–195.

Mitchell, K. J., Finkelhor, D., & Wolak, J. (2003). *Victimization of youths on the internet (The victimization of children: Emerging issues)*. New York, NY: Howard Maltreatment and Trauma Press.

Mitchell, K. J., Finkelhor, D., & Wolak, J. (2005). The internet and family acquaintance sexual abuse. *Child Maltreatment, 10*, 49–60.

O'Connell, R. (2003). *A typology of cyber sexploitation and online grooming practices*. Preston, England: University of Central Lancashire. Retrieved from http://www.uclan.ac.uk/host/cru/docs/cru010.pdf

O'Halloran, E., & Quayle, E. (2010). A content analysis of a 'boy love' support forum: Revisiting Durkin and Bryant. *Journal of Sexual Aggression, 16*, 71–85.

Osborn, J., Elliott, I. A., Middleton, D., & Beech, A. R. (2010). The use of actuarial risk assessment measures with UK internet child pornography offenders. *The Journal of Aggression, Conflict and Peace Studies, 2*, 16–24.

Quayle, E., & Taylor M. (2002). Child pornography and the internet: Perpetuating a cycle of abuse. *Deviant Behavior, 23*, 365–395.

Quayle, E., & Taylor, M. (2003). Model of problematic internet use in people with a sexual interest in children. *CyberPsychology and Behavior, 6*, 93–106. doi:10.1089/109493103321168009

Quayle, E., Vaughan, M., & Taylor, M. (2006). Sex offenders, internet child abuse images and emotional avoidance: The importance of values. *Aggression and Violent Behavior, 11*, 1–11.

Salter, A. C. (1988). *Treating child sex offenders and victims: A practical guide*. London, UK: Sage.

Seto, M. C., Hanson, R. K., & Babchishin, K. M. (2011). Contact sexual offending by men with online sexual offenses. *Sexual Abuse: A Journal of Research and Treatment, 23*, 124–145. doi: 10.1177/1079063210369013

Suler, J. (2004). The online disinhibition effect. *Cyberpsychology and Behavior, 7*, 321–326.

Sullivan, J., & Beech, A. (2002). Professional perpetrators: Sex offenders who use their employment to target and sexually abuse the children with whom they work. *Child Abuse Review, 11*, 153–167. doi:10.1002/car.731

Sullivan, J., & Sheehan, V. (2002). The internet sex offender: Understanding the behaviour and engaging the assessment and treatment issues. Paper presented to the 21st Annual Conference of ATSA (Association for the Treatment of Sexual Abusers). Montreal, Canada.

Sullivan, J., & Sheehan, V. (2016). What motivates sexual abusers of children? A qualitative examination of the spiral of sexual abuse. *Aggression and Violent Behavior, 30*, 76–87.

Webb, L., Craisatti, J., & Keen, S. (2007). Characteristics of internet child pornography offenders: A comparison with child molesters. *Sexual Abuse: A Journal of Research and Treatment, 19*, 449–465. doi:10.1007/s11194-007-9063-2

Webster, S., Davidson, J., Bifulco, A., Gottschalk, P., Caretti, V., Pham, T., & Grove-Hills, J. (2012). *European Online Grooming Project final report*. European Union. Retrieved from http://www.europeanonlinegroomingproject.com/wp-content/file-uploads/European-Online-Grooming-Project-Final-Report.pdf

Whittle, H. C., Hamilton-Giachritsis, C. E., & Beech, A. R. (2013). Victims' voices: The impact of online grooming and sexual abuse. *Universal Journal of Psychology, 1*, 59–71.

Whittle, H. C., Hamilton-Giachritsis, C. E., & Beech, A. R. (2014). 'Under his spell': Victims' perspectives of being groomed online. *Social Sciences, 3*, 404–426.

Whittle, H. C., Hamilton-Giachritsis, C. E., & Beech, A. R. (2015). A comparison of victim and offender perspectives of online grooming and sexual abuse. *Deviant Behavior, 36*(7), 539–564.

Whittle, H., Hamilton-Giachritsis, C., Beech, A., & Collings, G. (2013). A review of online grooming: Characteristics and concerns. *Aggression and Violent Behavior, 18*, 62–70.

Winder, B., & Gough, B. (2010). 'I never touched anybody-that's my defence': A qualitative analysis of internet sex offender accounts. *Journal of Sexual Aggression, 16*, 125–141.

Wolak, J., Finkelhor, D., & Mitchell, K. (2004). Internet-initiated sex crimes against minors: Implications for prevention based on findings from a national study. *Journal of Adolescent Health, 35*, e11–e20.

Wolak, J., Finkelhor, D., & Mitchell, K. (2009). *Trends in arrests of 'online predators.'* Crime Against Children Research Center. Retrieved from http://www.unh.edu/news/NJOV2.pdf

Wolak, J., Finkelhor, D., Mitchell, K., & Jones, L. M. (2011). Arrests for child pornography production: Data at two time points from a national sample of U.S. law enforcement agencies. *Child Maltreatment, 16*, 184–195. doi:10.1177/1077559511415837

Wolak, J., Finkelhor, D., Mitchell, K. J., & Ybarra, M. L. (2008). Online 'predators' and their victims: Myths, realities and implications for prevention and treatment. *American Psychologist, 63*, 111–128.

5 Treatment of Online Offenders: Current Best Practice and Next Steps

Sandy Jung

With the advent of the Internet, there have been many advantages and conveniences, but there have also been some menacing pitfalls as well. Abuse of this information highway has led to easy exploitation of vulnerable populations, such as children, teenagers and disenfranchised adults. The Internet has given impetus to online solicitation and the distribution and production of child pornography because of its anonymity, accessibility and affordability (Cooper, 1997). The number of incidents of juveniles and adults using the Internet to befriend and exploit children is rapidly increasing, yet Wolak, Finkelhor, Mitchell, and Ybarra (2008) note that sex crimes against youths have not increased (e.g., the United States showed decrease between 2004 to 2013, National Crime Victimization Survey; Truman & Langton, 2014). Wolak et al. (2008) speculate that 'sex offenders have migrated to the Internet from other environments, so that increases in online sex offending have been balanced by decreases in offline victimizations' (p. 121). Furthermore, child pornography cases accounted for 82% of the growth seen in referrals to US attorneys from 1994 to 2006 and has been described as the fastest growing offences (Motivans & Kyckelhahn, 2007) and has even grown among juvenile offenders (e.g., Finkelhor & Ormrod, 2004). Canadian crime statistics indicate decreases in almost all offences, except for child pornography cases, which increased by 21% from 2012 to 2013 (i.e., 2,177 to 2,668 crimes reported; Boyce, Cotter, & Perreault, 2014).

The use of the Internet by sexual offenders is a modus operandi that is ever-changing (Malesky, 2007) and has led to a losing race against technologically savvy offenders by criminal justice and treatment professionals. Identifying such offenders and detecting criminal activity is more difficult than it is for

Online Risk to Children: Impact, Protection and Prevention, First Edition.
Edited by Jon Brown.
© 2017 John Wiley & Sons, Ltd. Published 2017 by John Wiley & Sons, Ltd.

other forms of sexual offending. The term 'internet offending' can describe a range of internet-facilitated offences. Durkin (1997) proposed ways that individuals with a deviant interest in children may abuse the Internet, and they include the exchange of sexually abusive images, the location of potential victims for sexual abuse, inappropriate sexual communication (or sexual grooming) with potential victims and correspondence with other individuals who also have a deviant sexual interest in children. Whether we call such offenders 'child pornography offenders' or 'online solicitation offenders,' they comprise a group that is becoming more common in sex offender treatment settings. This chapter examines the current best practice of implementing treatment and intervention techniques with online sex offenders. Before examining interventions and treatments for these offenders, it is important to determine who are online sex offenders, whether these offenders are really different from other sex offenders, and what models may explain why offenders engage in online sexual exploitation behaviours. Several terms have been used in the literature and in practice. An overarching term, 'online sex offenders,' will be used interchangeably with 'online offenders' and includes 'internet sex offenders,' which has been used by some researchers. The term 'child pornography' will be used throughout this chapter as it is commonly termed in North America; however, it is recognised that many jurisdictions are moving to using more appropriate terms, such as 'child abuse imagery,' 'sexually abusive images,' and 'indecent images of children' (see Child Exploitation and Online Protection Centre, 2012).

ONLINE SEX OFFENDERS: CHARACTERISTICS AND COMPARISONS WITH CONTACT OFFENDERS

The resulting increase in online offending has led evaluators, treatment providers and criminal justice professionals to ask, 'who are these offenders' and 'are they different from non-online offenders?' Wolak, Finkelhor, and Mitchell (2004) reported that online child molesters are generally not paedophiles, but rather they more commonly target adolescents than young children. However, if we are to consider all online sex offenders, including those who use sexually abusive images from the Internet, the profile of online sex offenders becomes more complex.

Recent debates among researchers and clinicians is whether online offenders belong to a separate group of sex offenders or to a previously categorised one; for example, it was unclear if online offenders are merely child molestation offenders who are using a new technology to carry out their offences (Babchishin, Hanson, & Hermann, 2011). Some studies using small samples (e.g., Ns < 100) found that online sex offenders were mostly employed (Bates & Metcalf, 2007; Jung, Ennis, Stein, Choy, & Hook, 2013; Laulik, Allam, & Sheridan, 2007); more likely to be Caucasian (Tomak, Weschler, Ghahramanlou-Holloway, Virden, & Nademin, 2009; Webb, Craissati, & Keen, 2007); more likely to have experienced childhood physical abuse (Webb et al., 2007); more educated (Bates & Metcalf, 2007; Jung et al., 2013) and less likely to have abused drugs (Jung et al., 2013) than non-online offenders and/or contact offenders. However, discrepancies among these studies did not leave conclusive findings regarding the direction of differences in age and marital status. A US study by Faust, Bickart, Renaud, and Camp (2014) used a much larger sample of incarcerated offenders (428 online offenders versus 210 contact child molesters) to examine demographic variables. They found online offenders were more likely to be married, older, employed and Caucasian than contact offenders.

Beyond demographic comparisons, several studies examined psychological differences as measured on psychometric instruments. Using the Personality Assessment Inventory (PAI), Laulik et al. (2007) found their sample of 30 online offenders scored higher, on average, than the normative sample on several scales, including depression, suicidal ideation, schizophrenia, borderline features and anti-social features. More than 15% of the sample had scores in the clinical range for depression, suicidal ideation and borderline features. Bates and Metcalf (2007) found a smaller proportion of online offenders had scores above the normal range on scales that measured emotional congruence with children, sexualised beliefs about children and victim empathy deficits than contact offenders. Using the Minnesota Multiphasic Personality Inventory (2nd edition; MMPI-2), Tomak et al. (2009) found few differences between online offenders and contact child molesters on most of the clinical scales, except for the anti-sociality scale (i.e., psychopathic deviate, Pd) and the schizophrenia scale in which online offenders had lower means than contact child molesters. Similar findings from Jung et al.'s (2013) study demonstrated that child pornography offenders had lower scores on the anti-social egocentricity scale of the PAI than non-online/non-contact offenders (e.g., exhibitionistic and voyeuristic offenders). The difficulty with these small sample comparisons is the selection method, which limits the validity of the findings; for example, samples were not always matched (e.g., incarcerated child molester sample being compared to online offenders from the community; Tomak et al., 2009). Elliott, Beech, Mandeville-Norden, and Hayes (2009) compared a large community-based sample of online offenders ($N = 505$) and contact sex offenders ($N = 526$). They found that contact offenders had more distortions about victim empathy and sexualising children, higher levels of emotional congruence with children, and more externalised locus of control than online offenders, and online offenders had a greater ability to identify with fictional and fantasy characters.

Using aggregated data from 27 studies, Babchishin and her colleagues (2011) conducted a meta-analysis, which produced results that are more generalisable and less influenced by sampling error. Their findings revealed that online offenders (sample sizes ranged from 26 to 870; median = 100; $N = 4,844$) were less likely to be of a racial minority, to have experienced physical abuse, to endorse cognitive distortions sexualising children and to emotionally identify with children, and they were more likely to exhibit victim empathy and sexual deviancy than offline offenders (sample sizes ranged from 25 to 526; median = 104; $N = 1,342$).

In many of the studies reviewed, online offenders have excluded (e.g., Elliott et al., 2009) and included (e.g., Jung et al., 2013) online contact offending, such as online solicitation. An examination of differences between these online offenders with and without contact offending histories would provide some insight into variables that may lead online offenders to engage in contact offending. Using self-referred participants in Germany where there is no mandatory child abuse reporting law (Neutze, Seto, Schaefer, Mundt, & Beier, 2011), a sample of 137 participants diagnosed with paedophilia or hebephilia were classified into three categories: child pornography offenders ($n = 42$), child molestation offenders ($n = 45$) and a mixed group that included prior use of child pornography and contact offending ($n = 50$). Neutze et al. (2011) found that child sexual abuse offenders were older than child pornography offenders and a larger proportion of child pornography offenders were employed. Although high levels of psychological problems (e.g., emotional deficits, cognitive distortions, sexual self-regulation) were seen among all three groups, they were generally similar across the groups. The researchers suggest that the lack of differences may be because of sample composition, because self-referred persons tend to be more motivated and the variance in these measures may be more limited.

A Canadian study by Seto, Wood, Babchishin, and Flynn (2012) examined differences in risk among child pornography–only offenders with no identifiable victim ($N = 38$), solicitation offenders (i.e., solicited sexual contact from a minor; $N = 70$), and contact sexual offenders who scored lower risk on an actuarial measure ($N = 38$). The groups were more similar to each other in age, ethnicity, and their emotional identification with children than expected by the authors, but the two online offender groups had more education and were less likely to have lived with a lover. Also, the child pornography–only group was more likely to report paedophilic sexual interests than the other groups. Expanding their original UK sample (Elliott et al., 2009), Elliott, Beech, and Mandeville-Norden (2013) separated online offenders into a mixed contact/ online offender group ($N = 143$) and online-only offender group ($N = 459$) and found both groups were similar but differed from contact offenders ($N = 526$). The contact offender group had less victim empathy, more sexualising cognitions about children, more externalised locus of control and a higher level of impulsivity than the online groups.

In light of these and other additional studies, Babchishin, Hanson, and VanZuylen (2015) re-examined differences in their original meta-analysis but separated online offenders into two groups of online child pornography offenders ($N = 2,284$) and mixed offenders ($N = 1,086$) – the latter group with online and contact offences – and compared them with sex offenders against children

(N = 2,320) using 30 separate samples from published and unpublished works. Some differences were found. Online-only offenders tended to have higher income, were more likely employed and educated and were younger. Contact offenders tended to score higher on anti-social indicators than mixed offenders who demonstrated more anti-social behaviours than online-only offenders. The authors further asserted that their findings are consistent with the criminological model of routine activity theory: offenders who commit contact sex offences were found to have greater access to children compared to mixed offenders who had greater access than online-only offenders. Moreover, online offenders had greater access to the Internet than contact offenders. Intuitively, accessibility seems to be an important factor to examine, and clearly from Babchishin et al.'s (2015) meta-analysis this assumption is empirically confirmed.

These empirical findings shed some light on the characteristics of online offenders and the diversity of this group. It is important to note that existing studies face methodological difficulties with the limitations of such data. There is often selection bias in the inclusion of offenders in these samples that may be affected by the prosecution of such cases or by the inclusion of offenders with indiscriminant pornography downloading that is not necessarily child or adolescent focussed. Seto (2013) has indicated that some cases are easier to convict, such as sex offenders who have clearly accessed sexually abusive images of pubescent or pre-pubescent children or online sex offenders who solicit teens who subsequently report the offence. Hence, it would be neglectful to not recognise that differences found in these studies may reflect selection in studies that may be abated by meta-analytic endeavors but do not entirely eliminate bias.

TYPOLOGY OF ONLINE OFFENDERS

Increasing our understanding of online offenders allows for informed assessment and treatment decisions. Often the general sex offender literature has explored the presence of sex offender subtypes to help understand offending patterns, to build theories, and to identify and introduce interventions that prevent future offending. Offenders who sexually offend online are no exception. Early work on online offenders has led to typologies based on collecting behaviours (e.g., Hartman, Burgess, & Lanning, 1984). However, this is somewhat limiting given that child pornography offending is one of many sexually abusive behaviours conducted on the Internet by online sex offenders. Sex offender typology has typically stemmed from the identification of offender motives for committing offences. Consistent with general motivation theories of sexual offending behaviour, Quayle and Taylor (2002) initially proposed that compulsive Internet use is reinforcing and ineffectively changes negative mood states. Since then, there have been a few empirical examinations of online offenders' motivations conducted to date. It is important to note a challenge in examining motivations and explanations given by online offenders is recognising the 'social desirability' filter that such narratives go through (Winder & Gough, 2010). However, understanding underlying motives may help to identify processes across individuals and the triggers that could escalate to contact offending (Kloess, Beech, & Harkins, 2014).

So what are the motivations of these offenders to commit their sexual offending online? Seto, Reeves, and Jung (2010) examined the explanations provided by child pornography offenders who were at the stage of pre-conviction (police investigation) and post-conviction (psychological assessment for presentence hearing). A large proportion of offenders (80%) admitted they had deliberately accessed the sexually abusive images but fewer acknowledged a sexual interest in children (less than 50%). Explanations endorsed by nearly half of the sample reflected curiosity or accidental access to the materials, whereas less than a quarter attributed their crimes to pornography or internet addiction. The proportion of online offenders who used certain explanations for their behaviour was contingent on the context of their disclosure (whether it was to police at pre-conviction or to a psychologist at post-conviction). A second empirical endeavor was carried out by Merdian, Wilson, Thakker, Curtis, and Boer (2013), who used a qualitative design to identify themes in the narratives of child pornography offenders. They found three offence motivations that included emotional (e.g., use of child pornography as a source of relief and a means to escape negativity), sexual (e.g., a replacement for an adequate sexual object) and mediating factor explanations. The last refers to explaining what had triggered them to initially view the sexually abusive images (e.g., meant to find adult images but accidentally came across images of children, curiosity about female development).

Identifying motives for committing online offences can help develop a better understanding of online offenders. Krone (2004) proposed nine types of offending in increasing seriousness: browser, private fantasy (conscious creation of online text or image for private use), trawler (actively seeking images), non-secure collector (collecting through peer-to-peer networks), secure collector (collecting using secure networks that often require membership or exchange), groomer (cultivating online relationship with potential victims), physical abuser, producer and distributor. These subtypes of child pornography offenders were developed based on three aspects that included the type of involvement the offender has with the illicit material, the level of networking with other like-minded offenders and the level of security that the offender employs in his or her collecting behaviour. Briggs, Simon and Simonsen (2011) provide a parsimonious typology. They suggest that there may be two subtypes of online sex offenders (contact-driven versus fantasy-driven) who have real differences in their modus operandi, prevalence, characteristics and recidivism. Briggs et al. (2011) note that online sex offenders present a problem in treatment because they do not necessarily have a 'real' victim. They further propose that they may not have sexually deviant preferences or criminological behaviour but rather are socially isolated, dysphoric in mood, and have increased social isolation, and this may result in part because such features are inherent traits or a consequence of becoming more involved in the internet community (Briggs et al., 2011). Using existing models, Merdian, Curtis, Thakker, Wilson, and Boer (2013) set out to identify sub-groups and propose a typology that is based on the function of the child pornography (divides online offenders into fantasy-driven and contact-driven); the underlying motivation (financial, instrumental but non-monetary, generally deviant and paedophilic motivations) and the level of networking.

Other than identifying proposed subtypes, there is little empirical evidence to encourage the use of these typological groupings and to give way to specific treatments that use these subtypes. Because none of the existing typologies for internet sex offenders were devised on the basis of empirical research (e.g., cluster analysis), it is questionable as to whether they are reliable or generalisable across offenders.

THEORIES OF ONLINE OFFENDING

A psychological understanding of online offending is crucial for valid appraisal of risk for re-offending and for effective rehabilitative programming (Andrews & Bonta, 2010; Stinson, Sales, & Becker, 2008). It is through the generation and application of theoretical models that theorists, researchers, and clinical practitioners conceptualise the specific etiological factors thought to be associated with behavioural phenomena and design interventions to modify problematic behaviours and alter the probability that they will re-occur in the future. As emphasised by Elliott and Beech (2009), it would be flawed to dismiss decades of work developing etiological theories of sexual offending but it is equally important to re-examine these theoretical conceptualisations given that not all online offenders share clinical symptoms outlined in these theories. The following is a brief review of existing theories that have been applied to understand the processes among online offenders (for further discussion see Elliott & Beech, 2009; Seto, 2013).

Quayle and Taylor (2003) examined the explicit role that child pornography material plays in problematic internet use and propose that child pornography collecting behaviour is rewarding in and of itself for some individuals. From their interviews of 23 men with online offending histories, they found that downloading behaviour may be seen as a form of illness over which an offender has little to no control. Quayle and Taylor (2003) propose a theory that views online sex offending as part of a complex array of behaviours involving the Internet and therefore embraces legal and illegal activities. The use of the Internet for sexual purposes is neither novel nor unique to users of the Internet and can often empower users. Specific to online sex offenders, accessing sexually abusive images from the Internet enables them to function outside of the conventional social interactions by which they are limited and marginalised. Through this less pathological perspective, therapeutic assessment and intervention may be facilitated by changing problematic cognitions about the self, the material being viewed, and the function that viewing the materials serve.

A review paper by Jung, Ennis, and Malesky (2012) applied three existing theoretical models (that have previously been used to explain sexual offending) to child pornography offending and proposed that child pornography offending can be seen through various lenses, therefore informing intervention. The first, social learning theory, has a stronghold in the field of sex offender etiology and treatment and asserts that thoughts and behaviours are reinforced through online involvement with pro-paedophile groups, and limited or no negative consequences have a significant impact on increasing behaviour. Social learning theory–informed interventions incorporate elements of cognitive behavioural therapy (CBT), which is the primary treatment modality for sex offenders (Hanson et al., 2002). The second, the courtship disorder theory, emphasises the relational deficits of sexual offenders when engaging in the courtship process, which may lead to an alternative progression or escalation in behaviour for some online offenders (Jung et al., 2012). Given that child pornography offenders have been found to be less likely to establish intimate relationships, report experiencing more feelings of loneliness, and exhibit lower levels of dominance and warmth, treatment focusses on broader cognitive and social issues, such as enhancing relationship and interpersonal skills, providing offenders with the skills necessary to satisfy fundamental human needs and increasing one's sense of self-efficacy in the courtship process (e.g., encourage individuals to approach activities that have the potential for rejection). The third lens, behavioural economics, has been applied extensively to problematic behaviours that are characterised by poor self-control, including substance abuse and pathological gambling, and offers a unifying perspective and a set of operations that can be applied to any behavioural phenomenon in any situation, including sexual violence. It describes how offenders will weigh the decisions in acquiring sexually abusive images. This analysis provides a useful framework for raising 'the price of the commodity' through the fostering of victim empathy, humanising victims depicted in the images and challenging beliefs that offences are victimless. Jung et al.'s (2013) overview of these three lenses encourages the use of theoretically informed interventions with online sex offenders.

A widely adopted theory of sexual offending has also been applied to online sex offenders. The Pathways model refers to a comprehensive theoretical framework that integrates (or theory knits) several influential theories, namely, the Precondition model (Finkelhor, 1984), Quadripartite model (Hall & Hirschman, 1992) and Integrated model (Marshall & Barbaree, 1990), into a comprehensive etiological theory (Ward & Siegert, 2002). The Pathways model proposes that there are multiple pathways that lead to the sexual abuse of a child, and each pathway is influenced by developmental features, dysfunctional mechanisms and an opportunity to commit the crime. Five pathways are high-lighted and include (1) intimacy deficits, (2) distorted sexual scripts, (3) emotional dysregulation, (4) anti-social cognitions, and (5) multiple dysfunctional mechanisms. A study by Middleton, Elliott, Mandeville-Norden, and Beech (2006) empirically examined the 'fit' of 72 online sex offenders in these five pathways. They were able to place 60% of their sample into one of Ward and Siegert's five pathways with the most populated pathway being the intimacy deficits pathway and second largest group being the emotional dysregulation pathway. Middleton et al. (2006) concluded that the online offender population is not a homogeneous group and is diverse similar to other sex offender groups, such as rapists or child molesters. Although online offenders share similar psychological deficits to other sex offenders, nearly half did not have psychological deficits that were deemed similar to other sex offenders. Hence, the authors recommended that online offenders would benefit from the same treatment as contact sex offenders. Elliott et al. (2009) examined whether online and contact offenders were similar in clinically observable deficits according to Ward and Siegert's (2002) Pathways model. They concluded that contact offenders were more likely to have primary deficits related to the anti-social cognitions pathway than online offenders. They suggest that online offenders not having the same levels of distorted cognitions as contact offenders is encouraging because online offenders may be less likely to commit future contact sexual offences.

Without theories to explain the emergence and maintenance of sexually abusive behaviour, clinicians and researchers are limited in the development of an informed and cohesive understanding of online sex offender behaviour and consequently engaging in clinical work with this population.

INTERVENTION BEST PRACTICES WITH ONLINE SEX OFFENDERS

Many published works are available to treatment providers on empirically based treatment models and techniques for sex offenders. Relapse prevention dominated sex offender treatment practices (Laws, 1989) since the 1980s, and more recently, the Good Lives model (GLM; Yates, Prescott, & Ward, 2010) has become increasingly prevalent in most correctional and community treatment programmes. Practice guidelines are well-established and adopted by the Association for the Treatment of Sexual Abusers (ATSA, 2014). However, when it comes to online sex offenders, very little is known about treatment and supervision as it applies to these offenders (fact sheet retrieved from http://www.atsa.com/internet-facilitated-sexual-offending). The following section will focus on the application of the *principles of correctional rehabilitation* and two approaches that offers specific programming for online offenders: i-SOTP and Inform Plus.

PRINCIPLES OF CORRECTIONAL REHABILITATION

At the current time, a framework that provides an efficient and evidence-based approach to treating offenders, including sex offenders, is the Principles of Correctional Rehabilitation, otherwise known as the Risk-Need-Responsivity (RNR) model (Andrews & Bonta, 2010). Widely accepted in guiding offender management and rehabilitation, the RNR model is a theory of criminal conduct that comprises three principles, namely, (1) risk principle, which asserts that intensive services should be provided to higher-risk offenders, (2) need principle, which states that criminogenic needs should be targeted in treatment interventions, and (3) responsivity principle, which highlights the importance of providing interventions in a way that corresponds to the offender's abilities, personality, motivation and other characteristics that may inhibit the benefits of treatment. An expanded version of the RNR also stresses the importance of developing a therapeutic alliance with offenders, using structured and validated assessments and the involvement of the organisation to ensure adherence to the model and proper training to staff members (Andrews, Bonta, & Wormith, 2011). Adherence to the RNR principles has been empirically shown to be effective in reducing sexual recidivism risk among sexual offenders (Hanson, Bourgon, Helmus, & Hodgson, 2009).

Risk Principle

The first principle highlights the importance of matching the level of service to the offender's risk to re-offend with lower risk cases engaging in less intensive services and higher risk cases receiving more intensive rehabilitative services (Andrews & Bonta, 2010). The importance of using structured and validated measures in the assessment of risk becomes problematic in applying the RNR model to online offenders. The difficulty is the availability of a proper and validated assessment tool designed for use with online offenders. Seto (2013) states, 'it is not yet clear how to proceed in the risk assessment of pornography offenders with no history of contact' (p. 203). Several of the existing risk measures have been validated with online sex offenders who do have contact offences, such as the Static-99 (Hanson & Thornton, 2000) and the Risk Matrix 2000 (Thornton et al., 2003). However, these measures tend to overestimate risk for online offenders without contact offences (Osborn, Elliott, Middleton, & Beech, 2010), although the Risk Matrix 2000 seems to show promise for this population in its original (Barnett, Wakeling, & Howard, 2010; Wakeling, Howard, & Barnett, 2011) and revised formats (Osborn et al., 2010).

The Kent Internet Risk Assessment Tool (KIRAT) shows some promise in its preliminary findings. The measure was developed for use by police to prioritise their online offence cases (McManus, Long, & Alison, 2011) and is based on an examination of adult sexual offenders who have been formally convicted of offences that involve possession of indecent images of children, specifically comparing those with previous contact child offences and those with no evidence of any contact offences against children (Long, Alison, & McManus, 2013). The KIRAT measures variables that assess previous offending behaviour, offender's access to children and behaviours such as grooming and production of images (Long, Alison, & McManus, 2012). A retrospective study disseminated at a national conference (Long et al., 2012) showed that the tool had a good level of predictive accuracy ($AUC = .852$), but further studies that include prospective methodology are needed to examine its use as a risk assessment measure.

A few studies have made some attempts to investigate specific risk factors with samples of online sex offenders. As noted in the research by Long and his colleagues (2012, 2013) and Seto's review of the literature (2013), previous offences, access to potential victims, and grooming and production behaviours may be relevant. Faust, Renaud, and Bickert's (2009) presentation (as cited in Seto, 2013) reported that lower education, single marital status, having child pornography obtained through non-internet means, prior sex offender treatment and not having depictions of adolescent minors are variables found to be predictive of further sexual crimes. Well established in the general sex offender literature is that anti-sociality and sexual deviance are strong predictors of sexual violence, and Seto (2013) proposes that these findings are most likely to be fitting with online sex offenders as well. In applying Seto's motivation-facilitation model (2008), most online offenders may have the motivation (e.g., paedophilic and/or hebephilic interests), but they do not necessarily have the facilitative features that would increase their risk (e.g., anti-social patterns and tendencies).

A promising risk assessment tool to predict recidivism among child pornography offenders was recently examined and published by Seto and Eke (2015). The Child Pornography Offender Risk Tool (CPORT; pronounced 'seaport') is comprised of seven items: Young offender age, any prior criminal history, any contact sexual offending, any failure on conditional release, indication of sexual interest in child pornography material or prepubescent or pubescent children, more boy than girl content in child pornography, and more boy than girl content in other child depictions. In their examination of the CPORT, Seto and Eke obtained a sample of child pornography cases from police services where 88% involved online technology and 21% had also committed contact sex offending. Of the 286 offenders in their sample, 39% had new offences, 12% had new child pornography offences, and 16% had any new sexual offence. They found that the CPORT score predicted any recidivism ($AUC = .66$), any sexual recidivism ($AUC = .74$), and any contact sexual recidivism ($AUC = .74$). However, when the CPORT score was examined for the offenders who only had child pornography offences, the CPORT did not predict sexual recidivism.

Important to note is the caveat of very low base rates of sexual offending seen in the samples of online offenders with these preliminary findings. Research has reported consistently a lower likelihood for online sex offenders to sexually recidivate (e.g., 11% in 6 years follow-up, Eke, Seto, & Williams, 2011; 3% with targeted victim/1.6% CP offence in 4.8 years follow-up average, Faust et al., 2014; 7% in 2 years minimum follow-up, Jung et al., 2012; 4.6% in 1.5 to 6 years follow-up, Seto, Hanson, & Babchishin, 2011), especially when compared to contact child molestation offenders (12.7% of child molesters, Hanson & Bussiere, 1998; 13.7% of all contact offenders, Hanson & Morton-Bourgon, 2005). Similar numbers can be found with juvenile online offenders (e.g., 1.9%, Aebi, Plattner, Ernest, Kaszynski, & Bessler, 2014). Although a study by Bourke and Hernandez (2009) suggests that past hands-on offending as self-reported by offenders may be upwards of 85%, these findings have yet to be replicated. A meta-analysis by Seto et al. (2011) found remarkably lower rates of contact sexual offending in the histories of online offenders (12%). Hence, to identify risk predictors is difficult when there is little variance in the overall risk (Seto, 2013).

Need Principle

The need principle refers to the importance of assessing criminogenic needs and applying treatment that targets these identified needs (Andrews & Bonta, 2010). Given that effective treatment should be tailored to the type of offender and the risk he or she presents, a problem that is similar to the one seen with the risk principle emerges in that there is a lack of validated measures of risk and need factors for non-contact online offenders. However, given the empirical work that has examined the prevalence of criminogenic needs seen among online offenders, especially in comparison with child molestation offenders, some inferences can be made. There are some factors that are more likely to be areas of concern for online offenders as identified in the literature, such as intimacy deficits, emotional dysregulation, and anti-social associations and other areas in which there may be less importance to address in treatment for this group of offenders, such as anti-sociality.

As originally purported by Ward and Siegert's (2002) Pathways model and supported by Middleton et al.'s (2006) work, intimacy deficits and emotional dysregulation pathways appear to be more common among online offenders, and these deficits have been found to be prevalent among online offenders in multiple comparison studies. Intimacy deficits are found to be a core treatment target in more than half of US treatment programmes (64.6% of institutional and 65.7% of community programmes) and in most Canadian programmes (87.5 of institutional and 78.9% of community programmes; McGrath, Cumming, Burchard, Zeoli, & Ellerby, 2010). Often interpersonal or intimacy components of treatment focusses on skills building, and this is typically of a cognitive-behavioural nature with modeling, reinforcing and role-playing as part of the programme in developing appropriate intimacy behaviours. It is important in the process of treatment to analyse the opportunistic nature of using the Internet to groom victims (see Kloess et al., 2014, for further discussion) and to ensure more intensive treatment and supervision for those who use the Internet for fulfilling intimacy deficits and therefore for establishing a relationship with inappropriate partners.

Emotional dysregulation is frequently found in most North American treatment programmes as a core treatment target (i.e., institutional/community programmes in the United States, 83.5%/91.2%, and in Canada, 87.5%/94.7%; McGrath et al., 2010). There is a plethora of emotion-focussed modules for sexual offenders, but Quayle, Erooga, Wright, Taylor, and Harbinson (2006) have written specifically about therapy with online offenders and on emotional avoidance with accompanying exercises and worksheets that focus on increasing mindfulness skills to balance emotion, mind and reasonable mind (states of being in which thoughts, actions and feelings are under the primary influence of high emotional arousal or rational thought). Dialectical behaviour therapy, which has been shown to be empirically successful with borderline personality disorder, has some potential uses to address emotional dysregulation among sex offenders and even interpersonal difficulties as well (Shingler, 2004).

An area of concern for online sex offenders is their association with other anti-social and pro-offending associates through online networks or pro-paedophile forums. Malesky and Ennis (2004) examined the interaction between the members of an online community who endorsed paedophilic interests and found a diverse range of distorted cognitions that validated, romanticised and even idealised sexual relationships with children. Related to intimacy deficits, maintaining connections with other like-minded pro-offending individuals limits or even prohibits healthy relationships with pro-social adults. Having anti-social associates and companions has been indicated as an important risk factor in the general offending literature (Andrews & Bonta, 2010) and is a concern with online offenders in light of the influence that pro-paedophile communities have on encouraging anti-social patterns of thinking (Malesky & Ennis, 2004). Although it is not seen as a core treatment target in sex offender programmes, it is a relevant factor to assess, intervene and manage with this online offending population.

Intuitively, the regulation of internet access has been seen as a central consideration and a potential treatment target. Although Wolak et al. (2008) note that children and adolescents posting personal information does not increase their risk to online predators, they note that interactive behaviours, such as conversing online with unknown people about sex, creates more risk. So should online offenders be prohibited from internet use? A review of sentencing judgements showed that less than 50% of child pornography offenders received restrictions on their use of the Internet, and one judge further stated, "I was concerned that as the computer has become an integral part of our work and recreation in this society, caution must be exercised when considering prohibition of its use or possession altogether ... The computer was not the culprit in these circumstances any more than a typewriter" (p. 47; Jung & Stein, 2012).

Aebi et al. (2014) have indicated that dysfunctional internet use and sexually deviant arousal should be targets in treatment, based on their examination of juvenile child pornography offenders, and Quayle and Taylor (2003) have attributed problematic internet use as an etiological consideration. Hence, treatment should target appropriate use of the Internet, and not necessarily internet use, per se. d'Almeida Neto, Eyland, Ware, Galouzis, and Kevin (2013) call this the 'internet sex offender paradox', implying that restricting access to the internet does not enable skills practice (in using the Internet) and therefore treatment and internet use run in contrast with one another. The authors advocate for post-therapy brief online interventions to assist online offenders to put their skills into practice.

Sexually deviant interest is a critical risk factor for sex offenders in general and particularly online offenders. Given that most online offenders may have the motivation component of Seto's (2008) motivation-facilitation model, sexual deviance and persistence of sexual offending may be treatment targets for online offenders. At this time, sexual self-regulation is commonly addressed using pharmacological (e.g., anti-androgen medications; see Grubin, 2008) methods that markedly reduce sexual libido or psychological methods to address sexual preoccupation and cognitions, such as cognitive-behavioural approaches (e.g., relapse prevention; Laws, 1989).

Using a proper, validated assessment of the described needs and other criminogenic needs that are relevant to an online offender, it is important to focus treatment on these core areas. It is also noted by some authors that the use of child pornography may be attributed to curiosity (in the absence of paedophilic motivations or pro-paedophilic networking behaviours) and such offenders may have been evaluated as a low risk. In these cases, little or no treatment and minimal supervision may be appropriate.

Responsivity Principle

The responsivity principle ensures that rehabilitation is maximised by using cognitive social learning methods (e.g., reinforcement, modelling, skills building, cognitive restructuring) and tailoring interventions to suit the learning style, motivation, abilities, personality, mental health, demographics and strengths of the offender (Andrews et al., 2011). The general component of the responsivity principle refers to influence strategies that are used in the intervention and recommends that structured, cognitive-behavioural methods are used and that a therapeutic alliance is established. The specific component of the responsivity principle is a fine-tuning of the treatment to ensure that treatment is matched to the offender's characteristics that include his strengths, abilities, motivation, personality and demographic features (e.g., age, ethnicity). Therefore, appropriate assessment of these areas may be warranted when concerns are raised. For example, cognitive abilities may not be a deficit commonly seen among online offenders as the research has consistently found, but if an offender exhibits a learning disability, then proper psychometric measures of academic achievement may be suitable to identify areas of the programme that may prove more difficult for the individual.

Conclusion

The RNR model is currently part of best practices with adult male sex offenders as outlined by the empirical literature using distal outcome measures (i.e., recidivism) and organisations that focus on the prevention of sexual abuse (i.e., ATSA Practice Guidelines). Although data are not available on the specific application of RNR to online offenders, there is little dispute that adherence to these three principles and the expanded RNR model would affect positive change and outcomes for online offenders. The implementation of treatment that focusses on core treatment targets may need to be amended to suit online offenders depending on the assessment and identification of relevant criminogenic needs and specific areas of responsivity.

INTERNET SEX OFFENDER TREATMENT PROGRAMME (I-SOTP)

As with most correctional and criminal justice programmes, when there is a need, often a programme is developed to fulfill that need. Developed in response to phenomenal growth of online sex offenders in the criminal justice system, the Internet Sex Offender Treatment Programme (i-SOTP) was developed and accredited by the National Probation Service in England and Wales (Middleton, Mandeville-Norden, & Hayes, 2009). Treatment providers recognised a need to include material that was more specific to online offenders, such as sexual compulsivity, obsessional thinking and problematic internet use that stems from collecting behaviour, and this led to a review of empirical comparisons and identified intimacy deficits and problems with emotional regulation to be relevant (Middleton, 2008). However, given that not all offenders have these characteristics, the programme was made to be flexible and modular in its group format that is administered in 35 two-hour sessions (Middleton, 2008).

Consistent with the RNR model, the i-SOTP includes a process to identify criminogenic needs and to apply the appropriate dosage. Specifically, the i-SOTP uses the Risk Matrix 2000 (RM2000; Thornton et al., 2003) to determine if an offender is eligible. If the offender scored low, medium, or high risk using the RM2000 and was low in sexual deviance, he or she was deemed eligible for entering the i-SOTP. High-risk online sex offenders, particularly those who were high in sexual deviance, were placed in the longer and more generic sex offender treatment programmes. The i-SOTP also takes on a holistic approach rather than simply focussing on coping skills and managing high-risk situations as in the original relapse prevention model. In fact, the i-SOTP incorporates three contemporary models, namely, (1) model of change (Fisher & Beech, 1998), (2) model of problematic internet use (Quayle & Taylor, 2003), and (3) good lives model (Ward & Stewart, 2003), and is formatted into six modules with a different set of goals for each module.

The first module aims to increase motivation, decrease denial and identify and reduce the discrepancy between perceived pro-social and anti-social behaviours (e.g., by addressing distorted attitudes). According to Middleton (2008), the i-SOTP begins in this first module with a number of exercises that are designed to help offenders identify values that are important for themselves and how their behaviour has in some aspect not reflected these values. Establishing a discrepancy, hence building on the cognitive dissonance from this process, facilitates a focus on setting new pro-social goals. The second module challenges existing offence-supportive attitudes and behaviours. Through the analysis of the offence behaviour, offenders begin to challenge their offence-supportive cognitions and develop some ability to see the lack of functionality of their thinking. The third module endeavors to promote an empathic response to identifying that children depicted in the indecent images are real victims of child abuse. In this module, the victim experience is examined and victim awareness is increased. Middleton (2008) reported that facilitator feedback from the programme suggests that, once victim awareness is established, most internet sex offenders do not have difficulty in demonstrating appropriate empathy. There is an important linkage made between their viewing behaviour and child abuse.

The fourth module attempts to reduce the use of sex as a strategy for coping and emotional avoidance and to replace it with effective problem-solving strategies. This is the longest section of the programme and addresses socio-affective functioning, self-management and intimacy deficits by focussing on practicing skills. The goals of the fifth module are to develop adequate relationship, intimacy and coping skills and to improve self-esteem and internal locus of control. To address social adequacy and self-management deficits, offenders gain recognition of, and develop appropriate responses to, collecting and compulsivity issues. What is also targeted is their needs that are met through joining pseudo-communities online and replacing these behaviours with more appropriate behaviours to meet their needs. The sixth and last module aims to develop realistic relapse-prevention strategies and new pro-social lifestyle goals, therefore addressing self-management and socio-affective functioning. This module applies the new learning from the previous modules and incorporates the learning into relapse prevention or a 'new life plan.' Also, some exercises are undertaken to deal with deviant sexual fantasy.

Middleton et al. (2009) examined the effectiveness of the i-SOTP with 264 convicted offenders by measuring the pre-treatment and post-treatment scores on several psychometric measures. All scales from these measures showed reductions post-treatment with 53% of treated offenders demonstrating scores in the non-offending range. It is important to note that only a few of these variables are deemed psychologically meaningful variables (see Mann, Hanson, & Thornton, 2010), and these include cognitive distortions, emotional significance of children and impulsivity. Several of the variables, which are intended to assess the effectiveness of the modules given their relevance to the module's associated goals (e.g., measure of victim empathy and module three builds on empathic response) are not identified as criminogenic, although some may be useful responsivity variables and therefore may pose an obstacle to treatment effectiveness (e.g., distress, self-esteem; see Mann et al., 2010). Beyond proximal treatment change, there have been no further validation studies examining the effects of the treatment on post-treatment behaviour or criminal re-offending. However, the programme content highlights areas noted to be pathways in the development of sexual offending, namely, intimacy deficits, distorted sexualised cognitions and emotional dysregulation.

INFORM PLUS PROGRAMME AND SELF-HELP RESOURCES

Several educational resources are offered through the Lucy Faithfull Foundation in the UK (http://www.lucyfaithfull.org.uk). These resources are offered to online offenders, family and friends of offenders and people who are concerned about their inappropriate use of the Internet to access sexually abusive images. The premise behind each of these resources is to provide a safe environment to reduce further re-offending.

For individuals who have been arrested, cautioned, or convicted for internet offences that involve child pornography, the Inform Plus Programme offers a 10-week course for groups of six to eight persons with each session lasting 2.5 hours. The course provides an opportunity for individuals to explore their offending behaviours and develop strategies to avoid future online offending. On the Lucy Faithfull Foundation website, the programme claims to cover the behavioural process involved in this type of offending, the effects on child victims, the impact on the offender and those close to him or her, information about the criminal justice system and goals to achieve a positive future lifestyle. There is a cost to the participant and there is the opportunity to engage in one-to-one programming. A separate programme, called the Inform Programme, is a service for partners, relatives and friends of online offenders and is intended to dispel myths about online offending, explore questions about why the offender engages and continues to engage in this behaviour, consider criminal justice issues, help devise practical risk management strategies and provide emotional support. The course runs over five weeks and there is a cost to participants.

Also offered on through the same charitable foundation is a self-help programme (get-help.stopitnow.org.uk) for professionals and help-seeking individuals. According to the foundation's website and Seto (2013), the programme was originally developed by Ethel Quayle and her colleagues at the Combating Paedophile Information Networks in Europe (COPINE) Project. The programme is modular and aims to provide information about illegal images on the Internet, help individuals identify problematic internet use and assist individuals with learning techniques to help cope and change behaviours.

Similar to the Dunkelfeld Prevention Project in Germany (see Beier, Grund-mann, Kuhle, Scherner, Konrad, & Amelung, 2015), these programmes are intended to reach individuals who recognise that their behaviour is problematic and want to seek help. However, unlike the German project, these programmes have not yet been evaluated for their effectiveness, although a recent qualitative study offers some encouraging findings (Dervley, Perkins, Whitehead, Bailey, Gillespie, & Squire, 2017). Despite this limitation, the intentions are cost-effective and encouraging in its use of a medium that is readily useable by its intended audience (e.g., those who have problems with the internet; Seto, 2013).

CONCLUSION

The increasing prevalence of online offenders has led to a number of empirical endeavors to try to understand and describe this subtype of sexual offenders. The consistent message from this work suggests they are not markedly differ-ent from contact sex offenders with child victims, but what is notable is that they seem to include older and educated individuals who carry fewer anti-social behaviour patterns than their contact counterparts. Also, there appears to be diversity within this subtype of offenders; child pornography offenders were more likely to have paedophilic interests but less opportunity to access potential victims than contact offenders and online offenders with contact offences. The Internet is certainly a new medium to facilitate sex crimes, but the behaviour itself is still a form of sexual grooming with the potential to initi-ate child sexual abuse. The research thus far suggests that fewer online-only offenders are formally convicted for further sexual offences than con-tact offenders. Research is only beginning to examine the assessment and treatment of online offenders to determine best practices, and existing pro-grammes have yet to be examined for reductions in sexually criminal behav-iour for this population. At the current time, the RNR model is appropriate to effect changes in risk, but there is still a need to further develop and validate measures of risk and need for online sex offenders to appropriately assess treatment dosage and intensity. The i-SOTP and the in-person and online methods available through the Lucy Faithfull Foundation have promise, but methodologically sound evaluation research of these treatments is needed to establish whether these are effective treatment programmes in terms of proxi-mal and distal changes. For online offenders with a lower risk to commit con-tact sexual offences, intensive treatments would be an ineffective use of limited resources, and management and supervision may be more appropriate. More promising for online offenders at a moderate to high risk is the use of educa-tional programmes focussing on appropriate internet use and an assessment of criminogenic needs to target in treatment.

REFERENCES

Aebi, M., Plattner, B., Ernest, M., Kaszynski, K., & Bessler, C. (2014). Criminal history and future offending of juveniles convicted of the possession of child pornography. *Sexual Abuse: A Journal of Research and Treatment, 26,* 375–390. doi:10.1177/1079063213492344

Andrews, D. A., & Bonta, J. (2010). *The psychology of criminal conduct* (5th ed.). Cincinnati, OH: Anderson.

Andrews, D. A., Bonta, J., & Wormith, J. S. (2011). The risk-need-responsivity (RNR) model: Does adding the good lives model contribute to effective crime prevention? *Criminal Justice and Behavior, 38,* 735–755. doi:10.1177/0093854811406356

Association for the Treatment of Sexual Abusers (ATSA). (2014). *ATSA practice guidelines for the assessment, treatment, and management of male adult sexual abusers.* Beaverton, OR: Author.

Babchishin, K. M., Hanson, R. K., & Hermann, C. A. (2011). The characteristics of online sex offenders: A meta-analysis. *Sexual Abuse: A Journal of Research and Treatment, 23,* 92–123. doi:10.1177/1079063210370708

Babchishin, K. M., Hanson, R. K., & VanZuylen, H. (2015). Online child pornography offenders are different: A meta-analysis of the characteristics of online and offline sex offenders against children. *Archives of Sexual Behavior, 44*(1):45–66. doi:10.1007/s10508-014-0270-x

Barnett, G. D., Wakeling, H. C., & Howard, P. D. (2010). An examination of the predictive validity of the Risk Matrix 2000 in England and Wales. *Sexual Abuse: A Journal of Research and Treatment, 22,* 443–470.

Bates, A., & Metcalf, C. (2007). A psychometric comparison of internet and non-internet sex offenders from a community treatment sample. *Journal of Sexual Aggression, 13,* 11–20. doi:10.1080/13552600701365654

Beier, K. M., Grundmann, D., Kuhle, L. F., Scherner, G., Konrad, A., & Amelung, T. (2015). The German Dunkelfeld Project: A pilot study to prevent child sexual abuse and the use of child abusive images. *Journal of Sexual Medicine, 12,* 529–542. doi:10.1111/jsm.12785

Bourke, M., & Hernandez, A. (2009). The 'Butner Study' redux: A report of the incidence of hands-on child victimization by child pornography offenders. *Journal of Family Violence, 24,* 183–191. doi:10.1007/s10896-008-9219-y

Boyce, J., Cotter, A., & Perreault, S. (2014). *Police-reported crime statistics in Canada, 2013.* Ottawa, ON: Statistics Canada. Retrieved July 24, 2014, from www.statcan.gc.ca

Briggs, P., Simon, W. T., & Simonsen, S. (2011). An exploratory study of internet-initiated sexual offences and the chat room sex offender: Has the internet enabled a new typology of sex offender? *Sexual Abuse: A Journal of Research and Treatment, 23,* 72–91. doi:10.1177/1079063210384275

Child Exploitation and Online Protection Centre (CEOP). (2012). *A picture of abuse: A thematic assessment of the risk of contact child sexual abuse posed by those who possess indecent images of children.* Retrieved October 3, 2014, from http://ceop.police.uk/Documents/ceopdocs/CEOP%20IIOCTA%20Executive%20Summary.pdf

Cooper, A. (1997). The internet and sexuality: Into the new millennium. *Journal of Sex Education and Therapy, 22,* 5–6.

d'Almeida Neto, C., Eyland, S., Ware, J., Galouzis, J., & Kevin, M. (2013). Brief interventions: Solving the 'Internet sex offender paradox'. *Psychiatry, Psychology and Law, 20,* 183–187. doi:10.1080/13218719.2011.633329

Dervley, R., Perkins, D., Whitehead, H., Bailey, A., Gillespie, S., & Squire, T. (2017). Themes in participant feedback on a risk reduction programme for child sexual exploitation material offenders. *Journal of Sexual Aggression.* doi: 10.1080/13552600.2016.1269958 [Advanced online publication]

Durkin, K. F. (1997). Misuse of the internet by pedophiles: Implications for law enforcement and probation practice. *Federal Probation, 61,* 14–18. doi:10.4135/9781452229454

Eke, A. W., Seto, M. C., & Williams, J. (2011). Examining the criminal history and future offending of child pornography offenders: Extended prospective follow-up study. *Law and Human Behavior, 35,* 466–478. doi:10.1007/s10979-010-9252-2

Elliott, I. A., & Beech, A. R. (2009). Understanding online child pornography use: Applying sexual offense theory to internet offenders. *Aggression and Violent Behavior, 14,* 180–193. doi:10.1016/j.avb.2009.03.002

Elliott, I. A., Beech, A. R., & Mandeville-Norden, R. (2013). The psychological profiles of internet, contact, and mixed internet/contact sex offenders. *Sexual Abuse: A Journal of Research and Treatment, 25,* 3–20. doi:10.1177/1079063212439426

Elliott, I. A., Beech, A. R., Mandeville-Norden, R., & Hayes, E. (2009). Psychological profiles of internet sexual offenders: Comparisons with contact sexual offenders. *Sexual Abuse: A Journal of Research and Treatment, 21,* 76–92. doi:10.1177/1079063208326929

Faust, E., Bickart, W., Renaud, C., & Camp, S. (2014). Child pornography possessors and child contact sex offenders: A multilevel comparison of demographic characteristics and rates of recidivism. *Sexual Abuse: A Journal of Research and Treatment, 27*(5), 460–478.

Faust, E., Bickart, W., & Renaud, C. (2009, October). *Predictors of re-offense among a sample of federally convicted child pornography offenders.* Paper presented at the 28th Annual Conference of the Association for the Treatment of Sexual Abusers. Dallas, Texas.

Finkelhor, D. (1984). *Child sexual abuse: New theory and research.* New York, NY: Free Press.

Finkelhor, D., & Ormrod, R. (2004, Dec.). Child pornography: Patterns from NIBRS. *Bulletin of the Office of Juvenile Justice and Delinquency Prevention.* Retrieved April 11, 2009, from www.ojp.usdoj.gov/ojjdp

Fisher, D., & Beech, A. R. (1998). Reconstituting families after sexual abuse: The offender's perspective. *Child Abuse Review, 7,* 420–434.

Grubin, D. (2008). Medical models and interventions in sexual deviance. In D. R. Laws & W. T. O'Donohue (Eds.), *Sexual deviance: Theory, assessment, and treatment* (pp. 594–610). New York, NY: Guilford Press.

Hall, G. C. N. , & Hirschman, R. (1992). Sexual aggression against children: A conceptual perspective of etiology. *Criminal Justice and Behavior, 19,* 8–23.

Hanson, R. K., Bourgon, G., Helmus, L., & Hodgson, S. (2009). The principles of effective correctional treatment also apply to sex offenders. *Criminal Justice and Behavior, 36,* 865–891. doi:10.1177/0093854809338545

Hanson, R. K., & Bussiere, M. T. (1998). Predicting relapse: A meta-analysis of sexual offender recidivism studies. *Journal of Consulting and Clinical Psychology, 66,* 348–362. doi:10.1037//0022-006X.66.2.348

Hanson, R. K., Gordon, A., Harris, A. J., Marques, J. K., Murphy, W., Quinscy, V. L., & Seto, M. C. (2002). First report of the Collaborative Outcome Data Project on the effectiveness of psychological treatment for sex offenders. *Sexual Abuse: A Journal of Research and Treatment, 14*, 169–194.

Hanson, R. K., & Morton-Bourgon, K. E. (2005). The characteristics of persistent sexual offenders: A meta-analysis of recidivism studies. *Journal of Consulting and Clinical Psychology, 73*, 1154–1163. doi:10.1037/0022-006X.73.6.1154.

Hanson, R. K., & Thornton, D. (2000). Improving risk assessment for sex offenders: A comparison of three actuarial scales. *Law and Human Behavior, 24*, 119–136.

Hartman, C. R., Burgess, A. W., & Lanning, K. V. (1984). Typology of collectors. In A. W Burgess (Ed.), *Child pornography and sex rings* (pp. 93–109). Lanham, MD: Lexington Books.

Jung, S., Ennis, L. P., & Malesky, L. A. (2012). Child pornography offending seen through three theoretical lenses. *Deviant Behavior, 33*, 655–673.

Jung, S., Ennis, L., Stein, S., Choy, A. L., & Hook, T. (2013). Child pornography possessors: Comparisons and contrasts with contact and non-contact sex offenders. *Journal of Sexual Aggression, 19*, 295–310.

Jung, S., & Stein, S. (2012). As examination of judicial sentencing decisions in child pornography and child molestation cases in Canada. *Journal of Criminal Psychology, 2*, 38–50. doi:10.1108/20093821211210486

Kloess, J. A., Beech, A. R., & Harkins, L. (2014). Online child sexual exploitation: Prevalence, process, and offender characteristics. *Trauma, Violence, & Abuse, 15*, 126–139. doi:10.1177/1524838013511543

Krone, T. (2004, July). A typology of online child pornography offending. *Trends and Issues in Crime and Criminal Justice, 279*. Retrieved July 24, 2014, from www.aic. gov.au/publications/tandi2/tandi279.pdf

Laulik, S., Allam, J., & Sheridan, L. (2007). An investigation into maladaptive personality functioning in internet sex offenders. *Psychology, Crime & Law, 13*, 523–535.

Laws, D. R. (1989). *Relapse prevention with sex offenders*. New York, NY: Guilford Press.

Long, M. L., Alison, L. A., & McManus, M. A. (2012, Oct.). Risk assessment in online child exploitation: Kent Internet Risk Assessment Tool (KIRAT). In A. R. Beech (Chair), *The development of practical tools for the assessment, prioritization, and management of child pornography offenders*. Symposium presented at the conference of the Association for the Treatment of Sexual Abusers, Denver, CO.

Long, M. L., Alison, L. A., & McManus, M. A. (2013). Child pornography and likelihood of contact abuse: A comparison between contact child sexual offenders and noncontact offenders. *Sexual Abuse: A Journal of Research and Treatment, 25*, 370–395. doi:10.1177/1079063212464398

Malesky, L. A. (2007). Predatory online behavior: Modus operandi of convicted sex offenders in identifying potential victims and contacting minors over the internet. *Journal of Child Sexual Abuse, 16*, 23–32. doi:10.1300/J070v16n02_02

Malesky, L. A., & Ennis, L. P. (2004). Supportive distortions: An analysis of postings on a pedophile internet message board. *Journal of Addiction and Offender Counseling, 24*, 92–100.

Mann, R. E., Hanson, R. K., & Thornton, D. (2010). Assessing risk for sexual recidivism: Some proposals on the nature of psychologically meaningful risk factors. *Sexual Abuse: A Journal of Research and Treatment, 22*, 191–217.

Marshall, W. L., & Barbaree, H. E. (1990). An integrated theory of the etiology of sexual offending. In W. L. Marshall, D. R. Laws, & H. E. Barbaree (Eds.), *Handbook of sexual assault: Issues, theories and treatment of the offender* (pp. 257–275). New York, NY: Plenum.

McGrath, R., Cumming, G., Burchard, B., Zeoli, S., & Ellerby, L. (2010). *Current practices and emerging trends in sexual abuser management: The Safer Society 2009 North American survey*. Brandon, VT: Safer Society Press.

McManus, M., Long, M. L., & Alison, L. (2011). Child pornography offenders: Towards an evidence-based approach to prioritizing the investigation of indecent image offenses. In L. Alison & L. Rainbow (Eds.), *Professionalizing offender profiling: Forensic and investigative psychology in practice*. Abingdon, UK: Routledge.

Merdian, H. L., Curtis, C., Thakker, J., Wilson, N., & Boer, D. P. (2013). The three dimensions of online CP offending. *Journal of Sexual Aggression, 19,* 121–132.

Merdian, H. L., Wilson, N., Thakker, J., Curtis, C., & Boer, D. P. (2013). 'So why did you do it'?: Explanations provided by child pornography offenders. *Sexual Offender Treatment, 8,* 1–19.

Middleton, D. (2008). From research to practice: The development of the Internet Sex Offender Treatment Program (i-SOTP). *Irish Probation Journal, 5,* 49–64.

Middleton, D., Elliott, I. A., Mandeville-Norden, R., & Beech, A. R. (2006). An investigation into the applicability of the Ward and Siegert Pathways model of child sexual abuse with internet offenders. *Psychology, Crime and Law, 12,* 589–603. doi:10.1080/10683160600558352

Middleton, D., Mandeville-Norden, R., & Hayes, E. (2009). Does treatment work with internet sex offenders? Emerging findings from the Internet Sex Offender Treatment Programme (i-SOTP). *Journal of Sexual Aggression, 15,* 5–19. doi:10.1080/13552600802673444

Motivans, M., & Kyckelhahn, T. (2007, Dec.). Federal prosecution of child sex exploitation offenders, 2006. *Bureau of Justice Statistics Bulletin*. Retrieved August 8, 2014, from http://www.ojp.usdoj.gov

Neutze, J., Seto, M. C., Schaefer, G. A., Mundt, I. A., & Beier, K. M. (2011). Predictors of child pornography offenses and child sexual abuse in a community sample of pedophiles and hebephiles. *Sexual Abuse: A Journal of Research and Treatment, 23,* 212–242. doi:10.1177/1079063210382043

Osborn, J., Elliott, I. A., Middleton, D., & Beech, A. R. (2010). The use of actuarial risk assessment measures with UK internet child pornography offenders. *Journal of Aggression, Conflict and Peace Research, 2,* 16–24. doi:10.5042/jacpr.2010.0333

Quayle, E., Erooga, M., Wright, L., Taylor, M., & Harbinson, D. (2006). *Only pictures? Therapeutic work with internet sex offenders*. Lyme Regis, UK: Russell House Publishing.

Quayle, E., & Taylor, M. (2002). Child pornography and the internet: Perpetuating a cycle of abuse. *Deviant Behavior, 23,* 331–361.

Quayle, E., & Taylor, M. (2003). Model of problematic internet use in people with a sexual interest in children. *CyberPsychology and Behavior, 6,* 93–106. doi:10.1089/109493103321168009

Seto, M. C. (2008). *Pedophilia and sexual offending against children: Theory, assessment, and intervention*. Washington, DC: American Psychological Association.

Seto, M. C. (2013). *Internet sex offenders*. Washington, DC: American Psychological Association.

Seto, M. C., & Eke, A. W. (2015). Predicting recidivism among adult male child pornography offenders: Development of the Child Pornography Offender Risk Tool (CPORT). *Law and Human Behavior, 39,* 416–429. doi:10.1037/lhb0000128

Seto, M. C., Hanson, R. K., & Babchishin, K. M. (2011). Contact sexual offending by men with online sexual offences. *Sexual Abuse: A Journal of Research and Treatment, 23,* 124–145. doi:10.1177/1079063210369013

Seto, M. C., Reeves, L., & Jung, S. (2010). Explanations given by child pornography offenders for their crimes. *Journal of Sexual Aggression, 16,* 169–180. doi:10.1080/13552600903572396

Seto, M. C., Wood, J. M., Babchishin, K. M., & Flynn, S. (2012). Online solicitation offenders are different from child pornography offenders and lower risk than contact sexual offenders. *Law and Human Behavior, 36,* 320–330. doi:10.1037/h0093925

Shingler, J. (2004). A process of cross-fertilization: What sex offender treatment can learn from dialectical behaviour therapy. *Journal of Sexual Aggression, 10,* 171–180. doi:10.1080/13552600412331289050

Stinson, J. D., Sales, B. D., & Becker, J. V. (2008). *Sex offending: Causal theories to inform research, prevention, and treatment.* Washington, DC: American Psychological Association.

Thornton, D., Mann, R., Webster, S., Blud, L., Travers, R., Friendship. C., et al. (2003). Distinguishing and combining risks for sexual and violent recidivism. *Annals of the New York Academy of Sciences, 989,* 225–235. doi:10.1111/j.1749-6632.2003.tb07308.x

Tomak, S., Weschler, F. S., Ghahramanlou-Holloway, M., Virden, T., & Nademin, M. E. (2009). An empirical study of the personality characteristics of internet sex offenders. *Journal of Sexual Aggression, 15,* 139–148. doi:10.1080/13552600902823063

Truman, J. L., & Langton, L. (2014). *Criminal victimization, 2013.* Retrieved October 9, 2014, from http://www.bjs.gov/content/pub/pdf/cv13.pdf

Wakeling, H. C., Howard, P. D., & Barnett, G. D. (2011). Comparing the validity of the RM2000 scales and OGRS3 for predicting recidivism by internet sexual offenders. *Sexual Abuse: A Journal of Research and Treatment, 23,* 146–168. doi:10.1177/1079063210375974

Ward, T., & Siegert, R. J. (2002). Toward a comprehensive theory of child sexual abuse: A theory knitting perspective. *Psychology, Crime and Law, 9,* 319–351. doi:10.1080/10683160208401823

Ward, T., & Stewart, C. A. (2003). Good lives and the rehabilitation of sexual offenders. In T. Ward, D. R. Laws, & S. M. Hudson (Eds.), *Sexual deviance: Issues and controversies* (pp. 12–44). Thousand Oaks, CA: Sage.

Webb, L., Craissati, J., & Keen, S. (2007). Characteristics of internet child pornography offenders: A comparison with child molesters. *Sexual Abuse: A Journal of Research and Treatment, 19,* 449–465. doi:10.1177/107906320701900408

Winder, B., & Gough, B. (2010). 'I never touched anybody—that's my defence': A qualitative analysis of internet sex offender accounts. *Journal of Sexual Aggression, 16,* 125–141. doi:10.1080/13552600903503383

Wolak, J., Finkelhor, D., & Mitchell, K. J. (2004). Internet-initiated sex crimes against minors: Implications for prevention based on findings from a national study. *Journal of Adolescent Health, 35,* 424.e11–424.e20. doi:10.1016/j.jadohealth.2004.05.006

Wolak, J., Finkelhor, D., Mitchell, K. J., & Ybarra, M. L. (2008). Online 'predators' and their victims: Myths, realities, and implications for prevention and treatment. *American Psychologist, 63,* 111–128. doi:10.1037/0003-066X.63.2.111

Yates, P. M., Prescott, D., & Ward, T. (2010). *Applying the good lives and self-regulation models to sex offender treatment: A practical guide for clinicians.* Brandon, VT: Safer Society Press.

6 The Impact of Online Sexual Abuse on Children and Young People

Elly Hanson

We know from a rich and diverse research literature spanning several decades that child sexual abuse (CSA) often leads to negative outcomes for victims,[1] frequently over the long term. From recent qualitative research and supportive work with survivors there is reason to believe that image and/or online elements to sexual abuse add complexity and challenge to their recovery. This chapter attempts to pull together a picture of the negative impact of online sexual abuse drawing on all of these sources of knowledge. This includes exploration of why online and/or image elements in sexual abuse may worsen or complicate impact; why some children may be more negatively affected than others; how impact may change over time; where critical points of vulnerability may lie; and how emotions, meanings and experiences around online sexual abuse may play into subsequent difficulties. The chapter concludes by drawing out implications for work with children and families (see also Hanson, Chapter 7, this book) and suggesting directions for further research.

Whilst this chapter concerns itself with the negative impact of online sexual abuse, it does so with the recognition that many people do not experience significant psychological difficulties following sexual abuse, and of those who do, many go on to overcome them, with some reporting posttraumatic growth and 'thriving.' It is important to keep central that whatever the impact of online sexual abuse on an individual child and subsequent adult, it is a gross violation of his or her rights (UN Convention on the Rights of the Child; Reading et al., 2009).

Additionally, whilst the focus of this chapter is on the impact on direct victims of online sexual abuse, it is acknowledged that there can be highly negative consequences for their family unit and other individual members.

Online Risk to Children: Impact, Protection and Prevention, First Edition.
Edited by Jon Brown.
© 2017 John Wiley & Sons, Ltd. Published 2017 by John Wiley & Sons, Ltd.

OVERVIEW OF ONLINE SEXUAL ABUSE

There are several typologies of online CSA (Cooper, 2012; Martin & Alaggia, 2013; Shannon, 2008; Wolak & Finkelhor, 2011), and categorisations are likely to revise and expand as use of the Internet continues to evolve. A further typology, developed by Hamilton-Giachritsis, Hanson, Whittle and Beech (in press) is shown in Table 6.1 focussed on the abuse from the victim's perspective (versus, for example, criminal justice, policy, conceptual or offender perspectives). Offline sexual abuse, in which a victim experiences the threat of sexual

Table 6.1   *Types of technology-assisted child sexual abuse, categorised in view of victims' experiences*

Type of technology-assisted child sexual abuse	Further description and/or example	References for further discussion or description
1. Offline abuse shared with and viewed by unknown others	This is often the abuse depicted in child abuse images, also termed 'child pornography.' *Example:* Sexual abuse perpetrated by a victim's father shared via images and video with others online.	Leonard (2010) Martin & Alaggia (2013) Mitchell, Finkelhor & Wolak (2005)
2. Abuse committed online or offline shared with others in the victim's peer group	A young person (or persons) filming their abuse of a peer and sharing this with their friends for approval or status, or to shame (this includes male adolescents abusing female peers).	Beckett et al. (2013)
3. Contact abuse commissioned online	Perpetrators online direct perpetrators who are physically with the child to commit abusive acts. *Example:* Perpetrators in the UK watching and directing live streamed sexual abuse of children by perpetrators in the Phillipines.	National Crime Agency (NCA; 2014)
4. Offline sexual blackmail (imagery as leverage)	Child or young person is abused offline, images are taken and used as leverage in the continuation of the abuse. *Example:* 'If you tell, I will share this image with your friends and family.'	Gohir (2013)
5. Online sexual blackmail (imagery as leverage)	Sexual imagery of a child is ascertained online and then used as leverage in sexual abuse, which may be online, offline or both, *Example:* A child shares a sexual image with a person online; this person (the abuser) then threatens to share this imagery if the child does not produce further sexual images or comply with offline abuse.	Peachey (2013) Also see Figure 6.1

Table 6.1 *(continued)*

Type of technology-assisted child sexual abuse	Further description and/or example	References for further discussion or description
6. Online grooming	This term can include online sexual blackmail, but is more commonly used to describe perpetrators forging a close relationship with a victim online in order to gain the child's compliance in and secrecy around subsequent sexual abuse. *Example:* Perpetrator shows care and interest in child online who subsequently 'falls in love' and consents to online and/or offline sexual activity despite perpetrator being an adult and/or coercive and/or the child feeling uncomfortable.	Whittle, Hamilton-Giachritsis, Beech & Collings (2013a)
7. Sexual activity bought from a young person online	A child acting on their own volition advertising sexual services online for payment.	Jonsson & Svedin (2012) as cited in Sigurjónsdóttir (2012)
8. Sexual images created consensually shared nonconsenually	*Example:* A young person shares images with a romantic partner, the relationship ends and those images are shared by their ex-partner with peers.	Wolak & Finkelhor (2011) Ringrose, Gill. Livingstone & Harvey (2012)

Note: Exposure of children to online sexually explicit material and sexual harrassment or solicitations (e.g., a person starting up a conversation about sex online) have not been included in this typology as it was felt that the definition of online sexual abuse would become too wide (whilst recognising that exposure to such material and comments can be abusive and harmful). Additionally, children being sold by others online was not included as it was felt that this abuse is likely to either be captured in categories 1 and 2, or, if not, then the online/image element is likely to be less central to the victim's experience than in the forms of abuse described here.

images being distributed, is included, because even if in some cases this abuse does not strictly involve online activity, it carries with it the complexities of online sexual abuse related to the anticipated dissemination of images. Indeed 'technology-assisted' CSA may at times be a preferable term to 'online' CSA as it avoids a false dichotomy between online and offline worlds – often movement between the two in abuse is highly fluid; the two terms are used interchangeably in this chapter. Figure 6.1 depicts a chat log between a victim and an offender in technology-assisted sexual blackmail to provide an insight into the dynamics of this abuse, because it may be less well known than other forms.

We know little about how many children experience online sexual abuse and its different forms, because sexual abuse prevalence surveys do not typically ask participants specifically about online or recording elements. Adolescents appear

Figure 6.1 A chat log between a perpetrator of sexual blackmail and his victim demonstrating the processes involved.

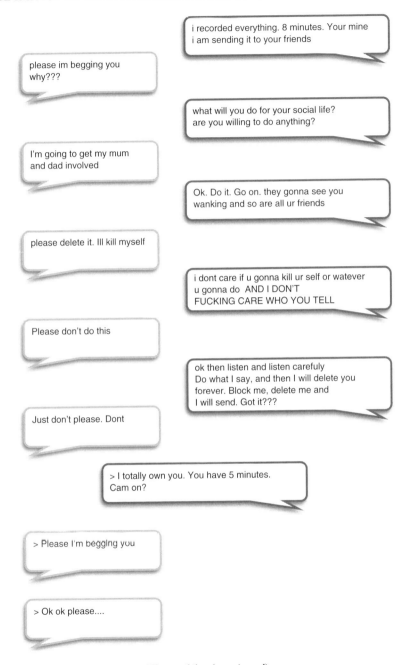

Figure 6.1   (*continued*)

to be more at risk of sexual abuse starting online and/or involving initially consensually created images (categories 5 to 8 in the typology) than younger children; this is likely to be because they use the Internet more frequently and their use is bound up with the increased risk-taking, impulsivity, sensation-seeking and sexual interest common to this life stage (Livingstone, Haddon, Görzig, & Ólafsson, 2010; Whittle, Hamilton-Giachritsis, Beech, & Collings, 2013b). However, some research suggests that younger children may be more at risk of sexual abuse with online elements that begins offline (for example categories 1 and 3 in the typology) – for example, analyses of online CSA images have found that the majority of children depicted in them are prepubescent (Bunzeluk, 2009; Quayle & Jones, 2011). Bunzeluk (2009) found that when images included violent and/or extreme assault (e.g., torture, degradation, bestiality) children were most likely to be under the age of eight. It should be noted, however, that sexual abuse images of adolescents may be less reported by the public or the focus of law enforcement because of potential uncertainty about whether they instead depict young-looking adults (Cooper, 2012).

Psychological difficulties during and following online grooming have been explored to a greater degree (Quayle, Jonsson, & Lööf, 2012; Whittle, Hamilton-Giachritsis, & Beech, 2013) than those associated with other forms of online sexual abuse. However, there is much we can say about the impacts of all forms of online abuse (and contributors to these) when we ground what research there is within the broader literature on sexual abuse generally. This is particularly true of categories 1 to 5 in the typology in Table 6.1, on which this chapter focusses. In sketching this emerging picture of impact, I also draw on observations made whilst working with the Child Exploitation and Online Protection Centre (CEOP), a command of the UK National Crime Agency since 2013.[2]

THE IMPACT OF CHILD SEXUAL ABUSE

There is now an accumulation of evidence from controlled studies that follow individuals over time (complemented by other research) demonstrating that CSA often negatively affects victims in child and adulthood and that subsequent difficulties are not explicable as solely the impact of commonly co-occurring adverse experiences, such as neglect.

A selection of CSA's highly evidenced harms is as follows:

- Intimate relationship difficulties, for example, breakups, dissatisfaction and avoidance (Colman & Widom, 2004).
- Sexual difficulties, for example, sexual aversion, sexual ambivalence (Noll, Trickett, & Putnam, 2003).
- Re-victimisation (Noll, Horowitz, Bonanno, Trickett, & Putnam, 2003).
- Self-destructive behaviour, for example, suicide attempts and ideation, self-harm (Fergusson, Boden, & Horwood, 2008; Yates, Carlson, & Egeland, 2008).

- Anxiety, depression and substance misuse (Kendler, Bulik, Silberg, Hettema, Myers, & Prescott, 2000).
- Physical health problems (Sickel, 2002)

Young people's descriptions of how technology-assisted sexual abuse has affected them echo many of these findings; Table 6.2 draws out some themes from their accounts.

Macro-level patterns support these qualitative findings and indicate substantial negative impact. Informal scoping by CEOP in 2013 found evidence of seven attempted suicides and seven completed suicides of young people in relation to online sexual blackmail. Given that these figures were gleaned from a brief exploration, it is likely that a more in-depth analysis that also included other forms of online CSA would uncover more such results.

A study exploring the impact of offline sexual abuse shared via images using survey and interview data found high rates of attentional, anger and irritability difficulties as well as sexual preoccupancy in child survivors (Svedin & Back, 2003). Some children discussed feeling deceived, ashamed, guilty, anxious and panicky and/or disgusted, specifically in relation to the images of their sexual abuse (Jonsson & Svedin, 2012). Very recently, Hamilton-Giachritsis,

Table 6.2 *The ways in which sexual abuse via online grooming and blackmail has affected young people*

Impact	Quotes from young people who have been sexually abused via online grooming
Relationship avoidance/difficulties	*'I'll never be able to be in a relationship … I mean, it would never work'* (Quayle et al., 2012, p. 94) *'I can't have a partner or children'* (Quayle et al., 2012, p. 95)
Depression	*'I was self-confident and now when this all happened, I got really depressed and it's still present in my life now … It's simply the case that I have to fight depression every day'* (Quayle et al., 2012, p. 94)
Hopelessness	*'I got to the point where I wanted to run into a brick wall and just keep running into it, I was crying myself to sleep and didn't want to wake up'* (young person victimised by online sexual blackmail talking to CEOP) *'I don't know. I don't see a future'* (Quayle et al., 2012, p. 94)
Self-harm	*'I was self-harming as well … I landed myself in hospital'* (Whittle et al., 2013, p. 62)
Shame, embarrassment, humiliation	*'I am embarrassed and humiliated and it's horrible because now my mum and dad know what happened'* (Whittle et al., 2013, p. 62) *'I felt so incredibly ashamed'* (Quayle et al., 2012, p. 57)

Note: All quotes from Hamilton-Giachritsis et al. (in press), Quayle et al. (2012) and Whittle, Hamilton-Giachritsis, and Beech (2013) throughout this chapter are from young people who had experienced technology-assisted sexual abuse.

Hanson, Whittle and Beech (in press) utilised both qualitative and quantitative methods to explore more fully the impact of technology-assisted sexual abuse on young people. Due to timings of writing and publication, this study's findings are not reviewed in depth here – instead it is recommended as a complementary text to this chapter. In short, they found no evidence that technology-assisted CSA was less impactful than fully offline CSA,3 despite some professionals perceiving it to be. Further their findings complement this chapter's analysis in suggesting that technology and online aspects to abuse can add to the complexity of its impact, for example by contributing to self-blame, anxiety, blame from others, and sense of ongoing trauma.

Characteristics of the sexual abuse and the social context it occurs within will affect how a given individual is affected (moderators), and this is via mediators, the social and psychological processes that lead from the abuse to its subsequent impacts. Moderators and mediators of sexual abuse, and their relevance to online CSA, are now discussed. Following this I consider how the online aspect is in itself a moderator and can play into specific psychological dynamics related to harm.

CHARACTERISTICS OF CSA THAT AFFECT IMPACT

Research has typically found that sexual abuse is on average more harmful the longer its duration, as well as when there is force, threats or sadism (Bulik, Prescott, & Kendler, 2001; Kordich Hall, Mathews, & Pearce, 1998; Steel, Sanna, Hammond, Whipple, & Cross, 2004). It is likely that these dimensions remain as important to impact when the abuse is online.

However, the applicability to online abuse of the finding that there is greater harm the greater degree of sexual contact (in particular penetration versus no penetration; Bulik et al., 2001; Collin-Vezina & Hebert, 2005) is questionable. Taken by itself this finding might suggest that online CSA is less harmful than offline CSA because on average it involves less contact. However, in the offline world degree of contact may be related to the power the offender has over the victim in a way that is not true of online and imaged abuse, and it may be this increased power that accounts for the increased impact of contact abuse in the offline world. In online abuse, offenders often cannot (because of physical separation) or choose not to (because of increased chance of detection) physically touch or penetrate. Rather, their power and the effectiveness of their strategies often lie in the degree to which they can achieve victim participation[4] in the abuse (explored further in the following sections).

SOCIAL CONTEXTUAL FACTORS THAT AFFECT IMPACT

FAMILIAL SUPPORT

How supportive family members are generally towards a child and how supportive they are specifically following the revelation of sexual abuse play important roles in determining longer-term impact. For example, Hong, Ilardi, and Lishner (2011) found that young adult survivors of CSA were more likely to experience borderline symptomatology (this includes reactions such as emotional lability, self-harm and extreme fear of abandonment) if they perceived general invalidation from their caregivers or if they perceived or anticipated invalidation specifically related to disclosure of the abuse. In those who did disclose the abuse, the co-occurrence of general and CSA-related invalidation appeared to exert a particularly toxic effect on later difficulties. It is unfortunate, given the potentially profound role supportive responses from familial and caregiving adults can play in victims' recovery from abuse (Bulik et al., 2001; Feiring, Taska, & Lewis, 1998), that in a large proportion of cases these responses are not adequately supportive (Allnock & Miller, 2013; Hershkowitz, Lanes, & Lamb, 2007). And it appears that children who experience sexual abuse with particular complexities, for example, involving rewards or an intrafamilial perpetrator or taking place over a longer period, are less likely to experience a supportive response (Hershkowitz et al., 2007; Schönbucker, Maier, Mohler-Kuo, & Landolt, 2014).

Parental reactions to revelations of online grooming are diverse (Quayle et al., 2012; Whittle et al., 2013). Similar to cases of other forms of sexual abuse, a number of victims report that their parents were not adequately supportive:

'I think she [Mother] just felt sorry for herself a lot of the time.' (Quayle et al., 2012, p. 80)

At times parental responses are harsh and punitive:

'My Dad came and he hit me! Yeah, he blamed me for that completely, that was all my fault, that wasn't the paedophile that groomed me that was my fault that was, I was the little whore.' (Whittle et al., 2013, p. 63)

There is a sense from some young people's accounts that the victim participation element to some forms of online CSA increases the risk that parents do not respond appropriately, resulting in increased negative impact. Hamilton-Giachritsis et al.'s (in press) and Whittle, Hamilton-Giachritsis and Beech (2013) research also indicate that a generally unsupportive family environment increases the impact of online CSA.

INTERACTIONS WITH THE CRIMINAL JUSTICE SYSTEM

Victims' experience of justice systems also has ramifications for recovery from CSA. When victims are interviewed multiple times, questioned harshly in an adversarial system and/or perceive police and lawyers to act unfairly, the impact of the sexual abuse may worsen (Kunst, Popelier & Varekamp, 2015; Troxel, Ogle, Cordon, Lawler, & Goodman, 2009).

Research by Quayle et al. (2012) and Hamilton-Giachritsis et al. (in press) indicates that poor police practice with victims of technology-assisted abuse is not uncommon. Despite some good practice (see also Whittle et al., 2013), worrying themes across a number of survivors' accounts include negative judgements being made about them, disbelief, inadequate investigation, repeated questioning and a sense that the police were not 'on their side.' This is all likely to worsen impact.

SOCIAL AND PSYCHOLOGICAL PROCESSES FOLLOWING ABUSE

Certain emotions, coping mechanisms and beliefs have emerged as key factors in the link between CSA and psychological difficulties (mediators):

• Shame (Andrews, 1995; Feiring & Taska, 2005; Kim, Talbot, & Cicchetti, 2009)
• Self-blame (Feiring & Cleland, 2007; Coffey, Leitenberg, Henning, Turner, & Bennett, 1996)
• Dissociation (Kaplow, Hall, Koenen, Dodge, & Amaya-Jackson, 2008; Yates et al., 2008)
• Social cognition difficulties (compromised ability to detect violations in social relationships; DePrince, 2005)

The characteristics of the abuse and its social context (moderators) may worsen impact because they heighten some or all of these mediators (e.g., victim participation increases self-blame, which in turn increases risk for psychological difficulty; Steel et al., 2004). In the remainder of the chapter a key argument is that the online and/or image element to the abuse is an additional negative moderator of impact – specifically, the technology dimension affects a variety of harmful social and psychological processes during and following the abuse.

COMPLEXITIES TO ONLINE SEXUAL ABUSE

Survivor, therapist and researcher accounts suggest that at least seven interrelated features of online CSA (summarised in Figure 6.2) may worsen or complicate its impact. Some of these apply more to some forms of online CSA than others, for example, *reach* may not be relevant to some victims of online grooming who do not sense that the perpetrator shared their images, whereas *victim participation* will not be relevant to some victims of offline abuse shared online.

EXISTENCE AND MAKING OF IMAGES

Shame and self-objectification are related to a person's sense of how they are viewed in the eyes of others and indeed themselves. In shame, a person sees her- or himself as an 'unattractive social agent' (Gilbert, 1998, p. 22); these

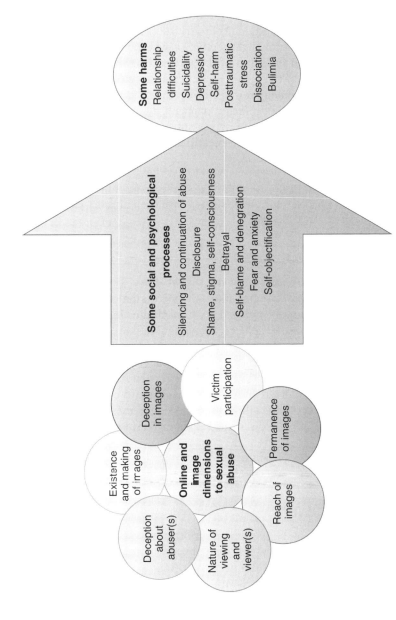

Figure 6.2 Online and image dimensions to sexual abuse and the processes following abuse they may affect.

people have an unwanted social identity and are motivated to hide this from others (Ferguson, Eyre, & Ashbaker, 2000; Gilbert, 1998). In self-objectification people have a salient mental viewpoint of themselves as an (often sexual) object and so, for example, in social interactions they may be preoccupied with how they look to those around them (Fredrickson & Roberts, 1997). Recording equipment, images and film (irrespective of whether they are permanent or shared) may increase in the mind of the victim the salience of a viewer's perspective of themselves. If the victim is acutely aware of themselves viewed as a sexual object, this would heighten self-objectification, and/or if they see themselves as somehow defiled or inferior, particularly in relation to the abuse, this is likely to trigger shame. Shame drives subsequent difficulties (discussed in the following sections), and self-objectification also appears to (American Psychological Association, 2007).

> 'It feels worthless, difficult ... mostly. I like start crying ... I mean I remember all the times I have had sex and all the times I have been filmed. I remember most of it.' (Quayle et al., 2012, p. 94)

DECEPTION IN THE IMAGES

Images are the abuser's account of the sexual abuse. They are therefore often constructed to convey certain lies about the victim that serve to increase abusers' (producers' and viewers') pleasure whilst minimising their discomfort and guilt. The impact of these deceits on the victim, however, adds a further layer of trauma. In particular, offenders often strategise to produce images in which victims are smiling and add captions to the images about the victim's acceptance and enjoyment. Victims can become preoccupied about how they are being inaccurately perceived by those viewing the pictures (Leonard, 2010) and their worries that others will assume their enjoyment or implicate them in the abuse can act to impede disclosure (Palmer & Stacey, 2004).

> 'I thought "I can't go to the police with a film where I'm smiling. They will just say I have myself to blame."' (Quayle et al., 2012, p. 57)

VICTIM PARTICIPATION

Child sex offenders may be particularly motivated to coerce, deceive or groom their victims to participate in their own abuse when this abuse is online. When there is physical separation, offenders will often depend on it for the abuse to take place, and even when this is not the case, victim participation in images may achieve a number of goals, in particular communicating, inaccurately, victim consent or enjoyment, and reducing the victim's likelihood of disclosure. Jonsson and Svedin (2012) found that it was common for victims of a number of types of online CSA to feel that they had been an active participant in their abuse.

In situations in which the actions of a person or persons drive the behaviour of another (even a child), people appear less capable of correctly assigning responsibility compared to situations in which a person is acting simply of his or her own accord. However inaccurate it is to do so, victims and others can become easily focussed on the behaviours of the victims, without giving due attention to the determining actions of the perpetrator(s) pulling the strings. This is likely to be behind the finding that victim participation increases self-blame and internalisation of the abuse. In turn these both contribute to a wide range of psychological difficulties (Steel et al., 2004).

PERMANENCE OF IMAGES

In many cases and across types of online CSA, it is not possible to fully retrieve images or footage of the abuse. Victims may be aware that their images may be or are still circulating on the Internet, and this can lead to feelings of on-going traumatisation. As Leonard (2010) articulates on the basis of her therapeutic work with two victims of online CSA, 'for them it is still present tense and they do not know what is happening with the picture but can only imagine, and are therefore traumatised further by the unknownness of the activity being performed' (p. 253). Similarly Cooper (2012) describes how victims she has spoken to are vigilant, fearful and non-delusionally paranoid about coming across images of their abuse online.

Von Weiler, Haardt-Becker, and Schulte (2010) found in interviews with 28 therapists who worked with victims of online CSA that the permanence of the images was the most challenging aspect of this abuse for them. It often evoked deep-seated helplessness that at times led to them questioning their ability to help the children they worked with. Preoccupying thoughts included 'I am hitting the boundaries' and 'in this situation healing becomes impossible' (p. 217). This raises the possibility that aspects of online CSA may additionally compromise recovery via their adverse impact on the therapeutic process.

REACH OF IMAGES

For victims, closely bound up with the complexities of the permanence and deceit of the images is their reach – which in the online world is the exponential number of people who may view them. Perpetrator-constructed abuse images stretch across time (permanence) and social space (reach), and as a whole this contributes to feelings of on-going traumatisation.

When abuse images have or might have been disseminated online to any number of unknown people, victims describe on-going watchfulness, anxiety about who has viewed the images (for example, worrying whether people they come into contact with have seen or viewed the images) and preoccupation with the context, motives and functions of abusers' viewing.

'The victims consider where the person is who is viewing the pictures, who else can see them, are they using them to justify abusing a child, are they making a child see them to create a sense that this is normal childhood behaviour, and who else is being harmed by the person looking at these pictures.' (Leonard, 2010, p. 254)

'One victim discussed with me her insomnia, years after the abuse had ended because she was aware that videos were on the internet. She described walking around her house looking out the windows many nights. When I asked her what she was searching for, she replied that she was looking for the people who would be looking back in at her.' (Cooper, 2012)

The power of the potential reach of online abuse images is also evident in how the threat of image dissemination is used a tool by offenders to silence victims and thereby continue abuse (Gohir, 2013). For example, in the numerous cases of sexual blackmail that CEOP has come across victims will comply with abuse rather than risk images of their abuse being seen by others. Discussions between CEOP or its partner agencies and victims reveal that when this threat exists many become consumed with preoccupying anxiety. At the same time, it is also critical to note that a number of young people do not show significant concern (e.g. Hamilton-Giachritsis et al., in press), and so impact should be explored rather than assumed.

NATURE OF VIEWING AND VIEWERS

Although the scenario of law enforcement personnel viewing abuse images can be upsetting to victims, it would seem that it is more impactful when abuse images have or might be seen by individuals gaining sexual or other perverse gratification from them or using them in abuse of other children or when they are viewed by family members or friends, for example, when shared to fulfil a threat in the context of sexual blackmail. *'I don't know what's out there and I don't know who's watching and I don't know what people are doing regarding to me and whether anyone's planning anything, that's what it makes me feel bad.'* Hamilton-Giachritsis et al. (in press)

Viewing by family and friends can feel acutely shaming (especially if the victim was coerced to perform humiliating acts) and, on a related note, victims may find (or fear) that this viewing leads increased judgement and blame if the images were deceptive or show participation.

DECEIT ABOUT THE ABUSER(S)

The online world affords more opportunity for individuals to deceive others about their identity, personality and motives than the offline world, and this is a feature offenders use to their advantage in online grooming and blackmail, with ramifications for victim impact. Figure 6.1 illustrates the use of deceit within online sexual blackmail. Even where abusers do not lie about their identity, they often deceive victims about the nature and exclusivity of their interest (Whittle, Hamilton-Giachritsis, & Beech, 2015). Deception and manipulation are used to disguise grooming and abuse as something normal and desirable until the victim is at a point at which he or she is trapped often by virtue of the manipulated attachment and dependency on the offender (Quayle et al., 2012).

> 'I don't think there's one thing that he said back then that I know now, that was the truth.' (Whittle et al., 2015, p. 548)

SALIENT FACTORS UNDERPINNING IMPACT

This section draws on those preceding to explore six social and psychological processes contributing to impact (summarised in Figure 6.2), which online and image elements of CSA impinge upon.

SILENCE AND THE CONTINUATION OF ABUSE

Technology-assisted CSA often comes to light via the discovery of images rather than a child disclosing. Even when confronted with the existence of abuse images, children may often deny that this abuse took place (Svedin & Back, 2003), and part of the reason for this may be the images themselves:

- In some forms of abuse (particularly online sexual blackmail but also in some cases of online grooming), children worry that disclosure will lead to their images being disseminated to family and friends.
- In cases in which images have been discovered, children may anticipate that confirming their identity in the images will lead to increased feelings of shame and guilt and related negative judgements, blame and disgust from others - at worst law enforcement actions against them.
- Even without threat of dissemination or discovered images, children may fear that disclosure will prompt image discovery, leading to the described array of emotions and consequences.

(These fears about disclosing are likely to exist alongside other anxieties common also to offline-only CSA, for example, worries about family disruption.)

Clearly in many cases this silencing effect of the images contributes to the continuation of the abuse. Indeed, as in blackmail, it is often a central aspect of the offender's strategy. Thus in some situations online and image elements increase the length of abuse, which in turn heightens impact.

DISCLOSURE

In parallel, when disclosure does take place, it often leads to a worsening of psychological difficulties and feelings of upset (Sigurjónsdóttir, 2012; Svedin & Back, 2003). Disclosure of CSA, generally, whilst it may lead to some positive consequences such as abuse coming to an end or abuse of other children being prevented, also often carries personal costs for children, such as emotionally difficult involvement in the criminal justice system and invalidation from family.

The flipside to the image-related fears that impede a victim's disclosure is the realisation of these fears following some disclosures. Disclosure can lead to others viewing the images, which in certain situations leads to negative feelings in survivors and judgements from others. For example, offenders at times fulfil threats and share sexual images of victims with the victims' friends and family, potentially prompting increased shame. Some parents, imagining or seeing CSA images of their child, become highly distressed, angry, ashamed and horrified (von Weiler et al., 2010). Without adequate support to help parents process these feelings, they can impede support of their child. Given the deceit often inherent in the images, others viewing them can sometimes develop erroneous and blaming perspectives, for example:

> 'an account was given of a judge who, looking at the picture, stated that it seemed the 15-year-old boy had participated willingly.' (von Weiler et al., p. 216)

At times this translates into actions that isolate the survivor:

> 'they found out and they, too, distanced themselves.' (Quayle et al., 2012, p. 84)
> 'People were calling me a slag, I couldn't get on the bus, that's why I couldn't go out the house… Just like anyone, some of them were from school, but then like, others were like people that they knew, or some people that I didn't even know… I started to think that it was true, like what they were saying' Hamilton-Giachritsis et al. (in press)

The existence of images when abuse comes to light can have some advantages, for example, if there is a criminal justice investigation, the compelling evidence within the images may obviate the pressures on the victim to go through the often distressing experience of being adversarially questioned about the abuse. The strength of image evidence may increase sentences and rates of conviction (von Weiler et al., 2010). Additionally, some parents describe the images helping them to accept the abusive nature of what took place and so support their child:

> 'one therapist recounted the case of a mother who could only support her son after seeing the images. Before this she has tried to excuse the offender, who was her brother, and explain his behaviour.' (Von Weiler et al., 2010, p. 219)

In many cases it is the images that bring the abuse to the attention of others. For some survivors this may heighten feelings of powerlessness – a sense that even the disclosure of the abuse was out of their control. For others, however, it may be better than feeling the responsibility of the disclosure and its impact (Nagel, Putnam, & Noll, 1997).

It is a complex picture, but it would seem reasonable to hypothesise that for a significant proportion of victims, online and image elements to the sexual abuse contribute to difficulties (such as anxiety, shame and blame from self and others) in the process of disclosure or revelation. A study that mapped online CSA victims' mental health at seven time points found poorest mental health at disclosure (Sigurjónsdóttir, 2012). It is likely to be a critical point at which survivors and their families would benefit from support to help avoid negative trajectories taking hold (for example, shame and self-blame fuelling isolation, depression and suicidality), and it offers unique opportunities for child protection and criminal justice professionals to counteract messages from the abuse.

SHAME

'I was ashamed, I felt I was not good enough for anything.'

'I felt like I was dirty.' (Sigurjónsdóttir, 2012, p. 17)

Shame[5] runs as a theme throughout this chapter – as we have seen, several dimensions of online abuse have the power to heighten victims' shame. Victims may feel ashamed that they believed an online groomer or blackmailer's lies, or that multiple people view images of their abuse, increasing the salience of the unwanted identity scripted for them within the abuse and imagery. Images that attempt to construe victims as accepting or enjoying the abuse, or depict particularly humiliating or degrading abuse acts have an increased power to shame.

Shame is a significantly negative consequence of abuse in and of itself. Certainly within Western cultures it is an intensely unpleasant emotional experience (Mesquita & Karasawa, 2004). Shame and fear of shame can be preoccupying and prompt people to avoid others and disclose little of themselves (MacDonald & Morley, 2001). Indeed Quayle et al. (2012) note a link between the shame experienced by victims of online grooming and nondisclosure about the abuse.

Shame following sexual abuse contributes to further harms over time for survivors. It predicts intrusions (such as nightmares, flashbacks and intrusive thoughts) six years later in young people (Feiring & Taska, 2005) and also accounts for the relationships between CSA and depression, bulimia, future family conflict and re-victimisation (Andrews, 1995, 1997; Kessler & Bieschke, 1999; Kim et al., 2005). Shame after CSA predisposes people to develop post-traumatic stress in response to further traumas (Andrews, Brewin, Rose, & Kirk, 2000), and it is closely related to the development of dissociation following sexual abuse (Talbot, Talbot, & Tu, 2004).

If, as argued here, online and image elements heighten shame following sexual abuse, it would be anticipated that they also increase risk for these subsequent shame-related difficulties. Working with survivors to reduce shame is likely to substantially reduce these harms over the longer term.

SELF-BLAME AND DENIGRATION

'then I only had myself to blame in some way.' (Quayle et al., 2012, p. 56)

'I really thought it was my fault and I still think its my fault.' (Quayle et al., 2012, p. 84)

Shame and self-blame are related but distinct. Shame is an emotional experience linked to an unwanted identity, whereas self-blame is the perspective that oneself is at least somewhat responsible for the abuse (this can feed into an unwanted identity, guilt and shame). It is also worth noting that self-blame is not at the opposite pole of perpetrator blame; they are separate perspectives.

As discussed, participation in the abuse can increase self-blame. Additionally other people accepting the perpetrator's story told through the images (for example, accepting that a victim's smile means his or her pleasure) may fuel their blame of the victim, which in turn can increase the victim's sense of blameworthiness (Draucker, 1995).

'She made me feel guilty. She said that it had been my fault because I had been too explicit, that I was to blame for having sought attention from other people.' (Quayle et al., 2012, p. 80)

If those near a survivor do not assertively communicate a non-blaming stance, survivors may interpret more neutral behaviour as confirmation of their belief that they were at fault:

'I don't know, in a way, it's hard to make people feel like they're not being judged for it, and it's not a bad thing they've done.' (Quayle et al., 2012, p. 84)

Deception, grooming, adaptive behaviour and lack of knowledge often play a part in how victims behave in the lead up to and commission of abuse, but in hindsight it may be difficult to fully appreciate this context and instead judge one's behaviour in isolation, fuelling self-blame:

'I was ashamed to say that I had had sex and I was ashamed of how stupid I had been.' (Quayle et al., 2012, p. 83)

Similar to shame, self-blame is difficult in and of itself, but it also contributes to longer-term difficulties, such as depression and intrusions (Coffey et al., 1996; Feiring & Cleland, 2007).

BETRAYAL

A sense of betrayal is encapsulated in the question for survivors: 'how could you do that to me?' Betrayal is greater when the victim trusted, loved or admired the perpetrator ('how could *you* do that to me?') and when the abuse is more severe or far-reaching ('how could you do *that* to me?').

It appears that many victims of online grooming initially engaged with their subsequent abuser because they felt that 'something was missing' from their lives (Quayle et al., 2012; Whittle, Hamilton-Giachritsis, & Beech, 2014), including emotional connection with others and attention.

> 'Young girls generally of a certain age, who don't have anyone to listen to them, who are alone, who see that their Mums and Dads are disinterested ... will natu-rally think it's good to look for people who seem to be interested and care on the internet.' (Quayle et al., 2012, p. 35)

In online grooming scenarios, the abuser deceives the victim into believing that he or she can be the 'missing part.' The horrific irony is that these young people who may be in most need of a loving relationship are entrapped instead into an abusive one – leaving them even more in need of what they first went searching for and with less confidence that they can find it.

> 'When I met him it was like this angel had come down to greet me ... I'd already developed the feelings, to how he was online, and I'd already kind of fallen for him. But he was an absolute dick in real life.' (Quayle et al., 2012, p. 48)

Grooming impersonates positive relationships, and so following this experi-ence it can be difficult for survivors to take steps to trust anyone intimately, even if, and at times in particular, when others are kind and caring.

> 'I don't trust people in general, I look still at all men as idiots that just want to take advantage of women.' (Sigurjónsdóttir, 2012, p. 17)

In sexual blackmail, betrayal is high often not because of the victim deeply trusted the offender, but because there is such a transformation from an ini-tially seemingly consensual sexual exchange into one in which the victim is controlled and enslaved. Dissemination of images, if it occurs, is a further layer of betrayal.

Victims of intrafamilial CSA shared online may experience some of the deepest feelings of betrayal in that someone they loved or trusted first sexually abused them and then shared this abuse for it to be seen by multiple others for an indefinite time.

Quotes from survivors throughout this chapter indicate how the betrayal in online CSA may preclude them from developing trusting relationships with others (see for example Table 6.2). The rich literature exploring betrayal trauma theory indicates that the betrayal dimension of sexual abuse can heighten a wide range of problems, including re-victimisation, panic, suicidality, anger and depression (DePrince, 2005; Edwards, Freyd, Dube, Anda, & Felitti, 2012).[6]

FEAR AND ANXIETY

Online or image elements to CSA can contribute to and drive a number of victim fears and anxieties. Sexual blackmail chat logs that I have read in my role at CEOP bear witness to the terror victims feel at the threat of images being disseminated, terror that drives many to comply with offender's demands for them to perform increasingly humiliating or intrusive acts. There is also preoccupying anxiety about when the offender will next come online and make a demand, and life becomes narrowly centred on this.

As discussed, in forms of online CSA in which images have been shared, survivors can develop a pervasive sense of threat, not knowing who has or will see them. Fear in traumatic situations, similar to shame, can lead to the development of posttraumatic stress disorder. The intrusive memories and emotion central to this disorder further engender a sense of on-going threat that survivors may respond to with hypervigilance and avoidance of people and places.

'Because I saw these images in my mind and that kind of thing ... I have cut a lot of classes afterwards, because I just couldn't get a grip and get over there. Because I was afraid that it would happen again.' (Quayle et al., 2012, p. 87)

PROMOTING RESILIENCE, REDUCING IMPACT, FOSTERING RECOVERY

There is a role for everyone in helping young people escape online sexual abuse and achieve wellbeing following it. We can contribute to creating environments in which children and young people are not vulnerable to online abuse,[7] feel able to disclose abuse or related worries and feel supported following disclosure or discovery.[8]

HELPING CHILDREN DISCLOSE

Alongside messages about how children and young people can increase their safety online, it is also important that they hear that if abuse does take place they are not to blame for it. Schools can take a leading role in stigmatising the viewing of images so that the threat of image dissemination is less powerful and actual dissemination is less harmful. Interested adults regularly asking children about how they are and how they are feeling provides opportunities for disclosure that might otherwise not arise (Allnock & Miller, 2013). Persistent, proactive care and concern is crucial in situations in which children's behaviour or mood worsen with no apparent cause.

SUPPORT FOLLOWING REVELATIONS OF ONLINE ABUSE

Children need to hear clear statements that they were not to blame, most importantly from their parents or caregivers. If they blame themselves, they need space to explore the dynamics of the abuse to challenge this perspective. They need their account of what happened to be actively believed, again especially by their parents. Parents are likely to support their children most effectively if they themselves also receive support in processing their feelings. Abuse often continues following disclosure, so proactive steps must be taken to prevent this possibility, whilst not overly restricting a young person's online world. If images might be or have been disseminated, young people are likely to benefit from space with someone outside of the situation to explore their fears, form a plan for coping with this situation (including how to respond to people who have seen the images) and help them psychologically separate their sense of self from the images (for further thoughts on support see Hanson, Chapter 7, this volume).

RESEARCH DIRECTIONS

It would be beneficial to have longitudinal studies charting the impact of technology-assisted abuse over time, and the routes to recovery and resilience. Within this and other research, it would also be valuable to explore potentially important but as yet under researched mediators of abuse impact, such as self-objectification.

CONCLUSION

This chapter has outlined how much that is true of the impact of offline sexual abuse is also likely to be true of the impact of online forms. However online and image dimensions, such as increased victim participation, deception in images and image dissemination, may complicate impact and recovery. Although we are at the early stages of understanding the processes involved, we know enough on which to build preventative efforts and approaches that foster resilience and support recovery. Central to these is preventing negative trajectories characterised by shame, blame, fear, distrust and isolation taking hold following abuse.

REFERENCES

American Psychological Association. (2007). *Report of the APA Task Force on the sexualisation of girls.* Retrieved from http://www.apa.org/

Allnock, D., & Miller, P. (2013). *No-one noticed, no-one heard: A study of disclosures of childhood abuse.* London, UK: NSPCC.

Andrews, B. A. (1995). Bodily shame as a mediator between abusive experiences and depression. *Journal of Abnormal Psychology, 104,* 277–285.

Andrews, B. A. (1997). Bodily shame in relation to abuse in childhood and bulimia: A preliminary investigation. *British Journal of Clinical Psychology, 36,* 41–49.

Andrews, B. A., Brewin, C. R., Rose, S., & Kirk, M. (2000). Predicting PTSD symptoms in victims of violent crime: The role of shame, anger and childhood abuse. *Journal of Abnormal Psychology, 109,* 69–73.

Beckett, H., Brodie, I., Factor, F., Melrose, M., Pearce, J. J., Pitts, J., ... & Warrington, C. (2013). *"It's wrong-but you get used to it": a qualitative study of gang-associated sexual violence towards, and exploitation of, young people in England.* University of Bedfordshire.

Bulik, C. M., Prescott, C. A., & Kendler, K. S. (2001). Features of childhood sexual abuse and the development of psychiatric and substance use disorders. *The British Journal of Psychiatry, 179,* 444–449.

Bunzeluk, K. (2009). *Child sexual abuse images: An analysis of websites.* Toronto, Canada: Canadian Centre for Child Protection Incorporated.

Coffey, P., Leitenberg, H., Henning, K., Turner, T., & Bennett, R. T. (1996). Mediators of the long-term impact of child sexual abuse: Perceived stigma, betrayal, powerlessness and self-blame. *Child Abuse and Neglect, 20,* 447–455.

Collin-Vezina, D., & Hebert, M. (2005). Comparing dissociation and PTSD in sexually abused school-aged girls. *Journal of Nervous and Mental Disease, 193,* 47–52.

Colman, R. A., & Widom, C. S. (2004). Childhood abuse and neglect and adult intimate relationships: A prospective study. *Child Abuse and Neglect, 28,* 1133–1151.

Cooper, S. W. (2012). The impact on children who have been victims of child pornography. Written testimony before the U.S. Sentencing Commission.

DePrince, A. P. (2005). Social cognition and revictimization risk. *Journal of Trauma and Dissociation, 6,* 125–141.

Draucker, C. B. (1995). A coping model for adult survivors of childhood sexual abuse. *Journal of Interpersonal Violence, 10,* 159–175.

Edwards, V. J., Freyd, J. J., Dube, S. R., Anda, R. F., & Felitti, V. J. (2012). Health outcomes by closeness of sexual abuse perpetrator: A test of betrayal trauma theory. *Journal of Aggression, Maltreatment and Trauma, 21,* 133–148.

Feiring, C., & Cleland, C. (2007). Childhood sexual abuse and abuse-specific attributions of blame over six years following discovery. *Child Abuse and Neglect, 31,* 1169–1186.

Feiring, C., & Taska, L. S. (2005). The persistence of shame following sexual abuse: A longitudinal look at risk and recovery. *Child Maltreatment, 10,* 337–349.

Feiring, C., Taska, L. S., & Lewis, M. (1998). Social support and children's and adolescents' adaptation to sexual abuse. *Journal of Interpersonal Violence, 13,* 240–260.

Ferguson, T. J., Eyre, H. L., & Ashbaker, M. (2000). Unwanted identities: A key variable in shame-anger links and gender differences in shame. *Sex Roles, 42,* 133–157.

Fergusson, D. M., Boden, J. M., & Horwood, L. J. (2008). Exposure to childhood sexual and physical abuse and adjustment in early adulthood. *Child Abuse and Neglect, 32*, 607–619.

Fredrickson, B. L., & Roberts, T. A. (1997). Objectification theory: Toward understanding women's lived experiences and mental health risks. *Psychology of Women Quarterly, 21*, 173–206.

Gilbert, P. (1998). What is shame? Some core issues and controversies. In P. Gilbert and B. A. Andrews (Eds.), *Shame: Interpersonal behaviour, psychopathology and culture* (pp. 3–38). Oxford, UK: Oxford University Press.

Gohir, S. (2013). *Unheard voices: The sexual exploitation of Asian girls and young women*. Birmingham, UK: Muslim Women's Network.

Hamilton-Giachritsis, C., Hanson, E., Whittle, H. C., & Beech, A. R. (in press). *"Everyone deserves to be happy and safe" A mixed methods study exploring how online and offline child sexual abuse impact young people and how professionals respond to it*. London: NSPCC.

Hershkowitz, I., Lanes, O., & Lamb, M. (2007). Exploring the disclosure of child sexual abuse with alleged victims and their parents. *Child Abuse and Neglect, 31*, 111–123.

Hong, P. Y., Ilardi, S. S., & Lishner, D. A. (2011). The aftermath of trauma: The impact of perceived and anticipated invalidation of childhood sexual abuse on borderline symptomatology. *Psychological Trauma: Theory, Research, Practice and Policy, 3*, 360–368.

Jonsson, L., & Svedin, C. G. (2012). Children within the images. In E. Quayle & K. M. Ribisl (Eds.), *Understanding and preventing online sexual exploitation of children* (pp. 23–43). Abingdon, Oxon, UK: Routledge.

Kaplow, J. B., Hall, E., Koenen, K. C., Dodge, K. A., & Amaya-Jackson, L. (2008). Dissociation predicts later attention problems in sexually abused children. *Child Abuse and Neglect, 32*, 261–275.

Kendler, K. S., Bulik, C. M., Silberg, J., Hettema, J. M., Myers, J., & Prescott, C. A. (2000). Childhood sexual abuse and adult psychiatric and substance use disorders in women: An epidemiological and co-twin control analysis. *Archives of General Psychiatry, 57*, 953–959.

Kessler, B. L., & Bieschke, K. J. (1999). A retrospective analysis of shame, dissociation and adult victimization in survivors of childhood sexual abuse. *Journal of Counseling Psychology, 46*, 335–341.

Kim, J., Talbot, N., & Cicchetti, D. (2009). Childhood abuse and current interpersonal conflict: The role of shame. *Child Abuse and Neglect, 33*, 362–371.

Kordich Hall, D., Mathews, F., & Pearce, J. (1998). Factors associated with sexual behavior problems in young sexually abused children. *Child Abuse and Neglect, 22*, 1045–1063.

Kunst, M., Popelier, L., & Varekamp, E. (2015). Victim Satisfaction With the Criminal Justice System and Emotional Recovery: A Systematic and Critical Review of the Literature. *Trauma, Violence, & Abuse, 16(3)*, 336–358.

Leonard, M. M. (2010). 'I did what I was directed to do but he didn't touch me': The impact of being a victim of internet offending. *Journal of Sexual Aggression, 16*, 249–256.

Livingstone, S., Haddon, L., Görzig, A., & Ólafsson, K. (2010). *Risks and safety for children on the internet: The UK report*. London, UK: LSE, EU Kids Online.

MacDonald, J., & Morley, I. (2001). Shame and non-disclosure: A study of the emotional isolation of people referred for psychotherapy. *British Journal of Medical Psychology, 74*, 1–21.

Martin, J., & Alaggia, R. (2013). Sexual abuse images in cyberspace: Expanding the ecology of the child. *Journal of Child Sexual Abuse, 22*, 398–415.

Mesquita, B., & Karasawa, M. (2004). Self-conscious emotions as dynamic cultural processes. *Psychological Inquiry, 15*, 161–166.

Mitchell, K. J., Finkelhor, D., & Wolak, J. (2005). The internet and family and acquaintance sexual abuse. *Child Maltreatment, 10*, 49–60.

Nagel, D. E., Putnam, F. W., & Noll, J. G. (1997). Disclosure patterns of sexual abuse and psychological functioning at 1-year follow-up. *Child Abuse and Neglect, 21*, 137–147.

National Crime Agency (NCA). (2014). *National strategic assessment of serious and organised crime 2014.* London, UK: National Crime Agency.

Noll, J. G., Horowitz, L. A., Bonanno, G. A., Trickett, P. K., & Putnam, F. W. (2003). Revictimization and self-harm in females who experienced childhood sexual abuse: Results from a prospective study. *Journal of Interpersonal Violence, 18*, 1452–1471.

Noll, J. G., Trickett, P. K., & Putnam, F. W. (2003). A prospective investigation of the impact of childhood sexual abuse on the development of sexuality. *Journal of Consulting and Clinical Psychology, 71*, 575–586.

Palmer, T., & Stacey, L. (2004). *Just one click: Sexual abuse of children and young people through the internet and mobile phone technology.* Barkingside, UK: Barnardo's.

Peachey, P. (2013, Sept. 20). Paedophiles blackmail thousands of UK teens into online sex acts. *The Independent.* Retrieved from http://www.independent.co.uk/news/uk/crime/paedophiles-blackmail-thousands-of-uk-teens-into-online-sex-acts-8827794.html

Quayle, E., & Jones, T. (2011). Sexualised images of children on the internet. *Sexual Abuse: A Journal of Research and Treatment, 23*, 7–21.

Quayle, E., Jonsson, L., & Lööf, L. (2012). *Online behaviour related to child sexual abuse: Interviews with affected young people.* Stockholm, Sweden: Council of the Baltic Sea States, ROBERT Project.

Reading, R., et al. (2009). Promotion of children's rights and prevention of child maltreatment. *The Lancet, 373*, 332–343.

Ringrose, J., Gill, R., Livingstone, S., & Harvey, L. (2012). *A qualitative study of children, young people and 'sexting': a report prepared for the NSPCC.* London: NSPCC.

Shannon, D. (2008). Online sexual grooming in Sweden: Online and offline sex offences against children as described in Swedish police data. *Journal of Scandinavian Studies in Criminology and Crime Prevention, 9*, 160–180.

Schönbucker, V., Maier, T., Mohler-Kuo, M., & Landolt, M. A. (2014). Adolescent perspectives on social support received in the aftermath of sexual abuse: A qualitative study. *Archives of Sexual Behavior, 43*, 571–586.

Sickel, A. E. (2002). The long-term physical health and healthcare utilization of women who were sexually abused as children. *Journal of Health Psychology, 7*, 583–597.

Sigurjónsdóttir, S. (2012). Consequences of victims' mental health after internet-initiated sexual abuse: A sexual grooming case in Sweden. Unpublished masters in psychology thesis, Stockholm University.

Steel, J., Sanna, L., Hammond, B., Whipple, J., & Cross, H. (2004). Psychological sequelae of childhood sexual abuse: Abuse-related characteristics, coping strategies and
attributional style. *Child Abuse and Neglect, 28*, 785–801.

Svedin, C. G., & Back, K. (2003). *Why didn't they tell us? Sexual abuse in child pornography*. Stockholm, Sweden: Save the Children Sweden.

Talbot, J. A., Talbot, N., & Tu, X. (2004). Shame-proneness as a diathesis for dissociation in women with histories of childhood sexual abuse. *Journal of Traumatic
Stress, 17*, 445–448.

Troxel, N. R., Ogle, C. M., Cordon, I. M., Lawler, M. J., & Goodman, G. S. (2009). Child
witnesses in criminal court. In B. L. Bottoms, C. J. Najdowski, & G. S. Goodman
(Eds.), *Children as victims, witnesses and offenders: Psychological science and the
law* (pp. 150–166). London: The Guilford Press.

von Weiler, J., Haardt-Becker, A., & Schulte, S. (2010). Care and treatment of child
victims of child pornographic exploitation (CPE) in Germany. *Journal of Sexual
Aggression, 16*, 211–222.

Whittle, H. C., Hamilton-Giachritsis, C. E., & Beech, A. R. (2013). Victim's voices: The
impact of online grooming and sexual abuse. *Universal Journal of Psychology, 1*,
59–71.

Whittle, H. C., Hamilton-Giachritsis, C. E., & Beech, A. R. (2014). In their own words:
Young peoples' vulnerabilities to being groomed and sexually abused online.
Psychology, 5(10).

Whittle, H. C., Hamilton-Giachritsis, C. E., & Beech, A. R. (2015). A comparison of
victim and offender perspectives of grooming and sexual abuse. *Deviant Behavior*,
36, 539–564.

Whittle, H. C., Hamilton-Giachritsis, C. E., Beech, A. R., & Collings, G. (2013a).
A review of online grooming: Characteristics and concerns. *Aggression and Violent
Behavior, 18*, 62–70.

Whittle, H. C., Hamilton-Giachritsis, C. E., Beech, A. R., & Collings, G. (2013b).
A review of young people's vulnerabilities towards online grooming. *Aggression
and Violent Behavior, 18*, 135–146.

Wolak, J., & Finkelhor, D. (2011). *Sexting: A typology*. Durham, NH: Crimes against
Children Research Centre.

Yates, T. M., Carlson, E. A., & Egeland, B. (2008). A prospective study of child maltreatment and self-injurious behavior in a community sample. *Development and
Psychopathology, 20*, 651–671.

NOTES

1 In this chapter the term 'victim' is predominantly used because there is a focus on
children who are being abused or suffering its impact, which can include the sense
of on-going abuse. 'Survivor' is also used to recognise the process of surviving and
recovering from abuse.

2 See www.ceop.police.uk for information about the roles and responsibilities of
this agency.

3   It is not possible to state that technology-assisted abuse is *more* impactful than
    offline forms, as each will have features that complicate impact. For example fully
    offline abuse is more likely to involve penetration which like participation can
    increase impact.

4   The term 'victim participation' refers to victims' behaviours forming a part of their
    own abuse – for example, victims sending sexual images because they have been
    manipulated or coerced by the offender, or victims sexually touching themselves or
    others under direction or grooming from offenders. It is not linked to responsibility
    for the abuse, although, as discussed further on in the chapter, it can lead to errone-
    ous conclusions about blame.

5   Space does not allow for a discussion of the differences between shame and its
    'relations' such as embarrassment, stigma, self-consciousness and humiliation –
    they all link to a sense of oneself in the eyes of others as inferior and therefore may
    all be heightened by image and online abuse elements. The focus here is on shame
    given the attention it has received in the research literature; however hypotheses
    about the relationship of these allied states to online and offline CSA, which should
    be explored in further research.

6   The betrayal typically explored within this research is the betrayal by a caregiver
    towards a child whom he or she has sexually abused. Further research is required
    to ascertain the range of difficulties linked to betrayal by a romantic attachment
    towards an adolescent (e.g., in online grooming).

7   See www.thinkuknow.co.uk for films and web pages aimed at reducing internet-
    related vulnerabilities.

8   See https://www.thinkuknow.co.uk/parents/articles/Finding-out-your-child-has-been-
    sexually-abused-or-exploited/ for an online article for parents who have found out
    their child has been abused. This aims to facilitate supportive responses.

7 Promising Therapeutic Approaches for Children, Young People and their Families Following Online Sexual Abuse

Elly Hanson

There are a variety of forms of online sexual abuse, including sexual abuse shared with others online, abuse commissioned online, sexual blackmail, online grooming, and buying sex from children[1] online (for an overview see Hanson, Chapter 6, this book). Each constitutes a violation of children's rights and can lead to victims[2] experiencing psychological difficulties at the time of the abuse and/or at some point following it. Potential difficulties in childhood or adolescence include mistrust and relationship difficulties; re-victimisation; depression, anxiety and posttraumatic stress; eating disorders; aggression; substance misuse and sexual risk-taking (see Hanson, Chapter 6, this book). In many cases, problems may emerge later, for example, once the person has reached late adolescence or adulthood (Trickett, Noll, & Putnam, 2011), and some people may experience little if any difficulty over their lifetime (Molnar, Buka, & Kessler, 2001). How a particular person is affected will depend on a variety of factors, including (in interaction) aspects of the abuse, the approach of family and professionals and the ways in which the child feels and thinks about the abuse. If sexual abuse has an online dimension this can add a layer of complexity for survivors – the dynamics of online abuse may heighten or lead to feelings of pervasive shame, self-blame, mistrust, fear or self-objectification, or the sense that the abuse is ongoing. Each of these feelings may then increase the risk of difficulties such as those just highlighted. (For full exploration of the impact of online sexual abuse, see Hanson, Chapter 6, this book.)

This understanding of impact has several implications for interventions aimed at preventing or resolving difficulties that may emerge following online sexual abuse. First, following abuse children who appear to be without

Online Risk to Children: Impact, Protection and Prevention, First Edition.
Edited by Jon Brown.

difficulty may still require and deserve intervention and support to avoid problems emerging at a later time point. For example, sexual abuse and responses to it can lead children to develop negative beliefs or threat-processing styles that, despite being relatively hidden, can contribute towards difficulties, such as posttraumatic stress disorder or re-victimisation in subsequent developmental stages or life circumstances (Andrews, Brewin, Rose & Kirk, 2000; Feiring & Cleland, 2007; Hanson, 2016; McCrory & Viding, 2015). Related to this, children have a right to support following adverse life experiences, whatever their impact (for example, Article 39 of UN Convention on the Rights of the Child; UN General Assembly, 1989). Second, because children and young people can be affected so differently by abuse, any intervention should be based on a good understanding of a young person's specific problems and the factors playing into them. Third, in most circumstances, alongside any direct work with children, treatments should help families and carers develop their supportive approach, and consideration should be given to work with other relevant systems near the child, for example, significant peer groups.

Drawing on an understanding of the impact of online sexual abuse and the evidence on effective interventions for sexual abuse generally, this chapter lays out some promising therapeutic methods, with a focus on addressing areas that may be particularly challenging or important when the sexual abuse has been online. The discussion is highly selective given space limitations, so, for example, methods for treating severe dissociation are not described, and there is a focus on treatments for adolescents (given that the majority of children in therapy following online sexual abuse are at this developmental stage). Much of what is covered is also relevant to the treatment of adult survivors. The evidence on effective therapeutic interventions for child victims of sexual abuse is discussed first.

EFFECTIVE AND PROMISING TREATMENT APPROACHES FOR PROBLEMS IN CHILDHOOD ARISING FROM SEXUAL ABUSE

Four meta-analyses, each with somewhat different methods and foci, have been conducted to ascertain the most effective forms of treatment for children and young people experiencing psychological difficulties following sexual abuse (Harvey & Taylor, 2010; Hetzel-Riggin, Brausch, & Montgomery, 2007; Sánchez-Meca, Rosa-Alcázar, & López-Soler, 2011; Trask, Walsh, & DiLillo, 2011). Taken together their results suggest that treatment is generally effective across a range of therapy types and problem areas (generally achieving medium to large effect sizes) and that therapy of longer duration tends to be more effective. The comparative effectiveness of different types of treatment depends on the measured problem; generally speaking, it appears that CBT and family-based treatments are particularly useful for treating posttraumatic stress, and an eclectic approach that draws on a variety of therapies such as CBT, abuse-specific and supportive therapy is most effective for improving social skills, sexualised behaviour and behavioural problems. Group and individual therapy may confer different advantages; for example, individual therapy appears to be more powerful in treating trauma symptoms and psychological distress (Harvey & Taylor, 2010; Hetzel-Riggin et al., 2007), whereas group therapy may be more useful for improving self-esteem (Hetzel-Riggin et al., 2007).

Meta-analyses summate the current research on effectiveness and provide broad brush-stroke pictures of the kinds of approach that are most likely to work in addressing particular problems. They are, however, necessarily limited in the detail that they can provide and by the extent of the therapy outcome research on which they are based.

Research indicates that trauma-focussed CBT (TF-CBT) is the most effective type of CBT for treating a broad range of difficulties following sexual abuse (Taylor, Graham, & Weems, 2015). This form of CBT involves several stages: (1) psychoeducation about trauma and developing anxiety management skills (for example, relaxation training); (2) cognitive restructuring (for example, challenging negative and maladaptive thinking); (3) building a narrative of the trauma and in-depth exploration of it; and (4) relapse prevention and planning for the end. In parallel there are sessions for parents helping them support their child's anxiety management and develop behavioural management strategies (Cohen, Mannarino, & Deblinger, 2006).

Other therapies have not yet been evaluated to the degree necessary to achieve prominence within a meta-analysis but are promising given the theory behind them and wider research.

A recently developed approach, which incorporates the core components of TF-CBT alongside other ideas from play and group therapies, is game-based CBT (Springer & Misurell, 2010). This is designed for children aged 5 to 13 years who have experienced sexual abuse, and it uses structured, therapeutic and developmentally appropriate games to deliver the core components of treatment. It is based on the rationale that pre-adolescent children often learn best through play and that structured games feel familiar to children and can prompt thinking and discussion about topics that might otherwise feel uncomfortable. There is also a parent group providing opportunities to discuss feelings about the abuse and to develop parenting and coping skills. Initial outcome studies show positive results across a range of cultures (Misurell & Springer, 2013; Springer, Misurell, & Hiller, 2012).

Eye movement desensitisation reprocessing (EMDR) is a further promising treatment approach, specifically focussed on resolving trauma symptoms (such as intrusive thoughts, memories and emotions related to the abuse). The hypothesised neuropsychological mechanisms of effect are somewhat similar to those within TF-CBT: it assists the child in adaptively integrating and processing trauma memories that are otherwise dysfunctionally stored and avoided, thereby causing intrusive symptoms. Children track therapist hand movements with their eyes whilst attending to trauma-related memories and feelings. There is solid evidence for its efficacy with adults across a range of traumas (Shapiro, 2012) and emerging evidence for its utility with child victims of sexual abuse in individual (Jaberghaderi, Greenwald, Rubin, Zand, & Dolatabadi, 2004) and group formats (Jarero, Roque-López, & Gomez, 2013). Jaberghaderi et al. (2004) found, albeit within a small sample size, that EMDR required fewer sessions than TF-CBT to achieve the same effects. A recent meta-analysis also found a small benefit of EMDR over TF-CBT for children who had experienced a variety of traumas (Rodenburg, Benjamin, de Roos, Meijer, & Stams, 2009). For some children EMDR may be especially beneficial because it requires less verbal skill and willingness to disclose and more closely follows the child's mind to the memories most in need of processing (in comparison with TF-CBT).

A therapy that takes the principle of child-led trauma processing even further is brainspotting (BSP: Grand, 2011; Grixti & Dean, 2015). Discovered in the context of EMDR, this therapeutic approach assists processing of trauma memories by drawing the person's attention to eye gaze positions that correspond to trauma-related bodily feelings and emotions.

Narrative therapy is also likely to be of value in treating a variety of abuse sequelae. As explored in subsequent sections, many problems develop from understandings of oneself and others that have been shaped by abuse – for example, children may isolate themselves and self-harm because they feel they are worthless. Narrative therapy, similar to cognitive restructuring in CBT, assists children and their families in developing more adaptive understandings of themselves and others. It makes particular use of playful, creative and strength-based techniques (Morgan, 2000) and recognises and challenges inequality and the misuse of power in survivors' lives (Mann & Russell, 2003). Descriptive studies demonstrate its utility specifically with young people experiencing sexual abuse–related difficulties (Ncube, 2010).

The rationale and evidence base of dialectical behaviour therapy (DBT) suggest it has merit in addressing some abuse-related problems in adolescents. DBT helps people adaptively regulate intense negative emotions and shift unhealthy relationship patterns through a blend of mindfulness and cognitive behavioural techniques that are heavily underpinned by a highly validating therapeutic relationship, a dual focus on helping people change and accepting themselves as they are (the central dialectic) and an 'irreverent' and playful style (Linehan, 1997, 2014). Recent studies have found that DBT reduces severe difficulties such as suicidal behaviour and self-harm in adolescents (Fleischhaker, Böhme, Sixt, Brück, Schneider, & Schulz 2011; Mehlum et al., 2014), mirroring the more well-established outcomes for adults. Furthermore a recently developed blend of DBT and trauma-focussed therapy (DBT-PTSD) significantly reduced PTSD in adult survivors of sexual abuse who were experiencing a range of complex difficulties (Bohus et al., 2013).

Other therapies that show promise in reducing sexual abuse sequelae include family therapy (Diamond, Creed, Gillham, Gallop, & Hamilton, 2012; Hetzel-Riggin et al., 2007) and animal-assisted therapy (Dietz, Davis, & Pennings, 2012; Schultz, Remick-Barlow, & Robbins, 2007).

In summary, a variety of therapies are effective or promising treatments for psychological difficulties caused by sexual abuse. The most effective therapy for a particular child will depend on the problems he or she is experiencing, the developmental stage and personality, preferences and strengths (Allnock, Hynes & Archibald, 2015). At the same time many therapies will achieve similar results, because they are underpinned by similar mechanisms of change. Implications of this analysis include (1) that a diversity of therapeutic approaches should be available to children and their families, (2) that the therapy offered to a particular child should be based on a good understanding of his or her particular difficulties and vulnerabilities, and (c) that more often than not an eclectic or integrative therapeutic approach is likely to be of the most benefit.

KEY TARGETS FOR CHANGE IN THERAPY

Therapy is most effective when it addresses the psychological or social factors underlying the overt problems that the child is currently experiencing or is at risk of experiencing in the future. Five such (interrelated) contributors that often need to be addressed in therapy, particularly following online sexual abuse, are explored here.

NEGATIVE BELIEFS

Sexual abuse can lead to children developing negative beliefs about themselves and others, such as 'I'm worthless,' 'I was to blame,' and 'there is no-one I can trust,' held explicitly and/or implicitly. Self-blame may be particularly high following some forms of online sexual abuse in which victims have been manipulated to participate (Hanson, Chapter 6, this book). These ways of thinking can in turn lead to a variety of other harms, such as social isolation, depression, anxiety and trauma symptoms (Coffey, Leitenberg, Henning, Turner, & Bennett, 1996; Feiring & Cleland, 2007; Reichert & Flannery-Schroeder, 2014). Therefore, helping children to come to more adaptive understandings of themselves and others is worthwhile in and of itself and has myriad positive knock-on effects. For example, McLean , Yeh, Rosenfield, and Foa (2015) found that two therapies for adolescents experiencing PTSD (client-centred therapy and prolonged exposure therapy – a form of CBT) achieved reductions in symptoms (such as hypervigilance and intrusive memories) through shifting these negative trauma-related beliefs.

SHAME

Shame, the feeling of being damaged or defiled in the eyes of oneself or others, is also common following sexual abuse and is often linked to (though separable from) blaming oneself for aspects of it. Shame is linked to PTSD, depression, bulimia, relationship conflict and aggression, and re-victimisation following sexual abuse (Andrews, 1995, 1997; Feiring, Simon, Cleland, & Barrett, 2013; Feiring & Taska, 2005; Kessler & Bieschke, 1999). It also contributes to dissociation, which has its own negative sequelae (Feiring, Cleland, & Simon, 2009; Yates, Carlson, & Egeland, 2008) and may be especially prevalent following online sexual abuse, given the making of images, their reach and permanence, and the high levels of victim 'participation' (see Hanson, Chapter 6, this book). When present, it constitutes a priority target for therapy, not least because if left unaddressed it can impede therapeutic progress (Hook & Andrews, 2005).

A SENSE OF ONGOING TRAUMA AND RELATED FEELINGS

Many children who have experienced online sexual abuse are left struggling with the reality of images of their abuse remaining online or the possibility of these images being disseminated in the future (see Hanson, Chapter 6, this book). They may worry intensely about who is viewing these images, how they will be judged by them, or, if they have not yet been shared, if and when they will be. These situations can create a sense of ongoing trauma, leading to hypervigilance, fear and shame (Cooper, 2012; Leonard, 2010). At times the desire to escape from it can prompt self-harm and suicidality. Many therapists find that the impact of this dimension of online abuse creates unique challenges in therapy. Difficult questions that they may grapple with include: Is it useful to explore memories of the abuse when the abuse feels ongoing? And, how can fear be resolved when it relates to current and future realities, not those of the past? (Martin, 2016; Von Weiler, Haardt-Becker, & Schultc, 2010).

Practitioners can be left identifying with children's feelings of helplessness, which in turn compromise the hope that facilitates therapeutic change. Their challenge is to find ways to help children overcome feelings of trauma and fear even when images are still circulating. As with each of these areas, some suggestions are proffered in the final main section of this chapter.

'It's not a distortion, really, not a cognitive distortion, if they are accessible, if people are looking. There is really nothing I can do to correct that.' (Martin, 2016, p. 380)

'How do you understand the term "creating safety in the present" when it might be the future that they are fearful of?' (Martin, 2016, p. 379)

FAMILY FACTORS

The support and validation that families, especially parents and carers, give to children in general, and specifically in relation to revelations of sexual abuse, profoundly influence how a child is affected by that abuse over the long term (Hong, Ilardi & Lishner, 2011). However, as Tavkar and Hansen (2011) state, 'often when a child who has been sexually abused is most needing their mother [non-abusive parents or carers], the mother's resources for coping with the disclosure and its aftermath are also being taxed' (p. 192). And many lack the reflective interpersonal spaces they require to work out what their child needs from them.

In situations of online abuse, parents may be particularly susceptible to seeing their child as blameworthy – the victim participation portrayed in images or chat logs is often taken at face value, and complex controlling dynamics are under-appreciated (Hamilton-Giachritsis, Hanson, Whittle & Beech, in press). In many cases the revelations of abuse make parents aware of the extent of their children's sexual knowledge, and they then struggle with their children's perceived loss of innocence (Leonard, 2015).

Parental support specifically of therapy is also important. This has an impact on its effectiveness (Taylor et al., 2015), and children benefit more when there is a family component to treatment (Tavkar & Hansen, 2011).

This all converges to suggest that therapeutic effectiveness will be improved by working with parents and carers to (1) develop their supportive approach to their child, (2) enhance their support specifically of their child's therapy, and (3) help them process and understand their own feelings about the abuse. There is also a strong case for providing therapeutic support to siblings of abused children, given the likely impact of the abuse on them and their contribution to a supportive family environment (Tavkar & Hansen, 2011).

SELF-OBJECTIFICATION AND BODY ESTEEM

Sexual abuse may lead to body shame, body dissatisfaction and self-objectification[3] (Kearney-Cooke & Ackard, 1999; Knowles, 2012), which may in turn contribute to other problems such as disordered eating and depression (Andrews, 1995, 1997). The focus on sexual *images* so often central to online sexual abuse may further heighten the risk of young people perceiving themselves as sexual objects and feeling negative towards their bodies (De Vries & Peter, 2013; Hanson, Chapter 6, this book).

Chronic distrust of others, dissociation and trauma processing strategy (i.e., avoidant or absorbed versus constructive; Simon, Feiring, & McElroy, 2010) are further factors that might be usefully targeted in therapy with the expectation of multiple positive knock-on effects.

This chapter now goes on to explore a few methods that hold promise in addressing the factors outlined here (and related others). These methods all fall within the broad group of effective and promising therapies previously outlined.

PROMISING METHODS OF FULFILLING KEY
(OVERLAPPING) THERAPEUTIC AIMS

ASSESSMENT AND FORMULATION

A nuanced understanding of a child's areas of difficulty, vulnerability, resilience and strength, and the thoughts, feelings and coping styles below the surface, assists in formulating a sensitive and responsive treatment approach. It may be best developed through using a variety of tools, such as ongoing careful listening to the child's verbal and non-verbal communication, gathering information from parents and teachers and age-appropriate psychometrics. The last can be used to explore salient problems, such as anxiety, sexualised behaviour and PTSD (e.g., the Trauma Symptom Checklist for Children; Briere, 1996) and more hidden relevant thoughts, emotions and coping styles (e.g., the Trauma Appraisal Questionnaire; DePrince, Zurbriggen, Chu, & Smart, 2010). This information is then used to build a working understanding of the factors playing into a child's struggles and concomitant ways forward.

Assessment is an ongoing process – we each disclose more as we come to feel safe. And a wise principle in all therapeutic work is refraining from assumptions about how particular life experiences have affected someone – for example, abuse images with online permanency may leave therapists feeling utterly powerless to help (Von Weiler et al., 2010), but not all children will make sense of this situation in the same way (for example, as a result of shorter future horizons) (Hamilton-Giachritsis et al., in press).

At the other end of the continuum in these circumstances some children will be at risk of suicidal behaviour. If this might be a possibility it is important to assess this risk, in part by compassionately exploring any suicidal, hopeless or despairing feelings and associated plans. Asking about suicidality does not increase risk but is typically experienced as a relief and often the beginning of its resolution.[4]

The assessment process involves giving as well as gathering information. In some cases of online abuse, children may not know all the details of their abuse, for example, that images of it have been shared. Careful thought should be given to how much a child is told, taking into consideration their developmental stage and the risks and benefits now and in the future of sharing or withholding. Sometimes professionals may feel that a child has a right to know; however, balanced against this can be the child's right to protection. Telling children, who are unlikely to otherwise find out, that images of their abuse are being shared constitutes a step in a pathway to a further layer of distress for the child. Therefore the disclosing organisation or person has a responsibility to make provision for this, for example, by providing a longer course of therapeutic help.

ENGAGEMENT AND BUILDING A STRONG THERAPEUTIC RELATIONSHIP

When there are trauma-related difficulties, a large proportion of children and their families drop out of therapy prematurely (Macdonald, Higgins, & Ramchandani, 2007; Saxe, Ellis, Fogler, & Navalta, 2012), so building engagement should arguably be the first goal of therapy (although methods to achieve it also work towards other goals in parallel).

At times engagement is compromised by logistical issues and wider stressful life circumstances. Victims of online sexual abuse may often be living in families struggling with multiple stressors (Whittle, Hamilton-Giachritsis, & Beech, 2013), and in these circumstances the young person and the family may find it hard to prioritise therapy. There are also numerous psychological factors (present prior to therapy or forming within it) that can compromise engagement, for example, perceptions that therapy will be ineffective and that difficulties are irresolvable, or, conversely, minimal; feelings that therapy will be stigmatising, blaming, pressurising, exposing or overwhelming, or a belief that the best approach is avoidance (Allnock, Hynes, & Archibald, 2015; Lindsey et al., 2014; Bolton-Oetzel & Scherer, 2003). It is often when difficulties are at their most intense that therapy can feel most risky or least feasible or likely to work.

If abuse images are circulating online (or might do so), young people may wonder how therapy can help them resolve what seems an ongoing fixed reality. And in some situations, especially those involving online grooming, they may have ongoing feelings of love or attachment towards the abuser, thwarting their ability to recognise the abuse and the difficulties it has caused them and therefore also the benefits of therapeutic help.

Thus engagement should never be assumed but reflectively facilitated at each stage of therapy. A number of methods have proven efficacy (Lindsey et al., 2014) – some should always be used, whereas the utility of others will depend on the specific treatment barriers at play:

- Making services accessible and affordable, for example, providing childcare when appropriate and offering sessions at convenient times.
- Prior to the initial session (e.g., via telephone) or during it, openly eliciting from young people and families any potential barriers to attendance and making a plan for addressing these.
- In collaboration with young people (and their families when appropriate), forging and working from an understanding of problems, strengths and goals.
- Providing information about therapy and how it works, as well as offering an explanation of any psychological difficulties that is non-stigmatising and non-blaming and instead normalises and offers hope.

- Recruiting informal helpers such as relatives to support therapy and pairing young people or families with others who may have experienced similar problems to share information and offer support.
- Helping young people and families to resolve crises or life problems that are compromising their ability to gain from therapy. This might involve problem-solving together (and teaching these skills), advocacy and coordination and liaison with other services.
- Addressing any specific barriers linked to culture, sexuality or disability.

A variety of operationalised approaches blend many of these methods (Ozechowski & Waldron, 2010; Saxe et al., 2012). Trauma systems therapy (TST) aims to increase engagement by providing psychoeducation, trouble-shooting and working with families to develop a highly specified plan of action. Preliminary evidence suggests that these technique, alongside a coordinated treatment plan (ensuring there is one lead provider) and family inclusion, can reduce drop-out rates in PTSD treatment from 90% to 10% (Saxe et al., 2012).

Most fundamental to engagement is a strong therapeutic alliance, and this is also key to broader therapeutic effectiveness (Shirk & Karver, 2003). Rapport between therapist and client is developed by the therapist being genuine, empathic, compassionate, hopeful and validating (Ackerman & Hilsenroth, 2003). Further interlocking therapist qualities include being flexible to the client's needs (on the basis that there are a variety of paths to wellbeing), drawing on their strengths and being assertive about change (Allnock et al., 2015; Bolton-Oetzel & Scherer, 2003; Linehan, 1997).

Ambivalence towards therapy may be particularly common in adolescence. When young people are unsure about whether they have problems in need of change (for example, they might feel this way about preoccupation with body image or a relationship with an abusive individual), it is most effective to dispassionately help them explore the issue and come to 'the reasons to change inside themselves.' Motivational interviewing helps people evaluate their situation and the possibilities for change and to strengthen their confidence in and commitment to change should they so wish to. It has proven efficacy in resolving ambivalence and thereby also contributes to positive outcomes (Jensen et al., 2011). Similarly narrative therapy contains lots of ideas and methods that help people to separate themselves from the problem and to see it in a more constructive way that opens up possibilities for positive change.[5]

Giving as much choice as possible also helps to increase adolescents' intrinsic commitment to therapeutic support in situations when they have at first felt compelled to attend. Ideally young people should have informed choice about their therapist, the approach and what topics are explored and how (Bolton-Oetzel & Scherer, 2003; Hamilton-Giachritsis et al., in press). It should be made clear that there is no expectation to discuss the facts of the abuse, and limits of confidentiality should be discussed up front and adhered to (Allnock et al., 2015; Hamilton-Giachritsis et al., in press).

A final point is that people may be most likely to engage in therapy at the point at which they have asked for help; this is part of the reason why long waiting lists may risk the effectiveness of therapy.

DEVELOPING POSITIVE BODY ESTEEM AND SEXUALITY

One promising approach to helping young people relate positively to their body is developing their appreciation of their body's functions and how their body sustains them in a diversity of ways. An intervention following this principle with proven efficacy invites young people to reflectively write about their body's senses, physical capacities, health, creativity, self-care and communicative abilities (Alleva, Martijn, Van Breukelen, Jansen, & Karos, 2015). Body appreciation and connection are also enhanced through creative, sensory and movement-based activities (e.g., dance, yoga, cooking, gardening) conducted mindfully and meditations focussed on body appreciation and acceptance (Tylka & Augustus-Horvath, 2011). Activities that demonstrate care and compassion towards one's body may be particularly important for addressing body shame (dovetailing with broader shame-combating approaches discussed in the following). Such activities can also assist with emotion regulation and 'grounding.'

Unfortunately many societal messages encourage self-objectification and body dissatisfaction, and so approaches may be most successful when they also assist young people in challenging and resisting such narratives. Examples of how this can be done include mapping out their existence and influence in young people's lives and collaboratively finding ways in which they can be avoided or challenged (for example, through conversations with friends, using positive self-mantras, social activism and avoiding certain media; Tylka & Augustus-Horvath, 2011). All of this also assists in building empowerment, helping to combat any abuse-related feelings of powerlessness.

Working to increase self-esteem in general is likely to have a knock-on effect on young people's feelings towards their body (O'Dea & Abraham, 2000). The Tree of Strength (Steiner-Adair & Sjostrom, 2006) is an example of an exercise designed to build self-esteem, it does so by focussing attention on the value of positive inner qualities. Young people can also be encouraged to think creatively about and explore in action multiple dimensions of who they are and what they enjoy doing. And as the therapeutic relationship develops, young people are more able to trust and 'hear' the therapist's unconditional positive regard and validation.

REDUCING THE IMPACT OF ABUSE IMAGES CIRCULATING AND THE THREAT OF THIS

First, in all cases in which images are circulating (or may do so in the future), steps should be taken to explore whether these images could be removed (practical guidance is discussed on CEOP's Thinkuknow website, https://www.thinkuknow.co.uk/, aimed at children, parents and professionals). And second, if young people are experiencing bullying or negative judgements, therapeutic work with them should be paralleled by work with their school, peer group or family.

Alongside this, therapeutic work with young people can help them come to a different relationship with the abusive images. The first step in this work may be 'acceptance' of their existence and what cannot be changed (in line with the principles of acceptance and commitment therapy; Greco & Hayes, 2008). The focus can then shift to the areas of life in which the young person is able to exert control. For example, the therapist and young person could collabora- tively develop a plan about how the young person might handle conversations with others who have seen the images and bring up the topic. This could include developing some mantras that the young person says to herself or himself or to others. Exploratory conversations and mapping areas of life in which a young person does feel a sense of control, including over his or her own body (e.g. in sport or dance), can help to strengthen this feeling. Breathing exercises can be used to focus attention on how the young person is connected to and in control of his or her body in the here and now. Empowerment (as well as self-esteem) might also be developed through exploring how this challenging situation has revealed strengths that he or she has and how the young person might draw on these in future situations.

New and adaptive conceptualisations of the images can be explored – for example, they can be thought of as images separate from oneself, communicat- ing only something about the offender and not the young person (they are the abuser's fantasy and deception). The sexual things that the young person is seen to be doing do not represent his or her sexuality – this can only be shared with whom and when she or he would like. Furthermore the young person has his or her body in the present and is in control of it; her or his existence in the present now is separable from the images. And the young person may come to see the images as a tiny fraction of the ever-increasing billions of sexual images in cyberspace. Creative approaches such as using art and poetry can develop these conceptualisations as well as imagery exercises and graphics that model them (for example pie charts showing the proportion of all online sexual images that involve the young person).

Traditionally trauma-focussed therapeutic techniques are only used when clients are in a place of safety. If they are experiencing an ongoing sense of fear related to images circulating and are not readily able to achieve a sense of safety from the previously discussed approaches, should trauma-focussed techniques therefore be avoided? In this scenario, bullying and negative responses from others notwithstanding, the person is physically safe from abuse and the lack of safety largely emanates from his or her relationship with the image. Trauma-focussed approaches (such as TF-CBT, EMDR and brain- spotting) may in fact be particularly useful in resolving this troubling relation- ship, because they often reach beyond other methods in helping people to revise their abuse-driven understandings of themselves and others and to reduce the dominance of the abuse in their life narrative. Through these achievements, they may reduce the threat posed by circulating images – so, in essence, rather than a sense of safety preceding trauma-focussed work, it may result from it.

For trauma-focussed therapy to be most useful, especially in situations of images circulating, it needs to prioritise the young person's choices and control. All methods can and should be adapted to different developmental stages. At times, young people may be reluctant to engage with trauma-focussed methods or to entertain less-threatening conceptualisations of the images. In contrast to persuasion and pressure, which are ineffective and unethical, inviting discussion with the reluctant part of the young person can open up a variety of onward avenues. This part is often trying to protect the young person in one way or another, and naming and exploring this can enable different parts to collaborate rather feel stuck in ambivalence.

OVERCOMING SHAME AND SELF-BLAME; BUILDING PRIDE AND MASTERY

A majority of children in therapy for sexual abuse–related difficulties report feelings of shame or self-blame (Deblinger & Runyon, 2005), and they may be particularly intense following online abuse involving images or 'victim participation.' When they are present, shame and self-blame should be primary targets for treatment.

A caring and respectful therapeutic relationship is the starting point for reducing shame. As Deblinger and Runyon (2005) state, 'actively listening and reflecting back client's worries and concerns can importantly contribute to enhancing feelings of validation and self-acceptance' (p. 370). This can set in motion positive spirals in which the child develops enough trust to disclose more of her or his feelings and experiences, which in turn provides the therapist with opportunities to further validate them and to open up conversations that shift shaming and self-blaming cognitions. Putting together a narrative of the abuse (for example, verbally, in writing or through pictures or poems), which is central to TF-CBT, can usefully facilitate such a spiral. However, if children are very shame-laden, they may not be able to open up enough to make the most of TF-CBT, and a less disclosure-dependent approach to trauma processing may be more useful (such as EMDR or brainspotting).

Psychoeducation, for example, provided in the form of games or exercises, can reduce shame in a variety of ways – by directly challenging beliefs that underpin shame (such as 'it was my fault' and 'the abuse means I am damaged goods'), by creating a sense of open communication about the abuse and by providing praise that enhances feelings of self-efficacy.

Especially when abuse has involved perpetrators' manipulating victims to perform sexual acts on themselves, it can be hard for victims to appreciate their lack of blame. In general across society, people use heuristics (mental short-cuts) in their judgements and one of these is that a person is in control of his or her actions. This is not the case for victims in abuse situations, and methodically mapping this out with clients can be transformative. Ways in which this can be done have been developed by Kubany and colleagues (Kubany & Ralston, 1998) and can be adapted to young people's developmental stage and the specifics of the abuse they have experienced. Also useful in this process are metaphors, analogies and evoking empathy for oneself (e.g., by first evoking empathy for a friend in the same situation).

At times, people may hold onto self-blame, because to let it go invites feelings of powerlessness. Therapists might usefully facilitate a conversation about this perceived dilemma and discuss how planning future actions to avoid significant risk (which increases true control) is separable from blaming oneself for the past.

Young people can also be invited to develop a more compassionate approach towards themselves, for example, by creating in their imagination a 'compassionate nurturer' who can counter self-attacking thoughts and be brought in to self-soothe during or following distressing flashbacks (Bowyer, Wallis, & Lee, 2014; Lee, 2010). Inviting people to explore any fears they might hold about being compassionate towards themselves is an important first step in this work.

Last, using animals such as horses and dogs[6] in therapy holds promise for reducing a variety of abuse-related difficulties, including shame. In the context of a relationship with an animal, children can experience profound unconditional positive regard, as well as develop emotion-regulation skills, a sense of pride and mastery and a deeper awareness of self and others in the present moment (countering dissociation).

FACILITATING SUPPORT FROM FAMILIES

Family-focussed interventions should be part and parcel of interventions for children who have experienced online sexual abuse, given the extent to which a family's approach affects their child's recovery and wellbeing.[7] Individual or group sessions for parents can be run in parallel to those for their children. Initially these might provide useful psychoeducation about online sexual abuse. Parents can be invited to reflect on any difficult feelings they might have towards themselves or their children (e.g., blame, anger, guilt) and to share, process and make sense of these feelings. This can be an important step in developing understandings of the abuse which are helpful to their child.

Parents should also receive guidance in how they can support and protect their child moving forwards – for example, ways in which they can demonstrate belief and validation, support their child's emotional processing, guide their child's engagement with the online world, and help shape their child's understanding of the abuse and its impact. Conjoint sessions towards the end of therapy can then provide an opportunity for parents to demonstrate much of this to their child. Without such guidance, it is easy for parents to adopt stances that are well-meaning but potentially harmful, for example, being overly restrictive, placing too much responsibility on the child to avoid future abuse or expressing aggressive intent towards the abuser, which can in fact lead children to feel isolated (Allnock & Miller, 2013; Deblinger & Runyon, 2005).

Finally, many of the themes and approaches discussed in this chapter for young people can be usefully adapted to work with parents, such as compassionate mind approaches for parents who find it hard to step out of blaming responses to themselves or their child and trauma-focussed approaches for those experiencing intrusive thoughts, images or emotions.

CONCLUSION

All children have a right to receive responsive therapeutic support (focussed on themselves and/or their families) following sexual abuse coming to light. Evidence suggests that therapy can reduce psychological difficulties caused by abuse and prevent them from developing at a later stage.

Although there is a large research literature demonstrating the effectiveness of a variety of therapeutic approaches in the treatment of sexual abuse–related difficulties, a number of promising approaches have not received adequate research attention (for example, narrative therapy), and we are at the early stages of understanding what methods are most useful for addressing specific difficulties that relate to online dimensions of abuse.

This chapter has provided an overview of the evidence and explored a number of methods that hold promise in addressing difficulties particularly pertinent to online abuse. The hope is that this will stimulate developments in therapeutic practice and further research endeavours, and that, ultimately, these in turn further increase the effectiveness of therapy so that more children and families are able to thrive and achieve well-being. For this goal to be achieved, such development needs to be matched with improvements in the accessibility and timeliness of therapeutic help, so that no child or family who would like such support is left wanting or waiting.

REFERENCES

Ackerman, S. J., & Hilsenroth, M. J. (2003). A review of therapist characteristics and techniques positively impacting the therapeutic alliance. *Clinical Psychology Review, 23*(1), 1–33.

Alleva, J. M., Martijn, C., Van Breukelen, G. J., Jansen, A., & Karos, K. (2015). Expand Your Horizon: A programme that improves body image and reduces self-objectification by training women to focus on body functionality. *Body Image, 15,* 81–89.

Allnock, D., Hynes, P., & Archibald, M. (2015). Self-reported experiences of therapy following child sexual abuse: Messages from a retrospective survey of adult survivors. *Journal of Social Work, 15*(2), 115–137.

Allnock, D., & Miller, P. (2013). No one noticed, no one heard. *A study of disclosures of childhood abuse.* London, UK: NSPCC.

Andrews, B. (1995). Bodily shame as a mediator between abusive experiences and depression. *Journal of Abnormal Psychology, 104*(2), 277.

Andrews, B. (1997). Bodily shame in relation to abuse in childhood and bulimia: A preliminary investigation. *British Journal of Clinical Psychology, 36*(1), 41–49.

Andrews, B., Brewin, C. R., Rose, S., & Kirk, M. (2000). Predicting PTSD symptoms in victims of violent crime: The role of shame, anger, and childhood abuse. *Journal of Abnormal Psychology, 109*(1), 69.

Bohus, M., Dyer, A. S., Priebe, K., Krüger, A., Kleindienst, N., Schmahl, C., ... & Steil, R. (2013). Dialectical behaviour therapy for post-traumatic stress disorder after childhood sexual abuse in patients with and without borderline personality disorder: A randomised controlled trial. *Psychotherapy and Psychosomatics, 82*(4), 221–233.

Bolton-Oetzel, K., & Scherer, D. G. (2003). Therapeutic engagement with adolescents in psychotherapy. *Psychotherapy: Theory, Research, Practice, Training, 40*(3), 215–225.

Bowyer, L., Wallis, J., & Lee, D. (2014). Developing a compassionate mind to enhance trauma-focused CBT with an adolescent female: A case study. *Behavioural and Cognitive Psychotherapy, 42*(02), 248–254.

Briere, J. (1996). *Trauma symptom checklist for children*. Odessa, FL: Psychological Assessment Resources.

Coffey, P., Leitenberg, H., Henning, K., Turner, T., & Bennett, R. T. (1996). Mediators of the long-term impact of child sexual abuse: Perceived stigma, betrayal, powerlessness, and self-blame. *Child Abuse & Neglect, 20*(5), 447–455.

Cohen, J. A., Mannarino, A. P., & Deblinger, E. (2006). *Treating trauma and traumatic grief in children and adolescents*. Guilford Press.

Cooper, S. W. (2012). *The impact on children who have been victims of child pornography*. Written testimony before the U.S. Sentencing Commission.

Deblinger, E., & Runyon, M. K. (2005). Understanding and treating feelings of shame in children who have experienced maltreatment. *Child Maltreatment, 10*(4), 364–376.

DePrince, A. P., Zurbriggen, E. L., Chu, A. T., & Smart, L. (2010). Development of the trauma appraisal questionnaire. *Journal of Aggression, Maltreatment & Trauma, 19*(3), 275–299.

De Vries, D. A., & Peter, J. (2013). Women on display: The effect of portraying the self online on women's self-objectification. *Computers in Human Behavior, 29*(4), 1483–1489.

Diamond, G., Creed, T., Gillham, J., Gallop, R., & Hamilton, J. L. (2012). Sexual trauma history does not moderate treatment outcome in attachment-based family therapy (ABFT) for adolescents with suicide ideation. *Journal of Family Psychology, 26*(4), 595.

Dietz, T. J., Davis, D., & Pennings, J. (2012). Evaluating animal-assisted therapy in group treatment for child sexual abuse. *Journal of Child Sexual Abuse, 21*(6), 665–683.

Feiring, C., & Cleland, C. (2007). Childhood sexual abuse and abuse-specific attributions of blame over 6 years following discovery. *Child Abuse & Neglect, 31*(11), 1169–1186.

Feiring, C., Cleland, C. M., & Simon, V. A. (2009). Abuse-specific self-schemas and self-functioning: A prospective study of sexually abused youth. *Journal of Clinical Child & Adolescent Psychology, 39*(1), 35–50.

Feiring, C., Simon, V. A., Cleland, C. M., & Barrett, E. P. (2013). Potential pathways from stigmatization and externalizing behavior to anger and dating aggression in sexually abused youth. *Journal of Clinical Child & Adolescent Psychology, 42*(3), 309–322.

Feiring, C., & Taska, L. S. (2005). The persistence of shame following sexual abuse: A longitudinal look at risk and recovery. *Child Maltreatment, 10*(4), 337–349.

Fleischhaker, C., Böhme, R., Sixt, B., Brück, C., Schneider, C., & Schulz, E. (2011). Dialectical Behavioral Therapy for Adolescents (DBT-A): A clinical trial for patients with suicidal and self-injurious behavior and borderline symptoms with a one-year follow-up. *Child and Adolescent Psychiatry and Mental Health, 5*(3), 1–10.

Grand, D. (2011). Brainspotting: A new brain-based psychotherapy approach. *Trauma and Gewalt, 3*, 276–285.

Greco, L. A., & Hayes, S. C. (2008). *Acceptance & mindfulness treatments for children & adolescents: A practitioner's guide*. Oakland, CA: New Harbinger Publications.

Grixti, M., & Dean, R. (2015). *Brainspotting with young people: An adventure into the mind*. Sattva.

Hamilton-Giachritsis, C., Hanson, E., Whittle, H. C., & Beech, A. R. (in press). *"Everyone deserves to be happy and safe" A mixed methods study exploring how online and offline child sexual abuse impact young people and how professionals respond to it*. London: NSPCC.

Hanson, E. (2016) Preventing revictimization. In L. Smith (Ed) *Clinical practice at the edge of care*. Palgrave Macmillan.

Harvey, S. T., & Taylor, J. E. (2010). A meta-analysis of the effects of psychotherapy with sexually abused children and adolescents. *Clinical Psychology Review, 30*(5), 517–535.

Hetzel-Riggin, M. D., Brausch, A. M., & Montgomery, B. S. (2007). A meta-analytic investigation of therapy modality outcomes for sexually abused children and adolescents: An exploratory study. *Child Abuse & Neglect, 31*(2), 125–141.

Hong, P. Y., Ilardi, S. S., & Lishner, D. A. (2011). The aftermath of trauma: The impact of perceived and anticipated invalidation of childhood sexual abuse on borderline symptomatology. *Psychological Trauma: Theory, Research, Practice, and Policy, 3*(4), 360.

Hook, A., & Andrews, B. (2005). The relationship of non-disclosure in therapy to shame and depression. *British Journal of Clinical Psychology, 44*(3), 425–438.

Jaberghaderi, N., Greenwald, R., Rubin, A., Zand, S. O., & Dolatabadi, S. (2004). A comparison of CBT and EMDR for sexually abused Iranian girls. *Clinical Psychology & Psychotherapy, 11*(5), 358–368.

Iarero, I., Roque-López, S., & Gomez, J. (2013). The provision of an EMDR-based multicomponent trauma treatment with child victims of severe interpersonal trauma. *Journal of EMDR Practice and Research, 7*(1), 17–28.

Jensen, C. D., Cushing, C. C., Aylward, B. S., Craig, J. T., Sorell, D. M., & Steele, R. G. (2011). Effectiveness of motivational interviewing interventions for adolescent substance use behavior change: A meta-analytic review. *Journal of Consulting and Clinical Psychology, 79*(4), 433.

Kearney-Cooke, A., & Ackard, D. M. (1999). The effects of sexual abuse on body image, self-image, and sexual activity of women. *The Journal of Gender-Specific Medicine: JGSM: The Official Journal of the Partnership for Women's Health at Columbia, 3*(6), 54–60.

Kessler, B. L., & Bieschke, K. J. (1999). A retrospective analysis of shame, dissociation, and adult victimization in survivors of childhood sexual abuse. *Journal of Counseling Psychology, 46*(3), 335.

Knowles, L. R. (2012). *Response to sexual trauma in relation to event centrality and objectified view of self* (Doctoral dissertation). University of North Texas, Denton, TX.

Kubany, E. S., & Ralston, T. C. (1998). Cognitive therapy for trauma-related guilt. *Cognitive-Behavioral Therapies for Trauma*, pp. 124–161.

Lee, D. A. (2010). Using a compassionate mind to enhance the effectiveness of cognitive therapy for individuals who suffer from shame and self-criticism. In D. Sookman & R. L. Leahy, *Treatment resistant anxiety disorders: Resolving impasses to symptom remission* (pp. 233–254). London, UK: Taylor & Francis.

Leonard, M. M. (2010). 'I did what I was directed to do but he didn't touch me': The impact of being a victim of internet offending. *Journal of Sexual Aggression, 16*, 249–256.

Leonard, M. M. (2015). *'Every ping gave me goosebumps': Working therapeutically with children/young people who were victims of online sexual exploitation*. Presentation at BASPCAN Conference, Edinburgh, Scotland, April.

Lindsey, M. A., Brandt, N. E., Becker, K. D., Lee, B. R., Barth, R. P., Daleiden, E. L., & Chorpita, B. F. (2014). Identifying the common elements of treatment engagement interventions in children's mental health services. *Clinical Child and Family Psychology Review, 17*(3), 283–298.

Linehan, M. M. (1997). Validation and psychotherapy. In A. C. Bohart & L. S. Greenberg (Eds.), *Empathy reconsidered: New directions in psychotherapy* (pp. 353–392). Washington, DC: American Psychological Association.

Linehan, M. M. (2014). *DBT® skills training manual*. New York, NY: Guilford Publications.

Macdonald, G., Higgins, J., & Ramchandani, P. (2007). Cognitive-behavioural interventions for children who have been sexually abused. *Evidence-Based Child Health: A Cochrane Review Journal, 2*, 1102–1147.

Mann, S., & Russell, S. (2003). Narrative ways of working with women whose lives have been affected by child sexual abuse. *Responding to violence: A collection of papers relating to child sexual abuse and violence in intimate relationships*. Adelaide, Australia: Dulwich Centre Publications.

Martin, J. (2016). Child sexual abuse images online: Implications for social work training and practice. *British Journal of Social Work, 46*(2), 372–388.

McCrory, E. J., & Viding, E. (2015). The theory of latent vulnerability: Reconceptualizing the link between childhood maltreatment and psychiatric disorder. *Development and Psychopathology, 27*(2), 493–505.

McLean, C. P., Yeh, R., Rosenfield, D., & Foa, E. B. (2015). Changes in negative cognitions mediate PTSD symptom reductions during client-centered therapy and prolonged exposure for adolescents. *Behaviour Research and Therapy, 68*, 64–69.

Mehlum, L., Tørmoen, A. J., Ramberg, M., Haga, E., Diep, L. M., Laberg, S., ... & Grøholt, B. (2014). Dialectical behavior therapy for adolescents with repeated suicidal and self-harming behavior: A randomized trial. *Journal of the American Academy of Child & Adolescent Psychiatry, 53*(10), 1082–1091.

Misurell, J. R., & Springer, C. (2013). Developing culturally responsive evidence-based practice: A game-based group therapy program for child sexual abuse (CSA). *Journal of Child and Family Studies, 22*(1), 137–149.

Molnar, B. E., Buka, S. L., & Kessler, R. C. (2001). Child sexual abuse and subsequent psychopathology: Results from the National Comorbidity Survey. *American Journal of Public Health, 91*(5), 753.

Morgan, A. (2000). *What is narrative therapy? An easy-to-read introduction.* Adelaide, South Australia: Dulwich Centre Publications.

Ncube, N. (2010). The journey of healing: Using narrative therapy and map-making to respond to child abuse in South Africa. *International Journal of Narrative Therapy & Community Work, 2010*(1), 3.

O'Dea, J. A., & Abraham, S. (2000). Improving the body image, eating attitudes, and behaviors of young male and female adolescents: A new educational approach that focuses on self-esteem. *International Journal of Eating Disorders, 28*(1), 43–57.

Ozechowski, T. J., & Waldron, H. B. (2010). Assertive outreach strategies for narrowing the adolescent substance abuse treatment gap: Implications for research, practice, and policy. *The Journal of Behavioral Health Services & Research, 37*(1), 40–63.

Reichert, E. L., & Flannery-Schroeder, E. (2014). Posttraumatic cognitions as mediators between childhood maltreatment and poorer mental health among young adults. *Journal of Child & Adolescent Trauma, 7*(3), 153–162.

Rodenburg, R., Benjamin, A., de Roos, C., Meijer, A. M., & Stams, G. J. (2009). Efficacy of EMDR in children: A meta-analysis. *Clinical Psychology Review, 29*(7), 599–606.

Sánchez-Meca, J., Rosa-Alcázar, A., & López-Soler, C. (2011). The psychological treatment of sexual abuse in children and adolescents: A meta-analysis. *International Journal of Clinical and Health Psychology, 11*(1), 67–93.

Saxe, G. N., Ellis, B. H., Fogler, J., & Navalta, C. P. (2012). Innovations in practice: Preliminary evidence for effective family engagement in treatment for child traumatic stress–trauma systems therapy approach to preventing dropout. *Child and Adolescent Mental Health, 17*(1), 58–61.

Schultz, P. N., Remick-Barlow, G., & Robbins, L. (2007). Equine-assisted psychotherapy: A mental health promotion/intervention modality for children who have experienced intra-family violence. *Health & Social Care in the Community, 15*(3), 265–271.

Shapiro, F. (2012). EMDR therapy: An overview of current and future research. *European Review of Applied Psychology, 62*(4), 193–195.

Shirk, S. R., & Karver, M. (2003). Prediction of treatment outcome from relationship variables in child and adolescent therapy: A meta-analytic review. *Journal of Consulting and Clinical Psychology, 71*(3), 452.

Simon, V. A., Feiring, C., & McElroy, S. K. (2010). Making meaning of traumatic events: Youths' strategies for processing childhood sexual abuse are associated with psychosocial adjustment. *Child Maltreatment, 15*(3), 229–241.

Springer, C., & Misurell, J. R. (2010). Game-based cognitive-behavioral therapy (GB-CBT): An innovative group treatment program for children who have been sexually abused. *Journal of Child & Adolescent Trauma, 3*(3), 163–180.

Springer, C., Misurell, J. R., & Hiller, A. (2012). Game-based cognitive-behavioral therapy (GB-CBT) group program for children who have experienced sexual abuse: A three-month follow-up investigation. *Journal of Child Sexual Abuse, 21*(6), 646–664.

Steiner-Adair, C., & Sjostrom, L. (2006). *Full of ourselves: A wellness program to advance girl power, health, and leadership.* New York, NY: Teachers College Press.

Tavkar, P., & Hansen, D. J. (2011). Interventions for families victimized by child sexual abuse: Clinical issues and approaches for child advocacy center-based services. *Aggression and Violent Behavior, 16*(3), 188–199.

Taylor, J. E., Graham, R. A., & Weems, C. F. (2015). Moderators and mediators of treatments for youth with traumatic stress. In M. Maric, P. J. Prins, & T. H. Ollendick (Eds.), *Moderators and mediators of youth treatment outcomes* (pp. 41–64). New York, NY: Oxford University Press.

Trask, E. V., Walsh, K., & DiLillo, D. (2011). Treatment effects for common outcomes of child sexual abuse: A current meta-analysis. *Aggression and Violent Behavior, 16*(1), 6–19.

Trickett, P. K., Noll, J. G., & Putnam, F. W. (2011). The impact of sexual abuse on female development: Lessons from a multigenerational, longitudinal research study. *Development and Psychopathology, 23*(2), 453–476.

Tylka, T. L., & Augustus-Horvath, C. L. (2011). Fighting self-objectification in prevention and intervention contexts. In R.M Calogero, S.E. Tantleff-Dunn & J. Thompson (Eds.), *Self-objectification in women: Causes, consequences, and counteractions*, pp. 187–214. Washington DC: American Psychological Association.

UN General Assembly. (1989, Nov. 20). *Convention on the Rights of the Child*. United Nations, Treaty Series, 1577, p. 3.

Von Weiler, J., Haardt-Becker, A., & Schulte, S. (2010). Care and treatment of child victims of child pornographic exploitation (CPE) in Germany. *Journal of Sexual Aggression, 16*(2), 211–222.

Whittle, H. C., Hamilton-Giachritsis, C., & Beech, A. R. (2013). Victims' voices: The impact of online grooming and sexual abuse. *Universal Journal of Psychology, 1*(2), 59–71.

Yates, T. M., Carlson, E. A., & Egeland, B. (2008). A prospective study of child maltreatment and self-injurious behavior in a community sample. *Development and Psychopathology, 20*(2), 651–671.

NOTES

1 The terms 'children' and 'young people' are used interchangeably in this chapter, although when 'young people' is used the focus is on adolescents.

2 Both the terms 'victim' and 'survivor' are used in this chapter. At times children are not yet 'survivors' because the abuse is still ongoing, and at others, even when it has physically stopped, a sense of present threat remains. 'Victim' also foregrounds the violation of rights inherent within abuse. However, 'survivor' emphasizes the strength inherent in living life following abuse and the process of moving forwards.

3 Self-objectification is the tendency to view oneself as an object under evaluation by others; so for example, during social interaction, people high in self-objectification may focus on how they look to those they are talking to, to the detriment of their focus on the conversation.

4 See, for example, resources from the Centre for Suicide Research at the University of Oxford.

5 To explore these ideas see the wide variety of articles at www.narrativeapproaches.com.

6 Wolves are also being used to help young people with complex difficulties; see, for example, www.wolfconnection.org.

7 For practical suggestions for sibling interventions see Tavkar and Hansen (2011).

8 Preventing Child Sexual Abuse Online

Stephen Smallbone and Richard Wortley

Online sexual abuse encompasses a broad range of problem behaviours, including online sexual harassment and bullying, unwanted 'sexting,' exposing children to age-inappropriate sexual material or conversation, online 'grooming' and sexual solicitation of children and the production, distribution and viewing of child pornography. The Internet and associated technologies may also be used to facilitate other types of sexual offences (e.g., the organisation of sexual exploitation and trafficking). We concentrate our attention in this chapter on online grooming and solicitation and internet child pornography. These are the two aspects of online abuse that seem to have attracted the most public concern, law enforcement attention and research interest.

The focus of our chapter is on how online sexual abuse may be further prevented. We say *further* prevented because the prevalence of online abuse would undoubtedly be greater without the many individual, social and technological barriers to these kinds of offences and the dedicated efforts to understand and respond to the problem. Although there is cause for concern and much more to be done, we should not disregard the factors that already limit the extent of the problem. Though the complexity and global reach of the Internet may tempt us to think that online abuse is 'out of control,' in fact the prevalence of contact sexual abuse seems to be on the decline (Jones, Finkelhor, & Kopiec, 2001; Radford et al., 2011). Presumably this is because of unprecedented levels of public (especially parental) awareness and concern, increased activity and capability of law enforcement and other relevant agencies and the resilience and good sense of many (particularly older) children to use the Internet safely.

Although there is now a substantial research literature concerned with online sexual abuse, there are as yet no definitive empirical demonstrations of 'what works' to prevent its various permutations. Our suggestions in this

Online Risk to Children: Impact, Protection and Prevention, First Edition.
Edited by Jon Brown.

chapter are therefore necessarily somewhat speculative. Nevertheless we are able to draw on existing empirical research and established conceptual frameworks as a guide. Our aim is to stimulate debate and to generate new ideas and research directions, rather than to simply review existing prevention programmes.

ORGANISING PREVENTION STRATEGIES

There are many potential players in the effort to prevent online sexual abuse, including parents, young people and their peers, schools, internet service providers, software and social media companies, advertising companies, credit card companies, advocacy groups, researchers, legislators, courts, police, child protection, corrections, youth justice and others. It may not be realistic to expect that all of these roles can be coordinated. However, from a public policy perspective it makes sense to develop a comprehensive, evidence-informed approach to identify weak points in the prevention 'armoury,' to support informal initiatives and to allocate resources to potentially effective activities (Findlater, 2014).

In this chapter, we propose a typology within which to organise prevention strategies for online sexual abuse (modelled on the prevention typology previously developed for application to contact sexual abuse – see Smallbone, Marshall, & Wortley, 2008). The typology is based on a fusion of the preventative health care model and the routine activities approach.

The preventative health care model was originally devised to set out prevention strategies according to three stages of the progression of disease (Goldston, 1987). Primary prevention strategies targeted the onset of disease, secondary prevention strategies targeted pre-clinical manifestations of the disease and tertiary prevention strategies targeted the disease once it has taken hold in the clinical phase. Adapted for crime prevention (Brantingham & Faust, 1976), primary prevention is conceived as population-wide measures designed to inhibit the onset of crime, secondary prevention refers to measures that target identifiable crime risks and tertiary prevention refers to measures to prevent re-offending once a crime has occurred. Thus, the preventative health care model (and its criminological adaptation) identifies *levels* of prevention.

The routine activity approach (Cohen & Felson, 1979) is a criminological model that sets out the three minimal elements that must converge for any crime to occur – a suitable victim, a likely offender, and a location or setting that lacks capable guardianship. These three elements are often represented as the sides of the so-called crime triangle (e.g., Clarke & Eck, 2003). Just as a triangle collapses if one of its sides is removed, so, too, crime cannot occur if any one of its three minimal elements is removed or neutralised. The routine activity approach, therefore, identifies *targets* for prevention.

Together, the preventative health care model and routine activity approach produce a 3×3 matrix involving three levels of prevention (primary, secondary and tertiary) applied to three crime-element targets (offenders, victims and settings[1]). The typology extends the original scope of both contributing axes. On the one hand, the addition of the routine activity approach to the preventative health care model makes it clear that prevention does not just involve interventions with potential or known offenders, too often the default position in criminology, psychology and law enforcement. That is, crime prevention is broader than changing criminal propensity, be that through developmental interventions (primary and secondary prevention) or arrest and rehabilitation (tertiary prevention). Prevention includes interventions that alter the criminogenic features of crime settings and offer protection to victims. Making a crime more difficult to perform, for example, will be sufficient to deter many opportunistic offenders and slow down the more determined.

On the other hand, with the addition of the preventative health care model, the routine activity approach is taken beyond its original focus on the immediate dynamics of the crime event. Interventions can also occur prior to and after the crime has occurred and in locations that are physically distant from the crime setting. Thus, interventions with victims, for example, can involve not just providing guardianship at the time of the offence (the usual routine activity approach response) but also efforts to bolster the resilience of vulnerable individuals to make it less likely that they will be victimised or re-victimised.

The matrix is shown in Table 8.1, with examples of prevention strategies for online sexual abuse. These examples are by no means intended to be exhaustive; rather, we hope they serve to illustrate the breadth of possible prevention approaches. Some of the examples are relevant specifically to grooming/solicitation (e.g., increasing online safety) or child pornography (e.g., warning messages); others (e.g., increasing perceived risk, preventing re-offending) are relevant to both. In the remainder of the chapter we outline the rationale and suggested approach for each of the examples in Table 8.1.

Table 8.1 *The 3×3 (level x target) matrix of prevention strategies.*

Prevention levels prevention targets	Primary	Secondary	Tertiary
(Potential) offenders	Increasing perceived risk	Warning messages	Preventing re-offending
(Potential) victims	Increasing online safety	Reducing vulnerabilities and risky behaviours	Preventing re-victimisation
Settings	Reducing availability	Blocking online transactions	Gathering intelligence

PREVENTION STRATEGIES

There can surely be no disagreement that it is more desirable to prevent online abuse before it would otherwise occur than it is to respond to victims, offenders and other affected persons after the fact. This is easier said than done, of course. Primary (universal) and secondary (selected) prevention require knowledge of risk and protective factors associated with the occurrence of the target problem, and unfortunately there is as yet little hard empirical evidence concerning risk and protective factors for online abuse. Similarly, knowledge of risk and protective factors associated with re-offending and re-victimisation required for tertiary (or indicated) prevention is also still undeveloped. There is, however, a strong conceptual basis for targeting certain factors across the primary, secondary and tertiary prevention spectrum, and evaluating outcomes of various interventions can in turn contribute to building the empirical 'what works' knowledge base. A comprehensive approach to prevention should, we argue, include a mix of primary, secondary and tertiary prevention activities targeting offenders, victims and settings.

PRIMARY PREVENTION

POTENTIAL OFFENDERS: INCREASING PERCEIVED RISK

The perceived anonymity afforded by the Internet may be one of the most significant drivers of online sexual abuse. According to the rational choice perspective, judgement of risk feeds into a cost-benefit analysis that determines whether an individual will proceed with a contemplated offence. Moreover, at a psychological level, sitting alone in front of a computer in the comfort of one's own home can create a sense of detachment and disinhibition that facilitates engagement in riskier behaviour than might be performed in the 'real world' (Suler, 2004). By contrast, prior to the widespread availability of the Internet, access to child pornography entailed significant effort and risk (Wortley & Smallbone, 2012). At the very least, obtaining child pornography would have involved some level of personal involvement with a distribution network and in some cases disclosure of personal details (e.g., a postal address) that might enable identification. Similarly, grooming and sexual solicitation of children in the 'real world' entails much greater effort and risk than using the Internet to do so (Seto, 2013). It follows that increasing perceptions of risk in the minds of potential abusers would reduce the probability of their engaging in these behaviours.

Of course, unless they make determined efforts to hide their identity (e.g., using remailers or encryption) people are not as anonymous online as they usually imagine. (The spate of advertisements one receives for products related to recent online purchases should be sufficient to disabuse internet users of the belief that they are anonymous.) However, a major problem for many police agencies is that they cannot investigate and arrest everyone whom they detect as potential offenders in the online environment. Investigations of child pornography offences, for example, can be very resource intensive, with each individual case requiring many hours of locating, examining and classifying seized material and developing the case for prosecution. To illustrate the scale of the problem, one international police operation – Operation Rescue – involved the investigation of a covert child pornography newsgroup with an estimated 70,000 members from five countries. Police were able to identify 640 members, and 184, including the group leader, were arrested. These kinds of figures indicate that the actual risk of being identified and arrested for online sexual abuse is low.

However it is important to distinguish between real and perceived risk. Another police operation – Operation Pin – initiated in 2003 by police in the UK (later expanded to include the FBI, the Australian Federal Police, the Royal Canadian Mounties and Interpol) involved setting up a bogus child pornography website. To reach the (non-existent) material, visitors to the site had to navigate through a series of web pages, each of which presented warnings that they were entering a child pornography site. The precise number of persons who took the final step was not made public, though numerous arrests were reportedly made. The key aim, however, was not to maximise the number of arrests but to increase the *perceived* risk in the minds of would-be offenders. This was done by openly advertising the launch of Operation Pin so as to create a sense of uncertainty about the safety of accessing child pornography websites generally – not just the bogus site set up for this particular operation.

Another way of increasing perceived risk is to publicise arrests and prosecution outcomes. The potential general deterrence effect of this kind of publicity has long been a central aim of the criminal justice system. The actual impact of general deterrence on preventing crime has been a matter of much debate among criminologists, though there seems to be general agreement that increasing the perceived risk of being caught is likely to have a greater impact than increasing the severity of punishment (Baron & Kennedy, 1998). It is certainly true that crime rates increase dramatically during police strikes (Nagin, 1978), blackouts (Muhlin, Cohen, Struening, Genevie, Kaplan, & Peck, 1981) and natural disasters (LeBeau, 1994) when policing resources are stretched. The general deterrence effect is probably even more relevant for the majority of online abuse offenders because, as most studies show, these offenders tend to be less anti-social and less criminally involved than general offender populations, and they may therefore be more sensitive to the risks of being caught (Wortley & Smallbone, 2012).

POTENTIAL VICTIMS: INCREASING ONLINE SAFETY

Sexual abuse, including online abuse, relies to a significant extent on children's vulnerabilities associated with their sexual naïveté and deference to adults. For older children, natural sexual curiosities and desires for romantic and sexual attention can be exploited. Another approach to primary prevention may therefore be to intervene in ways that may make children's Internet use safer. As public concern about online sexual abuse has increased, so too has a range of responses been developed to increase online safety. These fall mainly into three categories: (1) the use of internet filters and trackers, (2) house rules concerning children's Internet use, and (3) educating parents and children about online safety.

Many internet filter software programmes can now be installed on home computers to block specific websites, URLs, IP addresses and email addresses. Blocks can also be used to prevent the computer user from using specific words in Internet searches. Programmes are also available that enable parents to record and monitor their children's Internet use, track followers on social media (Facebook, Twitter, etc.), block Internet use for specified periods, and prevent children from posting personal information online. Prentky, Burgess, Dowdell, Fedoroff, Malamuth, and Schuler (2010) tested 11 commonly used filter programmes, and they reported that all performed equally well for their intended purpose. They noted, however, than none of the programmes monitored instant messaging or peer-to-peer activity.

Police and child protection advocates as well as internet filter vendors often recommend that parents establish house rules concerning their children's Internet use (Dombrowski et al., 2007; Young, 2008). These typically include the permanent placement or use of computers in open living areas accessible to direct monitoring, disallowing the use of smaller internet-enabled devices in private areas such as bedrooms and setting time limits on Internet use. Specific guidelines are often recommended for different age groups. For very young children, parents are typically advised to always sit with their children when they are using a computer, for example. For pre-teens and young teenagers, parents may insist on having access to passwords for email, chat-room and instant messaging accounts and to set rules limiting the time spent on Internet activities. For older teenagers it may be appropriate to negotiate specific rules and to engage in discussions about ethical social and sexual behaviour. As Young (2008) notes, however, enforcing such rules will become increasingly problematic as mobile technologies predominate.

Media portrayals of internet grooming and solicitation and unfortunately sometimes also police and child protection advocates tend to cast the online offender as a 'predator' and stranger who disguises his true identity and tricks young children into engaging in sexual conversation or luring them to some place to commit a sexual assault. Although isolated incidents such as this do occur, by far the more common scenario involves a 14- to 15-year-old girl (or sometimes boy) engaging online with a peer-aged or older male who does little to disguise his true identity or intentions (Wolak, Finkelhor, Mitchell, &

Ybarra, 2008). When the teenager does agree to meet in person, she or he tends to do so knowing that the other person is interested in sexual contact with her or him. Violence or abduction is apparently rare in these encounters (Wolak et al., 2008). This is not to say that such encounters are always harmless. Seto (2013) likens such scenarios to statutory sex offences in which the younger person agrees to the sexual activity but is deemed by law to be insufficiently mature to provide full and informed consent. This disconnect in the way online solicitation is often portrayed seems to be a weak point in current prevention efforts. Parents are already sensibly advised to keep lines of communication with their children open, to inquire in positive ways about their children's favourite Internet activities, and to encourage their children to come to them with any Internet-related concerns or problems. Helping parents to understand how more typical online sexual encounters can unfold, and how to identify particular vulnerabilities (e.g., loneliness, excessive emotional neediness, serious rule-breaking, sexual precociousness) in their teenage children, may be useful additions to present prevention efforts.

SETTINGS: REDUCING AVAILABILITY

In addition to our concerns for the children whose images have been used to produce pornographic material, there are two other reasons to reduce the volume of available material. First, reducing availability either by reducing the actual volume of material or by pushing existing material into harder-to-reach areas of the internet is likely to reduce the probability of casual or accidental encounters with the material. This is important because the scope of problem has almost certainly been widened because of the ease of accessibility provided by the Internet, and so making the material harder to obtain is likely to reduce the number of people accessing the material in the first place. Second, reducing availability also serves to increase the effort required by more committed users, many of whom may not be prepared to invest the additional effort required to obtain the material.

Police are assisted in the task of removing internet child pornography material by various groups such as the Internet Watch Foundation (IWF) and CyberTipline. Based in the UK, IWF claims that its work has led to the removal of 100,000 suspect URLs since it was established in 1996 and to have contributed to a significant reduction of child exploitation material hosted in the UK. The US-based CyberTipline has received 2.8 million reports of child exploitation material since 1998, providing information to relevant law enforcement agencies for investigation. Internet service providers may also independently remove material they become aware of.

Some of those involved in the distribution of child pornography have responded to these efforts with various adaptations. For example, some distributors of child pornography now split collections into smaller collections that are then hosted on a temporary basis across numerous sites (Internet

Watch Foundation, 2010). There is also some concern that active policing of the open web may drive dedicated offenders to deeper levels of the Internet, where they trade images in specific child pornography chat rooms and newsgroups. However, as we have previously argued (Wortley & Smallbone, 2012), these are expectable responses that should not be regarded as failures by law enforcement and affiliated agencies. Persisting in the efforts to reduce the availability incurs costs for offenders, making their activities increasingly risky and difficult. As noted, these efforts may have wide-reaching impacts on potential or casual viewers, as well as significant impacts on the more dedicated producers, distributors and users.

SECONDARY PREVENTION

POTENTIAL OFFENDERS: WARNING MESSAGES

As we have noted, because of the scale and complexity of the problem, police are unable to devote the resources needed to fully investigate every case of suspected online sexual abuse, particularly the suspected possession or viewing of child pornography images. Whereas many police agencies have been developing ways to prioritise the most serious or concerning cases for investigation, some have also considered alternative, wider-scale interventions. Perhaps the most significant of these has been the development of pop-up warning messages. In our prevention matrix (Table 8.1) these types of intervention are classified as offender-targeted secondary prevention, because they seek to prevent an offence before it occurs by targeting persons clearly at risk of doing so.

The Child Sexual Abuse Anti-Distribution Filter (CSAADF) implemented in Europe by the Cospol Internet Related Child Abusive Material Project (CIRCAMP) enables the insertion of a 'stop page' when access to a targeted website is denied. These stop pages can be inserted as an alternative to the usual 500-code server-error message. Following is an excerpt from a stop page used by Norwegian police:

Stop!

Your Internet browser is trying to contact an Internet site that is used in connection with the distribution of photos depicting sexual abuse of children, which is a criminal offence in accordance with the Norwegian Penal Code.

No information about your IP address or any other information that can be used to identify you will be stored when this page is displayed. The purpose of blocking access to these pages is only to prevent the commission of criminal dissemination of documented sexual abuse, and to prevent the further exploitation of children who have already been abused and photographed.

If you want more information, or if you wish to forward a tip to NCIS Norway, please go to the NCIS tip receival or phone us on ...

We have previously suggested (Wortley & Smallbone, 2012) that such warning messages could be designed with at least three purposes in mind. The first is to arouse the conscience of the viewer by crafting a message that emphasises the harms to children. These messages could draw attention to the potential harms of the original abuse and of the ongoing use of distributed images. In situational prevention terms this kind of approach aims to reduce the permissibility of the targeted behaviour, which seems to be the primary aim of the Norwegian police stop page. Second, messages could be designed to increase perceived risk in the mind of the (potential) offender. These kinds of messages may inform the viewer that their personal details will be captured if they proceed or that they are being 'watched' by police. Third, messages could focus on potential legal and psychological harms to the viewer himself and provide advice about where to go for help. The fact that up to a half of calls to the anonymous tip line Stop It Now are from offenders and potential offenders seeking help for their behaviour gives cause to believe that this third option can provide a useful service (Stop It Now, 2010).

Because there are as yet no evaluations of the effectiveness of various types of pop-up messages, it may make most sense for prevention purposes to design interventions to include all three types of message just outlined. A single message could aim to reduce permissibility, increase perceived risk and provide helpful advice. However, for research purposes, it would be helpful to trial different kinds of messages to see which are the most effective.

POTENTIAL VICTIMS: REDUCING VULNERABILITIES AND RISKY BEHAVIOURS

Though all children are to some extent vulnerable to sexual abuse, including online abuse, individual vulnerabilities vary widely. Secondary prevention is concerned with reducing vulnerabilities in and risky behaviours of those children who are already at increased risk of abuse or exploitation.

It is not yet clear whether vulnerabilities associated with online abuse are the same as those associated with contact sexual abuse. Certainly it seems that child pornography is often originally produced by older males already known to the child, including family members – circumstances that are common for other kinds of contact sexual abuse. In fact the production of child pornography often seems to involve the recording by known older males of sexual abuse that is already occurring (Wolak et al., 2011). Efforts to reduce children's vulnerabilities for contact sexual abuse may therefore also have an impact on reducing the original production of child pornography material. The most widely implemented child-focussed interventions in this regard are protective behaviours programmes. Although there is still limited evidence of the effectiveness of these programmes for preventing actual abuse (Finkelhor, 2009), it may be sensible to think about how these kinds of programmes might be adapted to target at-risk children. We have argued elsewhere (Smallbone, Marshall, & Wortley, 2008) that resilience-building programmes for at-risk children may be a viable adjunct or alternative to the resistance-training focus of protective behaviours programmes.

Little is yet known about the vulnerabilities associated more specifically with online grooming and solicitation. Emerging evidence indicates that the main at-risk group may be 14- to 16-year-old girls (Wolak, Finkelhor, & Mitchell, 2011), although Seto (2013) suggests that pubescent and adolescent males who may be struggling with their sense of sexual orientation may also be at risk. More research is needed to understand the particular kinds of vulnerabilities associated with online sexual encounters and how these vulnerabilities are exploited. We can surmise that either internalising factors, such as loneliness or emotional neediness, or externalising factors, such as serious rule-breaking or sexual precociousness, may increase the risk of online exploitation and abuse. Parents, teachers, child protection services and mental health services may be in positions to identify relevant vulnerabilities in children and adolescents.

The kinds of potential risk factors canvassed in this chapter may lead some children and youth to engage in risky online behaviours such as revealing too much about themselves online, visiting risky sites or responding to the sexual overtures of strangers. However, ordinary young people negotiating the personal and social turbulence of adolescence may also from time to time engage in risky online behaviours. Opportunities to prevent online abuse may arise when responsible third parties detect these kinds of risky behaviours.

Parents and, for older children, also peers are probably best placed to notice and respond to risky online behaviours. Parents may be supported in this by education programmes that provide frank, accurate and helpful advice. Casting the problem of online grooming and solicitation in terms of the devious and deceitful online 'predator' who preys on young children may be misleading and unhelpful for parents. Parent-focussed education programmes may need to counter this misconception and to instead help parents to understand how to notice and respond to signs of risky online behaviours particularly in their adolescent children.

Adolescent peers may be less susceptible to this stereotyped view of the problem because they are closer to the realities of their and their friends' online world. School-based responsible bystander programmes are now being developed as a prevention strategy for sexual violence more broadly (e.g., Banyard, Moynihan, & Plante, 2007). These approaches aim to effect responsible bystander intervention before (e.g., by helping peers to avoid high-risk situations), during (e.g., by interrupting a concerning incident), or after sexual violence has occurred (e.g., by providing timely and effective victim support). Programmes aim to increase recognition of risky situations, enhance perceived responsibility, overcome barriers to intervening with peers and build skills to intervene safely. Responsible bystander programmes could incorporate an additional focus on how to intervene when young people see their peers engaging in risky online behaviour.

Police may also play a role in reducing risky online behaviour. Many specialist police agencies are now very active on the Internet. In response to the problem of online solicitation, some police agencies will take on the persona of a child who has been the subject of unwanted sexual overtures in order to identify and arrest the suspected offender. Some police have taken this much further by routinely posing undercover as children to lure potential online 'predators.' Both of these kinds of circumstances may present opportunities to intervene with risky online behaviour. In the first instance, a child who has already been subject to online solicitation, as well as his or her parents, could be advised by police about how to reduce further risks in the child's online activities. The main, and possibly exclusive, focus for police understandably is on suspected offenders. However presumably police will also encounter risky behaviours by children – for example, they may notice a child using a provocative online name (e.g., one that draws attention to his or her age or that suggests sexual availability) or engaging in sexually provocative conversations. In these instances it may be possible for police to contact the child online, in a friendly and positive way, to advise him or her of the potential dangers of such behaviour and how to increase online safety.

SETTINGS: BLOCKING ONLINE TRANSACTIONS

Once a potential offender has committed to accessing child pornography, strategies can be put in place to make completing that task more difficult. One promising avenue is to make it more difficult for the potential offender to purchase selected images. The Financial Coalition Against Child Pornography (FCACP) was launched in 2006 with the goal of undermining the commercial viability of the child pornography industry. The usual and most efficient way for an offender to purchase child pornography is to use a credit card or some other form of e-payment system. FCACP is a grouping of 35 ISPs, credit card companies, banks and other online payment services, including American Express, Bank of America, MasterCard and PayPal. FCACP members use key word searches and web crawlers proactively to track commercial transactions involving child pornography and block payments for illegal downloads.

There is evidence that the activities of FCACP are changing the way that transactions involving child pornography are carried out, forcing child pornography distributors to adopt new and convoluted strategies to obtain payments. Distributors may, for example, direct purchasers to email a specified address to receive instructions on alternative payment methods, and ultimately purchasers may have to resort to mailing cash. From the offenders' point of view, these new means have the effect of increasing the effort required to obtain abuse images. The Financial Coalition Against Child Pornography (2011) claims that since the introduction of these restrictions on payment, there has been a 50% drop in the number of commercial child pornography sites and the cost of child pornography to purchasers has increased as much as 40-fold ($30 per month to $1,200 per month) since 2006.

TERTIARY PREVENTION

OFFENDERS: PREVENTING RE-OFFENDING

Priority for investigation and prosecution of online sexual offences should when possible be given to the most concerning cases, particularly to those in which contact sexual abuse is suspected or thought to be likely. For child pornography offences this may involve targeting producers, active distributers, network kingpins, those found with new (previously undiscovered) images and those found with more concerning (young age, violent, or especially degrading) images. It is important that, once detected, child pornography users are not allowed to continue their activities, even if doing so may build a stronger prosecution case. Doing so may increase risk by allowing the offender to become more psychologically involved with the material and to view additional and perhaps new images.

For online grooming and solicitation offences, priority may be given to offenders who have had online contact with younger children, those where there appear to be significant age gaps between the suspect and child, and those who seem to be grooming real children (as opposed to those lured in the first instance by undercover investigators). Indeed providing opportunities for people who believe they are engaging in online sexual discussions with children may be highly problematic. In one operation, undercover police posing as 13- to 14-year-old boys engaged online with 15 separate suspects, only three of whom provided sufficient evidence to be arrested (Grosskopf, 2010). Presumably those who were not arrested left the online conversation believing they had been in contact with a real boy. The effect of such police operations may be to encourage, rather than prevent, online offending, because for some of these 'suspects' this unwitting contact with online police may lead them to believe that children really *are* interested in having sexual conversations with them.

Even when targets are prioritised and carefully targeted, most online offenders will not be arrested. The question for those who are arrested and prosecuted becomes one of preventing further offending. Criminal justice system processes will involve additional considerations (e.g., retribution), but from a prevention point of view the task is to ensure there are no further offences. Decisions about how best to do this should be based on careful individual assessments.

Low sexual recidivism rates among online sexual offenders (Seto, 2013) indicate that simply being detected and arrested has a powerful deterrent effect on most of these offenders. However, distinguishing between those who may require further attention from those who may not is problematic. Risk assessments for online offenders are less well developed than are those for contact sexual offenders, and it is not yet clear whether standard risk assessment instruments based on research with contact sexual offenders are useful with online offenders. Some researchers have argued that modified versions of existing risk assessment scales may be helpful to distinguish higher and lower risk online offenders, even though the recidivism probability estimates associated with the original scales are unlikely to be valid (Seto, 2013; Witt, 2010). Elliot and Beech (2009) have argued that risk assessments for online offenders should include a specific focus on Internet use, including access to unsupervised Internet use and inappropriate online searching or other activities.

Ultimately, the purpose of risk assessment is of course to inform risk management. For higher risk offenders this may involve specific restrictions concerning access to the Internet or in some cases access to children. Both can present practical difficulties. Except perhaps for the highest risk offenders, prohibiting access to the Internet may be impractical and unreasonable given the increasing reliance on the Internet for a wide range of ordinary pro-social activities. One solution to this problem has been to develop computer monitoring software that can be installed on an offender's computer – this allows the offender to continue using the Internet but alerts a remote monitor when particular words or search terms are used. Prohibiting access to children, particularly the offender's own children, may be considered for offenders assessed as being of significant risk to these children. Even then, it may be feasible to develop safety plans that enable various kinds of limited or supervised involvement with children. Blanket prohibitions on access to children we believe should be avoided when possible.

Psychological treatment may contribute to risk management for some online offenders. Many clinical researchers and commentators seem to presume that psychological treatment is necessary in all or most cases, even though recidivism studies indicate that only a minority of online offenders go on to commit new sexual offences. Seto (2013) outlines a number of treatment approaches that may be helpful with online offenders assessed as requiring such interventions. A programme developed by Middleton, Mandeville-Norden, and Hayes (2009) specifically for online offenders is now available through probation services in the UK, although as far as we are aware there has yet been no outcome evaluation.

VICTIMS: PREVENTING RE-VICTIMISATION

Outcomes for victims of sexual abuse vary widely but for many abused children include severe short- and long-term harms. A longer duration of sexual abuse is one of a number of factors known to be associated with worse outcomes (Hebert, Parent, Daignault, & Tourigny, 2006). Though there has been very little research on the impacts specifically of online sexual abuse (see Svedin & Back, 2003, and von Weiler, Haardt-Becker, & Schulte, 2010, for relevant studies), it seems safe to presume that this is also the case for online abuse. Early detection and intervention should therefore be considered essential elements of a comprehensive prevention strategy.

Most services for sexual abuse victims are concerned primarily with ameliorating harms associated with the abuse. It seems self-evident that as many resources as are necessary are made available for this purpose. Though there is little available research that might point to problems associated specifically with various kinds of online abuse, we would presume that careful individualised assessments would give direction to therapeutic interventions when needed. One particularly concerning outcome of sexual abuse is an increased risk of further sexual victimisation, not only in the same circumstances as the original abuse but also in apparently unrelated circumstances and at later stages of life (Van Bruggen, Runtz, & Kadlec, 2006). In addition to focussing on the harms of the original abuse, therapeutic services therefore should also focus on preventing re-victimisation in the short and longer term.

For children and adolescents, the best-supported treatment approach for reducing psychological harms associated with sexual abuse appears to be trauma-focussed cognitive behavioural therapy (TF-CBT; Trask, Walsh, & DeLillo, 2011). Present-focussed CBT (PF-CBT; Classen, Palesh, & Aggarwal, 2006) is thought to be promising for reducing sexual re-victimisation (Classen et al., 2011). Specific rape risk-reduction programmes that target known personal and environmental risk factors have shown promise for increasing self-efficacy and enhancing risk perception and possibly also for reducing re-victimisation (Blackwell, Lynn, Vanderhoff, & Gidycz, 2003).

SETTINGS: GATHERING INTELLIGENCE

The investigation of online sexual abuse presents unique challenges for law enforcement agencies. The Internet is a complex, global network of networks with a decentralised structure that makes it difficult to screen content, enforce legislation, and track offenders. Investigators must cope with rapid technological advances that make it easier for offenders to avoid detection, and, as noted previously, the sheer volume of cases can simply overload investigative resources. In order to meet these challenges, police must acquire knowledge about modus operandi of online offenders; forge links with other police agencies, the internet industry and non-government organisations; develop technical expertise to counter the increasing sophistication of offenders and prioritise their efforts in order to make their task more manageable.

There is a range of technologies that may be deployed to aid the investigation process. Remote surveillance software applications enable investigators to analyze network traffic, capturing and extracting IP addresses, server and IRC passwords, websites accessed, email and graphic and video file transfers (Ferraro & Casey 2005). Seized computers and peripherals (printers cameras, storage devices) can be forensically examined not just to locate stored images but to reveal log files, browser history, and other online activity. In order to cope with the vast number of abuse image – numbering in the millions – that are now in circulation, image recognition software has been developed that identifies, assesses, links and catalogues images, dramatically reducing the time taken to accomplish these tasks and shielding investigators from the potentially traumatic effects of viewing images. Images can be matched against existing databases, images can be linked as part of a series based on the victims and perpetrators portrayed and clues to the location of the abuse may be gleaned. Finally, data-linking applications, such as the Child Exploitation Tracking System (CETS) enable police from different jurisdictions to share data and interrogate huge centralised databases in order to cross-reference evidence, identify offending patterns that link offenders across offences, track offenders across jurisdictions, link up investigations and analyse offender social networks.

When selecting cases on which to focus police resources, not surprisingly priority is usually given to the most serious offenders and, in particular, those actually involved in abusing children and producing pornographic images. The choice may be based on cross-referencing offenders with sex offender registries to increase the chance of targeting contact offenders. Greater attention may also be given to offenders who possess new or "first-generation" images because this may indicate that they produced the images themselves and are therefore also responsible for perpetrating child sexual abuse. The severity of the abuse image might also be used as the selection criteria; however, it should be noted that the correlation between the severity of the images possessed and involvement in contact offending is mixed and at best weak (Carr & Hilton, 2009).

As we argued previously in this chapter, investigation strategies need to be seen within a broader picture of preventing online child sexual abuse, not just in terms of bringing offenders to justice once they have committed a crime (as important as that is). The general deterrence effect of policing the Internet may have more overall impact on offending rates than the incarceration of individual offenders.

CONCLUSION

In this chapter we have set out a conceptual framework for organising prevention strategies that might be applied to combat online sexual abuse. We have
argued that prevention can be usefully thought of in terms of three levels:
primary prevention, broadly applied in order to inhibit online sexual abuse
before it occurs; secondary prevention, designed to counter known risks for
online sexual abuse and tertiary prevention, designed to prevent repeat offending. These levels of prevention can in turn be applied to three targets, which
comprise the essential chemistry for crime: the likely offender, the suitable
victim and the unguarded setting. We populated the resultant 3×3 matrix with
illustrative examples.

Our intention in presenting this matrix has been to demonstrate in a systematic way the breadth of potential strategies available for the prevention of
online sexual abuse and to stimulate a broader research agenda on the topic. In
particular, we want to encourage an understanding of online sexual abuse that
goes beyond the usual focus in the social sciences that privileges offender propensity above all other causes. A corollary of this view has been a focus on
catching and treating known offenders as the default prevention strategy. As
important as this task is, we believe that only by including victims and the
virtual environment in which offences take place can a comprehensive set of
prevention strategies be developed, ones that also take up the challenge of
stopping offending before it occurs.

We do not pretend that preventing online sexual abuse is an easy task. The
decentralised, global structure of the internet makes it notoriously difficult to
control (Wortley & Smallbone, 2012). The internet is a complex network of
networks, with no single controlling agency or storage facility, and crossing
international jurisdictional boundaries means that if one pathway is blocked or
website shut down there are many others to take its place. The essential 'ungov-
ernability' of the internet is compounded by technologies that help offenders
to avoid detection. P2P networks that allow offenders to communicate directly
with one another, anonymous remailers that strip the sender's identity from
email and file encryption that permits offenders to scramble or hide images
have been with us for some time (when 10 years is an age in internet time). The
newest emerging threat is that posed by the so-called darknet (Aked, 2011;
Bartlett, 2014).[2] The darknet refers to the collection of encrypted communication networks that exist at hidden levels outside of the observable internet.
Perhaps the best-known darknet is Tor (the Onion Router). After downloading free Tor software, a user is able to transmit encrypted data that cannot be
intercepted or read by unauthorised third parties, and the user remains anonymous and untraceable.

It is easy to become dispirited by the challenge to prevention that new technologies such as the darknet pose. Certainly, if the capabilities of Tor and similar networks were to be fully exploited by offenders, then the job of preventing
child sexual exploitation would become even more difficult. However, although

we need to take the threat of the darknet seriously, we should be equally care-ful not to overestimate the challenge that it poses. Offenders vary considerably in their determination to engage in online child sexual abuse and in their tech-nical proficiency to do so. Although there are offenders who exhibit both of these qualities, the evidence suggests that it is not the modal offender profile (see Balfe Gallagher, Masson, Balfe, Brugha, & Hackett, 2014, for a review). The majority of offenders, it seems, exercise few precautions to avoid detec-tion. Wolak et al. (2011), for example, found that a small minority of convicted offenders used identity protection technologies such as encryption (3%), anonymous remailers (1%) and P2P networks (28%).

We should be especially cautious of the argument that clamping down on child sexual exploitation in open areas of the internet will inevitably 'drive' offenders to the darknet. The experience of crime prevention more generally (i.e., outside of the cyber field) is that making crime more difficult, more risky and less rewarding results in reductions of crime with relatively little escalation or displacement (Guerette & Bowers, 2009). Just the same, crime prevention can never offer one-off solutions that will solve a crime problem once and for all. Rather, crime prevention is an arms race. Offenders are adaptive and many will find ways to circumvent the obstacles put in their way. In the process, however – as we saw with the blocking of online transactions of child pornog-raphy by FCACP – offenders can be slowed down as they are forced to less preferred modus operandi while new prevention strategies are devised and deployed to counter their adaptations.

REFERENCES

Aked, S. (2011). An investigation into darknets and the content available via anony-mous peer-to-peer file sharing. In *Proceedings of the 9th Australian Information Security Management Conference*, Edith Cowan University, Perth Western Australia, December 5–7. Retrieved from http://ro.ecu.edu.au/ism/106

Balfe, M., Gallagher, B., Masson, H., Balfe, S., Brugha, R., & Hackett, S. (2014). Internet child sex offenders' concerns about online security and their use of identity pro-tection technologies: A review. *Child Abuse Review*. doi:10.1002/car.2308

Banyard, V. L., Moynihan, M. M., & Plante, E. G. (2007). Sexual violence prevention through bystander education: An experimental evaluation. *Journal of Community Psychology, 35*, 463–481.

Baron, S. W., & Kennedy, L. W. (1998). Deterrence and homeless male street youths. *Canadian Journal of Criminology, 40*, 27–60.

Bartlett, J. (2014). *The dark net: Inside the digital underworld*. London, UK: William Heinemann.

Biddle, P., England, P., Peinado, M., & Willman, B. (2002, Nov.). The darknet and the future of content distribution. In *ACM Workshop on Digital Rights Management* (Vol. 6, p. 54). Washington, US: Microsoft Corporation.

Blackwell, L. M., Lynn, S. J., Vanderhoff, H., & Gidycz, C. (2003). Sexual assault revic-timization: Toward effective risk-reduction programs. In L. J. Koenog, L. S. Doll, A.

O'Leary, & W. Pequegnat (Eds.), *From child sexual abuse to adult sexual risk: Trauma, revictimization and intervention* (pp. 269–295). Washington, DC: American Psychological Association.

Bossler, A. M., & Holt, T. J. (2009). On-line activities, guardianship, and malware infection: An examination of routine activities theory. *International Journal of Cyber Criminology, 3*(1), 400–420.

Brantingham, P. J., & Faust, F. L. (1976). A conceptual model of crime prevention. *Crime & Delinquency, 22*(3), 284–296.

Carr, J., & Hilton, Z. (2009). Child protection and self-regulation in the internet industry: The UK experience. *Children and Society, 23*(4), 303–308.

Clarke, R., & Eck, J. E. (2003). *Become a problem-solving crime analyst: In 55 small steps.* London, UK: Jill Dando Institute of Crime Science.

Classen, C. C., Palesh, O. G., & Aggarwal, R. (2006). Sexual revictimization: A review of the empirical literature. *Trauma, Violence and Abuse, 6,* 103–129.

Cohen, L. E., & Felson, M. (1979). Social change and crime rate trends: A routine activity approach. *American Sociological Review,* pp. 588–608.

Dombrowski, S. C., Gischlar, K. L., & Theo Durst, T. (2007). Safeguarding young people from cyber pornography and cyber sexual predation: A major dilemma of the internet. *Child Abuse Review, 16*(3), 153–170.

Elliott, I. A., & Beech, A. R. (2009). Understanding online child pornography use: Applying sexual offender theory to internet offenders. *Aggression and Violent Behavior, 14,* 180–193.

Ferraro, M. M., & Casey, E. (2005). *Investigating child exploitation and pornography: The internet, the law and forensic science.* London, UK: Elsevier Academic Press.

Financial Coalition Against Child Pornography. (2011). *Report on trends in online crime and their potential implications in the fight against commercial child pornography.* Retrieved from http://www.missingkids.com/missingkids/servlet/PageServlet?LanguageCountry=en_US&PageId=3703

Findlater, D. (2014). Child sexual abuse: The possibilities of prevention. In A. Bentovim & J. Gray (Eds.), *Eradicating child maltreatment: Evidence-based approaches to prevention and intervention across services.* London, UK: Jessica Kingsley Publishers.

Finkelhor, D. (2009). The prevention of childhood sexual abuse. *The Future of Children, 19,* 169–194.

Goldston, S. E. (Ed.). (1987). *Concepts of primary prevention: A framework for program development.* Sacramento, CA: California Department of Mental Health.

Grosskopf, A. (2010). Online interactions involving suspected paedophiles who engage with male children. *Trends and Issues in Criminal Justice, 403,* 1–6.

Guerette, R. T., & Bowers, K. J. (2009). Assessing the extent of crime displacement and diffusion of benefits: A review of situational crime prevention evaluations. *Criminology, 47,* 1331–1368.

Hébert, M., Parent, N., Daignault, I. V., & Tourigny, M. (2006). A typological analysis of behavioral profiles of sexually abused children. *Child Maltreatment, 11*(3), 203–216.

Internet Watch Foundation. (2010). *2010 annual and charity report.* Retrieved from http://www.iwf.org.uk/accountability/annual-reports/2010-annual-report

Jones, L., Finkelhor, D., & Kopiec, K. (2001). Why is sexual abuse declining? A survey of state child protection administrators. *Child Abuse and Neglect, 25,* 1139–1158.

LeBeau, J. L. (1994). The oscillation of police calls to domestic disputes with time and the temperature humidity index. *Journal of Crime and Justice, 17,* 149–161.

Mesch, G. S. (2009). Parental mediation, online activities, and cyberbullying. *Cyber-Psychology & Behavior, 12*(4), 387–393.

Middleton, D., Mandeville-Norden, R., & Hayes, E. (2009). Does treatment work with internet sex offenders? Emerging findings from the Internet Sex Offender Treatment Programme (I-SOTP). *Journal of Sexual Aggression, 15*, 5–19.

Muhlin, G. L., Cohen, P., Struening, E. L., Genevie, L. E., Kaplan, S. R., & Peck, H. B. (1981). Behavioral epidemiology and social area analysis: The study of blackout looting. *Evaluation and Program Planning, 4*, 35–42.

Nagin, D. (1978). Crime rates, sanction levels, and constraints on prison population. *Law Journal, 12*, 341–366.

Prentky, R., Burgess, A., Dowdell, E. B., Fedoroff, P., Malamuth, N., & Schuler, A. (2010). *A multi-prong approach to strengthening internet child safety*. Needham, MA: Justice Resource Institute.

Radford, L., Corral, S., Bradley, C., Fisher, H., Bassett, C., Howat, N., & Collishaw, S. (2011). *Child abuse and neglect in the UK today*. London, UK: NSPCC. Retrieved from www.nspcc.org.uk/childstudy

Reyns, B. W., Henson, B., & Fisher, B. S. (2011). Being pursued online applying cyberlifestyle–routine activities theory to cyberstalking victimization. *Criminal Justice and Behavior, 38*(11), 1149–1169.

Seto, M. C. (2013). *Internet sex offenders*. Washington, DC: American Psychological Association.

Smallbone, S., Marshall, W. L., & Wortley, R. (2008). *Preventing child sexual abuse: Evidence, policy and practice*. Cullompton, Devon, UK: Willan Publishing.

Stop It Now UK and Ireland. (2010). *Stop It Now helpline report 2005–2009*. Retrieved from http://www.stopitnow.org.uk/files/Helpline%20Report%2009%20SM.pdf

Suler, J. (2004). The online disinhibition effect. *CyberPsychology & Behavior, 7*(3), 321–326.

Svedin, C. G., & Back, C. (2003). *Why didn't they tell us? Sexual abuse in child pornography*. Stockholm, Sweden: Save the Children Sweden.

Trask, E. V., Walsh, K., & DiLillo, D. (2011). Treatment effects for common outcomes of child sexual abuse: A current meta-analysis. *Aggression and Violent Behavior, 16*, 6–19.

Van Bruggen, L. K., Runtz, M. G., & Kadlec, H. (2006). Sexual revictimization: The role of sexual self-esteem and dysfunctional sexual behaviors. *Child Maltreatment, 11*, 131–145.

von Weiler, L., Haardt-Becker, A., & Schulte, S. (2010). Care and treatment of child victims of child pornographic exploitation (CPE) in Germany. *Journal of Sexual Aggression, 16*, 211–222.

Witt, P. H. (2010). Assessment of risk in internet child pornography cases. *Sex Offender Law Report, 11*, 1–16.

Wolak, J., Finkelhor, D., & Mitchell, K. (2011). Child pornography possessors: Trends in offender and case characteristics. *Sexual Abuse: A Journal of Research and Treatment, 23*, 22–42.

Wolak, J., Finkelhor, D., Mitchell, K. J., & Ybarra, M. L. (2008). Online 'predators' and their victims: Myths, realities, and implications for prevention and treatment. *American Psychologist, 63*, 111–128.

Wortley, R., & Smallbone, S. (2012). *Internet child pornography: Causes, investigation and prevention*. Santa Barbara, CA: Praeger.

Young, K. (2008). Understanding sexually deviant online behavior: From an addiction perspective. *International Journal of Cyber Criminology, 2*(1), 298–307.

NOTES

1   As originally conceived, the setting in the routine activities approach refers to a physical place. When applying routine activities to internet-assisted crime, the setting is extended to include the virtual world of cyber space (e.g., Bossler & Holt, 2009; Mesch, 2009; Reyns, Henson, & Fisher, 2011).

2   Although darknet capabilities have existed since the early days of the Internet, and the term itself was popularized by Biddle et al. in 2002, the implications for child sexual exploitation are only now being realised. An (albeit unsystematic) examination of half a dozen or so well-known books on internet child sexual exploitation, published as recently as 2012, found almost no reference to the darknet or related terms. Likewise, a Google Scholar search using the terms 'darknet' and 'child sexual exploitation' produced no more than a handful of articles.

9 Promoting Child Protection Principles in Complex Abuse Investigation Involving Online Offending

Zoe Hilton

It is recognised that the advent and widespread take up of the Internet and its associated technologies – and their increased use in offending against children – has meant that law enforcement agencies face new challenges that they traditionally have not been well equipped to deal with.[1] The emergence of the Internet on a mass scale has enabled offenders to network with each other with far greater ease and share images and videos of child sexual abuse – often in conjunction with chat that contains sexual abuse fantasies as well as distorted justifications about such abuse being normal or harmless. In recent years we have seen a rise in the popularity of the live streaming of abuse, with children abused in one location to be viewed in another, and we have seen the building of relationships within offending networks, supportive of encouraging offenders to travel to particular locations to abuse specific children.

The challenges for law enforcement in this context are considerable. The successful delivery of operational activity to pursue and deter offenders involves not only effective cross-border collaboration in a range of different judicial, legal, policing and social care contexts but also in many cases the development of a constructive and shared understanding with industry partners who hold key information. All of these issues layer further complexity on what would anyway be defined as 'complex' child abuse inquiries (as involving more than one offender and victim), and these cases require continuous risk management of victim welfare and understanding of how investigative activity must be planned throughout to avoid any direct risks of personal harm to children.

Online Risk to Children: Impact, Protection and Prevention, First Edition.
Edited by Jon Brown.
© 2017 John Wiley & Sons, Ltd. Published 2017 by John Wiley & Sons, Ltd.

This chapter recognises some of the challenges and complexities faced by law enforcement agencies in ensuring that their international operational activity to disrupt and pursue child sex offenders supports the protection, safeguarding and welfare of children. The chapter presents some of the key principles that have been promoted by the Child Exploitation and Online Protection Centre (CEOP) Command of the NCA to ensure that whatever jurisdiction the work is undertaken in the activity is ethical and consistent in relation to children. In developing these principles the CEOP Command has drawn on specific operational experience and has benefited from the feedback of colleagues from a range of agencies across the world. This chapter will also outline some anonymised case examples in which an understanding and application of these principles has been important.

One of the key elements of the (CEOP) Command's approach has been its recognition and support of partnerships. In particular for CEOP the partnership with the National Society for the Prevention of Cruelty to Children (NSPCC), and the placement of an NSPCC team within CEOP, working alongside law enforcement officers has not only provided day-to-day operational support on safeguarding issues but also helped to promote a culture within the Command in which child welfare issues are given constant consideration.

DEFINITIONS

The World Health Organisation, in association with the International Society for the Prevention of Child Abuse and Neglect, defines child sexual abuse in general terms as follows:

'The involvement of a child in sexual activity that he or she does not fully comprehend, is unable to give informed consent to, or for which the child is not developmentally prepared, or else that violate the laws or social taboos of society. Children can be sexually abused by adults or other children who are – by virtue of their age or stage of development – in a position of responsibility trust or power over the victim.'

The Council of Europe Convention on the Protection of Children against Sexual Exploitation and Sexual abuse defines sexual exploitation as the behaviour described in articles 18 to 23 of the convention (see Annex 1).

Child sexual abuse and exploitation violates the rights of children and has been shown to be directly and independently linked to a number of harmful outcomes. These include sexual risk-taking and sexually harmful behaviour, re-victimisation, intimate relationship difficulties, general distrust and fear of others, parenting difficulties, low self-esteem, poor academic achievement, posttraumatic stress disorder, eating disorders, mood disorders, depression, self-destructive behaviours (including suicide ideation), drug and alcohol addiction, aggression, personality disorders and physical health problems.[2] It has been shown that there is significant variation in the degree to which each of these difficulties is likely to be experienced depending on the characteristics of the abuse, the reaction and support of the victim's social network and his or her other life experiences. It is also influenced by how the victims themselves understand and respond to the abuse.

Recognising the variety of different legal frameworks that govern different territories, it is helpful to use the International Convention on the Rights of the Child 1989 in promoting child protection activity. The United Nations Convention on the Rights of the Child (UNCRC) is the most widely ratified international human rights treaty in the world, setting out what all children and young people need to be happy and healthy. The UNCRC has the status of a binding international treaty and, by agreeing to the UNCRC, governments across the world have committed to promoting and protecting children's rights by all the means available to them. It is therefore a key reference point in considering and advocating for the needs of children in any international operational work.[3]

KEY PRINCIPLES FOR OPERATIONAL ACTIVITY

CEOP seeks the following key working principles for law enforcement to promote in working with victims:

a. Enable the gathering of best evidence from vulnerable children.
b. Enhance, rather than detract from, their wellbeing and welfare.
c. Manage and reduce risk to them.
d. Ensure that victims are supported and safeguarded regardless of their willingness to participate in the investigation or criminal justice process.

Underlying assumptions include the following:

• In most circumstances, (a), (b), and (c) are compatible aims and working towards them achieves a 'win-win' – so, for example, when victims' welfare and safety are thought about and addressed, the quality of their evidence and the likelihood of their participation in the criminal justice process tends to improve.
• Whether they participate or not (d) their right to support is an important principle in line with Article 39 of the UNCRC.
• These principles focus on the needs of the victims of child sexual abuse and exploitation. However, they are relevant to all serious crimes against children including those that are likely to have had substantial impact on their psychology and relationships. These include trafficking and all crimes against children involving violence and exploitation.

INCORPORATING CHILD PROTECTION PRINCIPLES INTO OPERATIONAL PLANNING

When undertaking operational planning for investigations into child sexual exploitation and abuse that cross different jurisdictions, it is recognised that there will be variations in different countries in terms of the following issues:

- The nature, capability and capacity of statutory child protection services.
- The role played by non-governmental organisations in child protection.
- The legislation and duties that law enforcement and other partners are working under.
- The procedures by which investigations are undertaken.
- The cultural narratives about child sexual abuse and cultural responses to victims.

Notwithstanding these variations, it is desirable for all law enforcement agencies to aim to produce a bespoke child protection plan that sits alongside the operational plan for any investigation into child sexual exploitation and abuse.

This plan should highlight the relevant national childcare legislation and best practice so that officers are clear about the child protection framework they are operating under as well as the relevant criminal charges. When there is limited relevant national legislation, investigators should consider their duties to child victims under the UNCRC. This includes the duty under Article 3 to ensure that a child's best interests are a primary consideration in all decisions that affect him or her as well as the duty under Article 39 to provide support and aftercare to victims of exploitation.

PRINCIPLES OF WORKING

In the development of the child protection plan, it is recommended that the following principles or approaches are adopted[4]:

i. *Recognising the impact of abuse and barriers to disclosure* (aims a and b). All strategies should recognise that child sexual exploitation and abuse can have a long-lasting and deleterious effect on victims (see 'Key Principles for Operational Activity'). Research has demonstrated that the act of disclosure is rarely purposeful or clear – this can be for a whole range of reasons, including the impact of shame and fear, as well as how we remember traumatic experience. Instead we may expect the accounts of children in these circumstances to be fragmented and inconsistent, and in almost all cases the disclosure will be partial at the outset. The potential for children to speak out against families and communities involved in hands-on abuse or the facilitation of abuse may be limited. The implications for operational practice mean that each potential victims needs individual assessment and detailed interview planning with consideration of how he or she can be made to feel as at ease or comfortable as possible. It may help to actively address any ways in which the victim is psychologically or materially dependent on the offender – unless these are addressed, disclosure may conflict or appear to conflict with the child's best interests.

ii. ***Recognising the deliberate silencing of victims*** **(aims a and b).** Linked to this, investigators may benefit from an understanding of how offender strategies explicitly aim to ensure that child victims of exploitation and abuse hold their silence. This includes targeting children with particular vulnerabilities, gradually desensitising them, using their sense of confusion and shame, forcing them to take an 'active' role in the abuse so they feel responsible, and threatening them with the 'dire' consequences of disclosure. When the Internet has been used we see particular emphasis by offenders on persuading victims that they have been active, through forcing them to produce or view material that depicts their own abuse and playing on their feeling of complicity. This was very evident in case Study A outlined further on.

iii. ***Understanding the cultural barriers.*** An additional challenge to this can be the specific cultural barriers to the disclosure of abuse in many countries. It is useful to challenge pervasive cultural attitudes that might lead to victim blaming (such as honour-based cultures) through appropriate counter-narratives drawn from the same culture. Investigators should keep an open mind as to how to overcome a range of barriers – and should seek to communicate an attitude that is protective, non-blaming and non-judgemental.

iv. ***Pausing to plan*** **(aims a and b).** The planning of individual engagement needs careful consideration and needs to be informed by individual needs and the situation of the child as well as the evidential requirements of the legal system under which the investigation is operating. All planning decisions about children's engagement and welfare need to be reviewed dynamically throughout the investigation as more information becomes available. Investigations can be expensive and time-consuming, and they rightly carry a legitimate sense of urgency with officers feeling under personal and professional pressure to achieve resolution for child victims. It can be difficult when under pressure to 'pause and plan' in order to consider the impact of actions on not only the immediate safety of a child but also on his or her psychological welfare – yet a planned approach is consistent with children's best interests and usually more likely to enable an approach that will facilitate successful engagement.

v. ***The importance of planning for interview*** **(aims a and b).** Interviews should be conducted by those with specific relevant training in interviewing children, and ideally children will also have access to someone who is independent and can explain and support them through the process.

A child protection strategy should consider and research the availability of these from the outset. Interrogative-style interviews of child victims should be avoided because these violate the rights of victims as well as being counterproductive and silencing.

vi. ***The importance of planning for the identification of services*** **(aims a, b, c and d).** It is important to plan the process from end to end when considering the approach to victims that is likely to enhance and facilitate their engagement with the investigation and criminal justice system. This includes detailed planning from the point of first contact to communication and safety planning throughout. The specialist support services required are likely to include medical support, emergency accommodation, financial assistance, education, therapeutic care and potentially longer-term assistance in moving to a different location.

vii. ***The value of partnerships and sharing information*** **(aims a, b, c and d).** When possible it is recommended that there is close collaboration between law enforcement and those state agencies whose primary remit is the care and welfare of children, because this will assist with information sharing as well as access to specialist alternative care and support. Information sharing between agencies has been shown to be critical to the safeguarding and protection of children, because relevant information about the health, safety or welfare of children is often held by agencies other than law enforcement. Such agencies may hold a wealth of relevant information about the child that can assist in planning and assessment as well as being able to offer longer-term support beyond the life of the investigation.

viii. ***Recognising the role of NGOs*** **(aims a, b, c and d).** Law enforcement agencies are also encouraged to consider working with voluntary sector partners and NGOs. Whilst there may be resistance to working with non-law enforcement agencies in some jurisdictions, these should be overcome when it is clearly in the best interests of the child. In particular in jurisdictions where there is limited access to support from state agencies or partners there should be planning with relevant local or international NGO partners and clear protocols agreed in advance. Legitimate concerns about the security of information needs to be balanced against the risk of not being able to engage or support victims in a way that enhances their safety and wellbeing.

ix. ***Recognising the responsibility to safeguarding and protect throughout*** **(aims c and d).** It is important that the investigation makes reasonable efforts to identify all of the potential victims within the scope of an investigation and not merely a sufficient number for a prosecution. This is so that all victims get an opportunity to share their experiences and be offered safeguarding support. It should be recognised, however, that this can be particularly challenging in internet-based investigations because there are potentially very large numbers of victims, and sometimes the extent of the intelligence about their involvement is limited. In order to approach this proportionately and ethically the investigation team should seek to map the key victims and the relationships between them in the same way that they would seek to understand the full extent of the offending network. In relation to developing a victim and witness management strategy, selection and prioritisation process, it is important that no victim who has been engaged is left without the offer of support, even when his or her account is deemed not useful to the investigation. It is important to understand that the process of providing evidence to the investigation can in itself be traumatic whether or not the evidence is used, and having raised those issues for the individual victim he or she may need further psychological support.

x. ***Respecting victims and not forcing disclosure*** (**aim d**). The wishes and feelings of victims must be respected and when victims clearly indicate that they do not want to disclose or be part of the investigation, they should not be bullied or pressured to participate or repeatedly re-interviewed by different officers. Some victims are not psychologically ready to accept and represent their own abuse to others. The interview must be conducted by those experienced in doing so and be respectful, professional and caring – accepting the account the victim wishes to give. In internet-related CSA investigations it is not in a child's best interests to show images of his or her own abuse in order to prompt a disclosure, and this could in fact further his or her distress.

xi. ***Ensuring the risk management of operational tactics*** (**aims a, b and c**). At no point in the investigation should victims be treated as 'evidence' rather than vulnerable children, and it is not acceptable to allow a child to be harmed, or potentially harmed, in the conduct of an investigation. This principle requires detailed and ethical planning for the use of surveillance techniques and covert operations. All possible actions to prevent the 'live time' abuse of children must be taken. It is not acceptable to allow children to be raped or sexually assaulted as a means to gather evidence and no investigative team should be complicit in any action that results in harm to a child. This is relevant in internet-related investigations in which offenders are using technologies that hide their identity or location and further engagement is required, as well as offline when prosecution may be easier when offenders are caught in the act of abuse.[5]

xii. ***Understanding the necessity of sustained support*** (**aims b and c**). A common challenge in the investigation of child sexual exploitation and abuse is how to protect vulnerable victims from being influenced or intimidated by their abusers following a disclosure and the need to prevent a child from being bullied, threatened or put at risk of losing his or her life as a result of coming forward. It is common for victims of child sexual exploitation and abuse to withdraw their disclosures when they are returned to the families and communities where they were initially vulnerable – and this challenge should be anticipated and planned for within any child sexual exploitation investigation.[6] In particular high-risk cases, alternative sources of care and support will be essential, for example, when the offender is running an institution providing care for victims or tangible financial support to them or their families.

xiii. *Exploring alternatives to relying on children's evidence alone* (aim b and c). Investigative or operational tactics that reduce the pressure on children to directly give evidence in sexual exploitation and abuse investigations (or that reduces the pressure of reliance on that testimony) should be explored. Although some victims may feel empowered by testifying, other may feel that testifying is difficult and stressful. In addition, victims of child sexual abuse and exploitation may recant their statement. Developing fulsome corroborating testimony may obviate the need to call the victim as a witness or assist in making a credibility determination. This may include fully exploring online material as well as any forensic or crime scene evidence that may be available.[7]

xiv. *Ensuring a rights-based approach* (aims a, b, c and d). It is important to keep the needs and rights of victims at the centre of the operation and when necessary to challenge partners who fail to do this. Other than in extreme circumstances when it is the only means of providing for safety, incarceration of victims should always be avoided. It should never be used as a means of holding a victim until he or she provides a disclosure. This is not only the responsibility of law enforcement but also of all parts of the criminal justice system.

CAPACITY AND CAPABILITY BUILDING

A key aspect in upholding and implementing the principles of safeguarding and welfare of children is the availability of experienced and well-trained staff members who will act in a professional and caring manner towards children. To enable this, when it is not already in place, countries should be encouraged to put in place dedicated and specialist units to manage these investigations and people who are available to advise and support colleagues working on complex child sexual exploitation and abuse investigations. The CEOP Command of the NCA has found that as a specialist centre there has been potential to build expertise in the area of online offending and complex child abuse and build on learning about what is effective and likely to work.

Training for relevant officers helpfully includes how to use the principles in practice as well as more broadly a series of modules that lay the foundations for how child safeguarding can be considered in all law enforcement activity:

   i. Understanding of children's rights and child development and how to spot the indicators of abuse.
  ii. Impact of the key crimes on victims linked to its relevance for investigations, such as understanding the ways victims can give their best evidence.

iii. The behaviour and strategies of sex offenders and those seeking to exploit children.

iv. Multi-agency training and best practices for working among different professions, such as with health and social care as well as with other criminal justice agencies.

v. Interviewing of child victims.

vi. Interviewing of offenders.

vii. Covert internet investigation.

viii. Working with industry.

ix. Key learning from online and offline investigations into child sexual exploitation and abuse – guidance for operational planning and strategic considerations.

OPERATIONAL EXAMPLES

CEOP Command of the NCA has led and collaborated on a range of international cases involving organised networks of offenders, multiple child victims, and the use of travel and technologies to offend across different jurisdictions and/or to exploit environments where children are particularly vulnerable to abuse. The following are a couple of operational examples that illustrate some of the challenges and complexities in relation to victim support in such contexts.

CASE STUDY A

In case study A, a small network of offenders based overseas were involved in the online grooming and abuse of about 300 UK victims (as well as victims from other countries). The abuse occurred exclusively online through sexual abuse activity captured via webcam; there was never any meeting in the real world in which any of the offenders actually met with their victims (the small group of offenders were known to each other in the real world but never left their country or met victims in the real world). The offenders used a range of online identities to confuse and bully victims, engaging them to begin with (in most cases) in sexual chat that developed into extreme blackmail and hacking of accounts. The grooming technique in this case was to persuade the children (mainly girls aged 13 to 17) to engage in minor sexual activity over webcam then threatening full exposure to friends and family if they failed to engage in more serious sexual activity.

Unfortunately initial sexual activity or sexual posing by the victims was used for the vast majority of cases to extort more severe and harmful sexual performances via webcam, including acts of self-penetration and acts involving the contact abuse of other young people. The challenges in relation to victim support in this case involved understanding the distress of the victims and the extent to which they felt terrified and trapped by the hacking of their online lives and their constant fear of exposure. This anxiety, resulting in self-harm (and one attempted suicide) and evident for many in the hours of chat logs between offenders and victims – made approaching victims in a sensitive and planned way essential. The nature of the offending and its 'severity' was also important to convey to local services in the UK, where the ongoing safeguarding support for victims needed to be provided.

One of the key challenges in this case was working across borders to try to safeguard victims at current risk without having the capability to act against the offender as swiftly and immediately as if the offender was UK based. There was also significant data communications work with internet service providers and platforms to resolve the identities of some of the highest-risk victims and to ensure their contact and support whilst at the same time seeking to apprehend and the arrest the offender with the assistance of law enforcement in the country of the offenders. CEOP deployed officers to assist with this, supporting an arrest or prosecution in the country, as well as supporting the assessment of risk posed to local children. This kind of investigation was new to the offenders' home country, so legal provisions needed to be identified that could cover these offences (for example, exploring their anti-blackmail legislation) because the domestic legislation for sexual offences had to be extended or interpreted in a particular way to include interactions via webcam. In safeguarding terms the UK victims were also supported to engage in the foreign prosecution via written affidavits, but it was also necessary to challenge some of the perceptions about the victims in the case in the country where the offenders were being prosecuted, because these perceptions were based on an honour-based culture in which these child victims should not have been engaging with strangers on the Internet. In the UK a further part of the safeguarding strategy involved a public media appeal (with the support of the NSPCC helpline) to highlight the modus operandi by the offenders and to ensure any victims whom it had not been possible to identify via technical means were identified and safeguarded.

CASE STUDY B

Case study B involved a network of offenders operating in the UK and a number of other English-speaking countries who were in touch with each other communicating and facilitating the live streaming of child abuse activity from a country in Southeast Asia. This was a particularly challenging network with many offshoots to the investigation; in particular, one of the most serious offenders travelled to a third country where he was offending against street children who were particularly poor and destitute and arranging the abuse of children from a remote village (and this became a separate operation).

Within the main network there was an arrangement whereby money was exchanged with a group of offenders in the country where the victims were based in return for the local group facilitating the abuse of children in return for the payment. The key victims were young children who were known to the local facilitators via family and community networks. The challenge here was to prevent and pursue the offending, within the international network (and identify and safeguard domestic victims), and pursue the in-country facilitators whilst also working with local agencies to safeguard the overseas victims.

This case presented many challenges. Although there was some evidence capture from the technology used, it was also important to obtain a disclosure of abuse from the children in order to secure the arrest and prosecution of the offenders locally. This was only made possible by working closely with an international NGO based locally and engaging in detailed joint planning about how individual victims should be interviewed and the framework of support that could be put around them in the short and long term, because the case relied on the children having the resilience and willingness to give evidence against the community (and in some cases family) members. It was necessary for a number of them to do this consistently over a period of time and subsequent to an assessed return to non-offending family and community – with risks managed by local social services and support for them provided via NGOs. The network of activity was disrupted because the key facilitators were arrested and prosecuted.

ANNEX 1

COUNCIL OF EUROPE CONVENTION ON THE PROTECTION OF CHILDREN AGAINST SEXUAL EXPLOITATION AND SEXUAL ABUSE

Article 3 – Definitions

For the purposes of this Convention:

a. 'child' shall mean any person under the age of 18 years;
b. 'sexual exploitation and sexual abuse of children' shall include the behaviour as referred to in Articles 18 to 23 of this Convention;
c. 'victim' shall mean any child subject to sexual exploitation or sexual abuse.

Article 18 – Sexual abuse

1. Each Party shall take the necessary legislative or other measures to ensure that the following intentional conduct is criminalised:
   a. engaging in sexual activities with a child who, according to the relevant provisions of national law, has not reached the legal age for sexual activities;
   b. engaging in sexual activities with a child where:
      • use is made of coercion, force or threats; or
      • abuse is made of a recognised position of trust, authority or influence over the child, including within the family; or

- abuse is made of a particularly vulnerable situation of the child, notably because of a mental or physical disability or a situation of dependence.
2. For the purpose of paragraph 1 above, each Party shall decide the age below which it is prohibited to engage in sexual activities with a child.
3. The provisions of paragraph 1.a are not intended to govern consensual sexual activities between minors.

Article 19 – Offences concerning child prostitution

1. Each Party shall take the necessary legislative or other measures to ensure that the following intentional conduct is criminalised:
   a. recruiting a child into prostitution or causing a child to participate in prostitution;
   b. coercing a child into prostitution or profiting from or otherwise exploiting a child for such purposes;
   c. having recourse to child prostitution.
2. For the purpose of the present article, the term 'child prostitution' shall mean the fact of using a child for sexual activities where money or any other form of remuneration or consideration is given or promised as payment, regardless if this payment, promise or consideration is made to the child or to a third person.

Article 20 – Offences concerning child pornography

1. Each Party shall take the necessary legislative or other measures to ensure that the following intentional conduct, when committed without right, is criminalised:
   a. producing child pornography;
   b. offering or making available child pornography;
   c. distributing or transmitting child pornography;
   d. procuring child pornography for oneself or for another person;
   e. possessing child pornography;
   f. knowingly obtaining access, through information and communication technologies, to child pornography.
2. For the purpose of the present article, the term 'child pornography' shall mean any material that visually depicts a child engaged in real or simulated sexually explicit conduct or any depiction of a child's sexual organs for primarily sexual purposes.
3. Each Party may reserve the right not to apply, in whole or in part, paragraph 1.a and e to the production and possession of pornographic material:
   - consisting exclusively of simulated representations or realistic images of a non existent child;
   - involving children who have reached the age set in application of Article 18, paragraph 2, where these images are produced and possessed by them with their consent and solely for their own private use.

4. Each Party may reserve the right not to apply, in whole or in part, paragraph 1.f.

Article 21 – Offences concerning the participation of a child in pornographic performances

1. Each Party shall take the necessary legislative or other measures to ensure that the following intentional conduct is criminalised:
   a. recruiting a child into participating in pornographic performances or causing a child to participate in such performances;
   b. coercing a child into participating in pornographic performances or profiting from or otherwise exploiting a child for such purposes;
   c. knowingly attending pornographic performances involving the participation of children.
2. Each Party may reserve the right to limit the application of paragraph 1.c to cases where children have been recruited or coerced in conformity with paragraph 1.a or b.

Article 22 – Corruption of children

Each Party shall take the necessary legislative or other measures to criminalise the intentional causing, for sexual purposes, of a child who has not reached the age set in application of Article 18, paragraph 2, to witness sexual abuse or sexual activities, even without having to participate.

Article 23 – Solicitation of children for sexual purposes

Each Party shall take the necessary legislative or other measures to criminalise the intentional proposal, through information and communication technologies, of an adult to meet a child who has not reached the age set in application of Article 18, paragraph 2, for the purpose of committing any of the offences established in accordance with Article 18, paragraph 1.a, or Article 20, paragraph 1.a, against him or her, where this proposal has been followed by material acts leading to such a meeting.

NOTES

1   Davidson, J. (2010). Legislation and policy: Protecting young people, sentencing and managing internet sex offenders. In J. Davidson & P. Gottschalk (Eds.), *Internet child abuse: Current research, policy and police practice.* Routledge. Davidson, J., Quale, E., & Morganbasser, L. (Eds.). (2010). Special issue: Child sexual abuse and the internet; Offenders, victims and managing the risk. *Journal of Sexual Aggression,* 16(1).
2   Elly Hanson – Research summary for CEOP (What do we know about CSA) (2009).

3   The articles of the Convention that are most relevant to these principles are summarised here:

> Article 2: The Convention applies to everyone whatever their ethnicity, gender, religion, abilities, whatever they think or say, whatever type of family they come from.
> Article 3: The best interests of the child must be a top priority in all things that affect children.
> Article 12: Every child has the right to say what he or she thinks in all matters affecting him or her and to have his or her views taken seriously.
> Article 13: Every child must be free to say what he or she thinks and to seek and receive all kinds of information.
> Article 16: Every child has the right to privacy.
> Article 19: Governments must do all they can to ensure that children are protected from all forms of violence, abuse, neglect and bad treatment.
> Article 34: Governments must do all they can to ensure children are protected from all forms of sexual abuse and exploitation.
> Article 39: Children who are neglected, abused, exploited, tortured or who are victims of war must receive special help to help them recover their health.

4   This discussion of child protection principles has emerged from operational activity from the online as well as offline environment. However, these should be relevant to any case in which a child has or children have been the victims of sexual abuse and/or exploitation.

5   Operational requirements may lead to circumstances in which children may be produced or presented as victims for potential abuse. It is unlikely that prior to the point of production the location or identity of a child would be known, and this may be the first opportunity to protect the child. In these circumstances the operational plan must be clear that action is taken to remove the child from danger at the earliest opportunity.

6   In a sample of 257 children with substantiated child sexual abuse Malloy, Lyon, and Quas (Malloy, L. C., Lyon, T. D., & Quas, J. A. [2007]. Filial dependency and recantation of child sexual abuse allegations. *Journal of the American Academy of Child and Adolescent Psychiatry, 46*(2), 162–170.) found that 23% retracted their disclosures at some point in formal and informal interviews. The act of retraction appears to be linked to lack of support from the non offending caregiver, a familial relationship with the abuser, younger child age and more frequent abuse rather than the degree of evidence for child sexual abuse.

7   Notwithstanding this, all investigative tactics and decisions must be considered in line with the needs and rights of children, including those discussed under point 9 as well as for example decisions with regards to medical examination.

10 Staying Safe Online

Dido Harding

As one of Britain's leading internet service providers, TalkTalk believes passionately in the ability of the Internet to change lives for the better. We see it every day, with customers using the Internet to change how they live, work and play. At its best it can advance human knowledge and understanding, enable businesses to thrive and spread prosperity and bring families and communities together. That's a tremendous force for good. Similar to every other transformational technology, however, we have to ensure we harness its potential safely. Industry has the resource, expertise and, I believe, a duty to play a leading role in this process. It's a big responsibility, but if we get it right, we can ensure British children are the biggest beneficiaries of the most exciting technology in the world. That's a prize worth striving for.

TECHNOLOGY IS CHANGING THE RULES – OR IS IT?

If you ask parents about child safety, one of the most frequent issues they raise is that new technology is changing the rules of parenting. As a parent, it certainly feels like today's issues are less familiar and more complex than when we were children. 'Charley says "don't talk to strangers"' is a refrain that will resonate with other parents who, similar to me, had their childhood TV viewing interrupted by a variety of public information films designed to warn them about various childhood perils – from crossing the road to playing near railway lines or near open water.

One of the perceptions is that the risks in those early public information films were simpler to manage because they were familiar. Parents had grown up being taught about the risks of crossing roads, so they found it easier to pass those lessons onto their own children. It's certainly true that some of the risks were inter-generational, but it's also true that new risks emerged. Some of these were driven by changes in social attitudes. For instance those early public

Online Risk to Children: Impact, Protection and Prevention, First Edition.
Edited by Jon Brown.
© 2017 John Wiley & Sons, Ltd. Published 2017 by John Wiley & Sons, Ltd.

information films also warned about not talking to strangers. Until then, many parents would have encouraged their children to respect their elders and be polite when spoken to. Suddenly parents found themselves reversing that advice and encouraging children to walk away, not to engage and to refuse sweets. It was a departure from the advice of yesteryear.

It's also easy to forget that even then new technologies were giving rise to parenting challenges. Faster trains and more cars obviously led to increased risks for children, but I can also remember films warning us not to play in disused fridges. It sounds bizarre to think of fridges in the context of child safety now, but, in a society with more electrical goods, this was a new, unforeseen danger that parents had not had to contemplate before.

In many respects then, the Internet and its associated risks are just the latest in a long line of issues parents have had to understand and help their children navigate. Similar to their 1970s counterparts, the parents of today have to come to terms with a risk they themselves never experienced as children. That doesn't diminish the challenge, but it reminds us that we have adjusted to new technology before and, with the right support, we can do it again.

What is unique about today's technology is the pace of change. As Martha Lane Fox said during the 2015 Richard Dimbleby lecture, it took 38 years for the radio to reach 50 million users in the UK, television took 13 years, but the web took just 4. Even parents who feel familiar with the online world can be left confused by the pace of change within it. Just as parents think they've conquered YouTube and Facebook, they realise their children have moved onto Snapchat, Instagram and WhatsApp. Whilst innovation is a wonderful thing, some parents are left feeling left behind and blind to the risks their children might encounter.

EMBRACING OPPORTUNITIES

What's striking in talking to parents about the online safety challenge, however, is that despite their concerns, they remain determined that their children don't miss out on the benefits of being online. Even parents who feel left behind by the explosion in devices, apps and services recognise that being online is essential for their children to succeed.

Indeed the scale of the safety challenge we face is a reflection of how enthusiastically Britain has embraced the Internet. It's also a reflection of how competition and regulation has succeeding in making the Internet accessible and affordable.[1] Over 80% of premises are now online, with superfast broadband set to be available to 95% of homes by 2017.

Britons have been some of the most enthusiastic adopters of digital technology in the world. In 2014 nearly three-quarters of UK adults bought good and services online, over half banked online and UK adults now spend more time using electronic devices each day than they do sleeping. So even though some parents might be nervous about the challenges of the internet age, the majority of us recognise the benefits of being online.

The benefits are particularly apparent in education. I remember school projects used to involve time in the school library, poring over battered encyclopaedias and hoping the books weren't too old and the facts not too outdated. That's not a risk for today's children. They have access to the most incredible array of knowledge at the touch of a button, at their desk, on the sofa or on the bus (perhaps making it easier than teachers might like to finish homework at the last minute!). The range of online teaching and study resources doesn't just support higher attainment, but through educational games and interactive content, they bring subjects to life and make learning fun. That's not something you want children to miss out on.

The Internet also gives young people the chance to use their skills, ideas and creativity to make their own content and possibly aspire to be the next tech success stories. Nick D'Aloisio, a teenager from Wimbledon, developed the app 'Summly,' which summarises news stories, while revising for his mock GCSEs in 2011. After attracting investment from Hong Kong billionaire Li-Ki Shing, the 17-year-old sold the app to Yahoo! for almost $30 million, making him one of the youngest tech millionaires ever. Nick embodies how young people embrace the Internet with enthusiasm, seeing its rich potential. Nick describes himself 'as a net native ... born when the Internet was founded and have only known a world with Internet. Young people are just not aware of the constraints, so why not go build a social network, for example?' For Nick the worst thing his parents could have done would have been to make their digitally native son afraid to experiment online.

Even for those children not lucky enough to follow in Nick's footsteps, technology and digital skills are essential to future employment prospects. Basic online skills are already becoming as essential as basic maths and English in the workplace, and young people leaving school or university without them will struggle to secure the jobs they might like. Indeed, the same innovation that can leave parents confused is driving the growth and jobs essential for Britain's future. Between 2009 and 2012, when the rest of the economy was struggling, the number of tech and digital companies in London grew by 76% to nearly 90,000, accounting for nearly a third of all new London jobs during that period. Some of those jobs will have been designing the very apps that parents sometimes struggle to keep up with. It's a reminder that what some parents think of as dangers are viewed as opportunities by our digitally native children.

Parents are therefore faced with a digital twist of the age-old parenting dilemma. They're ambitious for their children and want them to seize the opportunities available, but they're nervous about what their children may encounter. It's the same difficult balance that parents face when their children develop their independence in the real world, by going on their first holiday with friends, or waving goodbye as they go off to university: excitement, pride, but a nagging concern.

INDUSTRY'S RESPONSIBILITY

Just because it's perfectly natural for parents to worry about striking the right balance doesn't mean they should have to face that dilemma on their own. The technology industry has a responsibility to help and we are uniquely well placed to do it.

When I first joined TalkTalk in 2010, there were still some in the industry who adopted the 'dumb pipe' school of thought. They thought that internet service providers merely provided a connection to the Internet and that consumers were responsible for how they used it and what content they accessed. Spurious comparisons were prevalent, such as car dealerships selling cars but not being responsible for whether they were driven safely.

TalkTalk took a different view. We know that consumers rightly expect far more from companies than they ever have done. They expect their supermarkets to source sustainably, their clothes shops to have robust supply chains and drinks companies to use recyclable packaging. Corporate social responsibility has transformed from being an optional extra to a business imperative, and this applies to technology companies as much as anyone else. When consumers make technology purchases they're not just driven by product and price. They want to know that a company understands their concerns and will help them to address the challenges the Internet delivers.

Supporting our customers and helping to reassure their concerns is not just the right thing to do morally but also the smart thing to do commercially. We know the fear of technology is a barrier for some people getting online. It's one of the reasons why over ten million UK adults lack basic online skills. Persuading those people of the benefits of being online is harder than marketing to digitally native young adults, but it would be foolish for any technology company to ignore such a large potential market of new customers. That creates a huge commercial incentive for companies to transform their products and services to reflect customer concerns. A lot of British families need more than a 'dumb pipe'; they need products, services and advice to help them use their connection effectively and safely.

It hasn't always been easy to convince everyone in the sector to embrace a more rounded concept of responsibility to customers. There will always be some laggards. I'm pleased, however, that the major players in the sector, covering the vast majority of the market, have come round to TalkTalk's way of thinking. It means the 'dumb pipe' argument is now as out-dated as the dial-up internet its proponents used to sell. That's good news for consumers and good news for those us who think the industry should be embracing its responsibilities.

INDUSTRY ACTION

The industry now agrees it has a role to play in helping to protect customers. The key question is what that help should look like. As with most complex questions, there isn't a single, simple answer, not least because as technology rapidly evolves, we have to continually modify how we help consumers keep up with it. Broadly, however, there are three ways industry can help: using our resources in the products and services we offer and the expertise we have.

RESOURCES

Resources matter. Britain is blessed with some of the world's leading children's charities and experts, including the NSPCC. We work closely with many of them and are continually amazed by their commitment, knowledge and passion for making Britain a better, safer place to grow up. That requires funding though and I'm proud that companies in the UK have risen to the challenge.

For instance, as far back as 1996, when the Internet was still in its infancy, Britain's ISPs established an independent charity, the Internet Watch Foundation (IWF) to help make the Internet safer. The IWF was the first hotline for members of the public to anonymously report websites containing potentially illegal images, in particular images of child sexual abuse, in a secure way. With the support of industry, the IWF has grown and now operates a 'notice and takedown' service that alerts ISPs and hosting companies to child abuse images so it can be removed from their networks. It also provides unique data to law enforcement partners in the UK and abroad to assist with investigations into distributions, and as a result, child abuse image content has now been virtually eradicated from networks in the UK.

When the IWF was formed in 1996 nearly one-fifth of global child abuse imagery was hosted in the UK. Today it stands at less than 1%.[2] There are 100,000 URLs containing criminal content that have been removed, and child abuse content is now typically taken down within an hour in the UK. More importantly, the IWF has helped the police to rescue 12 children in the last three years We recently significantly increased our contribution to the IWF, enabling it to start proactively searching the Internet for known child abuse imagery rather than relying on referrals from members of the public. The IWF has been at the forefront of Britain's efforts to be a global leader in online child safety and that's only been possible because of industry committing the resources needed to make it happen.

The UK's four leading ISPs went even further in 2014, committing additional resources to a multi-year funding deal with some of the other charities pioneering ways to keep our kids safe. This included Lucy Faithfull / Stop It Now, which runs a helpline for adults seeking support to stop abusive behaviour or for friends and family concerned about potentially abusive behaviour. Adults trying to access child abuse imagery known to the IWF are diverted to a splash page, which explains that the content they're trying to access is illegal and provides the Lucy Faithfull helpline number. Some abusers know their behaviour is wrong and want to stop it, but they struggle to manage and control it. Lucy Faithfull experts help abusers recognise their behaviour and seek professional help to stop it.

The four leading ISPs also signed multi-year funding deals in 2014 with Marie Collins Foundation, which carries out pioneering work with the victims of child abuse, as well as Childnet International, which works with children from 3 to 18 to understand child behaviour online and offer safety advice. These charities do incredible work, often in very challenging circumstances, and by committing resources, industry is helping to ensure that work can continue.

PRODUCTS AND SERVICES

One of the most significant ways industry can support online child safety is through the products and services we offer. Technology innovation doesn't just mean producing new apps and functionality; it also means developing ways for people to use the internet more safely. That's exactly what we did in 2011, when we were the first ISP to launch a whole-home filtering system, called HomeSafe.

HomeSafe is available for free to all TalkTalk households, and enables parents to filter potential age-inappropriate content. Once activated, HomeSafe prevents any device connected to the home Wi-Fi network, such as laptops, tablets, smartphones and games consoles, from accessing content that a parent has chosen to filter.

TalkTalk's experience with HomeSafe tells us there are three principles that have to underpin products designed to help customers: choice, flexibility and simplicity.

Its crucial parents feel like they have a choice about what products they use to protect their family. We recommend to customers that they use HomeSafe if they have children and present them with an unavoidable choice about whether to turn it on. We have always resisted those who would like filters to be on by default, not because we don't think they're a good idea for families, but because we feel strongly that parents ought to make an active decision.

The risk with a default on approach is that parents aren't forced to consider the issue; they don't engage. By making them think about whether or not they need filters, we make them consider internet safety and can direct them to expert advice. TalkTalk pre-ticks the 'on' box, a little bit like terms and conditions are sometimes pre-ticked when shopping online, but the final choice is with the individual. Customers told us they liked that approach: 80% said it was a good thing, and 60% said they wouldn't have applied filters in their home if we hadn't asked them about it.

Products also have to be flexible, recognising that there are no 'one size fits all' solutions to internet safety. We know that every home is different. Children mature at different ages and only parents know what content is appropriate for their child. Some content is clearly inappropriate, such as pornography, but with other content, such as social media, there are shades of grey. Some parents will be content to let their 13-year-old use Facebook, whilst others may be more cautious. Ultimately it's for parents to decide what's right for their family, and flexible products such as HomeSafe give them the tools they need to make that call.

That flexibility underpinned the design of HomeSafe. Media coverage of filtering systems has typically focussed on pornography, often dubbing them 'porn filters.' Whilst pornography is one of the categories we allow parents to filter, HomeSafe is much broader than that and reflects the range of concerns parents might have. It enables parents to block categories such as suicide and self-harm, weapons and violence, gambling and alcohol and tobacco. It also enables parents to be flexible with when filters apply. For instance, the Home-work Time feature means parents can restrict access to potential sources of distraction, such as social media sites, whilst their children are completing homework immediately after school, but then enabling access later in the evening or at weekends. We also enable parents to filter individual websites that may be causing concern. For instance parents may permit their children to use most social media websites but want to block a particular site where a child has had a negative experience. HomeSafe enables parents to find the right level of protection for their home.

For products to work, they also need to be simple. We know parents are far less likely to use filters where they have installed software or update it; often people find it confusing or difficult. That's why we specifically designed Home-Safe to make it as easy as possible. It doesn't require a download or update; instead, a simple click of the mouse switches it on. It updates automatically and because it applies to every device connected to the home network, parents only ever need to make one decision about what content to filter rather than installing software and configuring individual devices.

The response from customers demonstrates that they value the support filters offer. When presented with an unavoidable choice, just over a third of new TalkTalk customers choose to activate them. Whilst HomeSafe led the way, I'm pleased that the rest of the industry has followed suit. The UK's three other major ISPs have now also launched free filtering services, meaning over 90% of UK households now have access to free filtering technology to protect their families.

We need to be honest as an industry, however, about the limitations of filter-ing technology. Whilst it can help parents feel more confident and comfortable with their child's Internet use, it should never be completely relied on. We are continually refining the system but all technology is fallible. The vast majority of content will be caught and blocked, but no matter how hard we try, some will also be incorrectly classified and will slip through the net.

It isn't just a case of missing things that should be caught. We also have to acknowledge problems caused by over-blocking, where filters incorrectly restrict access to content that should be available. For instance, some youth charities offering sex and relationship advice have found their services miscategorised as unsuitable for young people. What's crucial, then, is that robust reporting processes are in place, so organisations can report miscategorisation and know it will be rectified quickly. All of the ISPs have processes in place, but we now have agreed on a single reporting tool, meaning charities or other organisations now need to report concerns about over-blocking only once.

The fact filters aren't perfect is a good example of why they should only be part of the toolkit parents use to keep their children safe. We encourage our customers to think of the online world in the same way they do the real world. When a young child first starts visiting the park on his or her own, parents spend time talking to the child about where he or she will be, any 'out of bounds' areas, staying together with friends and not talking to strangers. Its crucial parents apply these practices to the digital world. That means taking the time to talk to their children about the sorts of websites they visit, whom they talk to online and appropriate boundaries for sharing personal information and pictures. These are the conversations that help mould what children do online and how safe they are, with filters acting as an additional safety net.

It isn't just the ISPs. With the explosion of smartphone access, it's crucial that mobile operators offer products to prevent phones being used to access inappropriate content. Whilst a smartphone connected to the home Wi-Fi network would be subject to ISP filters, those restrictions wouldn't apply away from the home. Parents need to know that the content they filter at home doesn't suddenly become available on an iPhone in the school playground. That's why the UK's mobile operators launched a self-regulating code of practice on mobile content, providing a filter to protect children from age-inappropriate content. The operators drew on the experience of the British Board of Film Classification (BBFC) to balance differing views on what is and is not acceptable content for parents. The mobile operators use the classification body to provide their framework for mobile content. Individuals who disagree with how mobile content has been classified by the content provider can also ask the BBFC to view the content and decide whether it's suitable for under 18s or not.[3]

The array of products and services designed to better protect children online is expanding constantly. That's testament to a shift in how industry approaches the issue. Before, safety products, such as anti-virus software that had child filters included, were bought separately from hardware or internet connections and applied retrospectively; now, safety functionality is increasingly being designed into products and services from the outset. That's a huge advance for parents and demonstrates a commitment by industry to put safety at the heart of its products.

EXPERTISE

The third major contribution industry can make is through the expertise we have and the advice we can offer. We know that parents want to play an active role in helping their child to use the Internet safely. They want to have the conversations about responsible online behaviour with their children and not simply rely on filtering technology. We recognise, however, that many parents lack the information they need to lead those conversations. When questioned in 2014, 74% of parents wanted more advice to help them keep their children safe online. They told us they didn't know where to go to access reliable advice and wanted a single source of information. That's why Britain's main ISPs united in 2014 to launch Internet Matters, a ground-breaking, not-for-profit organisation dedicated to offering parents all the advice they need.

Internet Matters acts as a one-stop hub, offering simple, easy and practical advice on a range of online safety issues, including cyberbullying, sexting, grooming and inappropriate content. It doesn't preach to parents, but helps them to learn about, talk about and deal with typical issues their children might encounter online. It also offers a range of age guides, helping parents to decide what behaviour is appropriate at what age. Much like filters, it isn't prescriptive, because each family is different. Instead it seeks to give parents guidelines that empower them to make the right decisions for their family.

Take cyberbullying as an example. It's something nearly a third of parents said they're worried about.[4] That's not surprising, given there was an 87% rise in reported instances of cyberbullying between 2012 and 2013.[5] It can be particularly difficult to tackle because it's hard to get away from, with bullies able to use text messages and social media to target victims in their own home. Internet Matters gives parents tips on how to talk to their children about it, including staying calm so children can talk openly and praising them for doing the right thing in sharing the problem. It then gives parents advice on how to deal with the issue, including not replying to posts, keeping evidence of messages and applying tools to block accounts causing concern. Those steps may sound obvious to child safety experts, but to many parents – particularly those with little experience of social media – Internet Matters provides an essential guide that can put them back in control of otherwise difficult situation.

We know, however, that it isn't just parents that need support. Schools also have a vital role to play in keeping children safe online. As well as teaching children essential digital skills in the classroom, Internet Matters research shows that 70% of parents look to schools for advice on internet safety in the home.[6] Whilst teachers are skilled in judging risks to children, it's unfair to expect them to be experts in the nuances of technology and online content. That's why Internet Matters expanded its work into schools, offering free teaching resources to as well as guidance for teachers to share with parents. Internet Matters was also an active champion of the NSPCC Share Aware campaign, aimed at helping parents to talk to 8- to 12-year-olds exploring online for the first time. It's a great example of how Internet Matters can help support other charities seeking to advance the online safety agenda.

Industry doesn't have a monopoly on good advice. Quite the opposite: we need to work with the charities and services that have more experience and expertise than we do. We can, however, use our understanding of technology to supplement the vital work of Britain's child safety experts and use our customer reach to help ensure we reach as many families as possible.

THE FUTURE CHALLENGE

In the same way that the risks children of the 1970s faced in the real world quickly changed, so the risks of today rapidly change. It's easy to say that technology companies best understand the risks that new services can bring, but in truth people will develop ways to use services that developers never envisaged. For example, YikYak was conceived as an online campus-based social forum but one that didn't require a previous relationship or friendship connection, similar to other social media sites. YikYak enabled users to post relevant, timely content to others on campus, but it was quickly abused by some users, who posted anonymous bullying content.[7] More positively, when Larry Page and Sergey Brin first conceived Google, they probably didn't imagine that, by aggregating search queries, it would one day become a useful tool for health services around the world seeking to predict and respond to influenza epidemics. As big data become more accessible in the future, people will find evermore inventive ways to apply information, many of which are impossible to predict now.

We will never be able to anticipate and address every risk. New apps, new trends will mean parents will always be trying to keep up with what their children are doing and the challenges this brings. Attempting to stifle that innovation would not only be ineffective but also would put at risk the jobs and growth opportunities that Britain's technology sector provides. The Internet will increasingly underpin almost every aspect of our lives; the challenge is to help people adjust so they can maximise the benefits and mitigate the risks. That's not a job one company, charity, government or parents can do alone. It's a collective challenge, one that will require all of us to use our resources, products and expertise to continually refine our approaches. That's an enormous challenge but one Britain's technology sector is committed to.

NOTES

1   Office for National Statistics, UK
2   https://www.iwf.org.uk/about-iwf

3   http://www.bbfc.co.uk/what-classification/mobile-content
4   Ofcom Children and Parents: Media Use and Attitudes Report (Oct 2014) p. 138, Figure 98.
5   Childline (2014).
6   http://www.internetmatters.org/educate/schools.html
7   http://www.theguardian.com/technology/2014/oct/21/yik-yak-anonymous-app-college-campus-whisper-secret#comments

11 UK Policy Responses and Their International Relevance

Claire Lilley

Between 2012 and 2014 hardly a day went past without coverage in the UK media about an allegation of child sexual abuse. The revelations about Jimmy Savile and others demonstrated the scale of so-called historical sexual abuse, but the Ian Watkins and the Little Teds Nursery cases highlighted the new ways in which sex offenders use digital technology to abuse children, and the tragic suicides of children including Daniel Perry, linked to sexual images on social media sites, highlighted the vulnerability of young people online. The issue of internet child sexual abuse began to be recognised as a significant issue in the UK, and every week seemed to bring a new, technologically mediated phenomenon into the public consciousness: sexting, revenge pornography, self-harm selfies, live streaming of abuse to order from developing countries, sexual blackmail, the hacking of personal images – the list continues to grow.

At the same time, our understanding of offenders and victims also grew through research studies such as the EU Kids Online project and the European Online Grooming project, with the UK and North America leading the way on the development of a robust evidence base.

The UK's national policing lead agency for the issue – the Child Exploitation and Online Protection centre (COEP) – stated in their 2013 annual threat assessment that an estimated 50,000 individuals are involved in downloading and sharing child abuse images in the UK (with police chiefs more recently saying this is likely to be a significant underestimate), and the head of CEOP admitted that the police did not have enough capacity to arrest all the people they know are downloading these images.

Internet child sexual abuse is a global phenomenon with no respect for national boundaries, so it is imperative that UK public policy responses link with international efforts to tackle this type of crime, the scale of which is beginning to be understood. International leadership and capacity building is needed, and the UK is playing a key role in this.

Online Risk to Children: Impact, Protection and Prevention, First Edition.
Edited by Jon Brown.

DEFINITIONS AND TERMINOLOGY

There is no single, specific criminal offence or agreed definition of internet child sexual abuse. There is broad agreement about the definition of online child sexual exploitation from the Child Exploitation and Online Protection Centre (CEOP)[1], the Department for Education[2] and children's charity Barnardo's[3]. However, these definitions are limited to internet child sexual *exploitation* and are incomplete as definitions of internet child sexual *abuse* because they do not specifically include crimes related to child abuse images.

The NSPCC adopted the following definition for internet child sexual abuse in 2014:

> 'Online child sexual abuse is the use of technology to manipulate, coerce or intimidate a child, to engage in sexual activity that is abusive and/or degrading in nature. Online child sexual abuse is characterised by an imbalance of power and lack of choice resulting from physical, emotional and/or social vulnerabilities. As with other forms of sexual abuse, online abuse can be misunderstood by the child and others as being consensual, occurring without the child's immediate recognition or understanding of abusive or exploitative conduct; although it is emphasised that no child under the age of 18 can consent to being abused or exploited. Online child sexual abuse includes, but is not limited to, the grooming of children for sexual purposes, including sexual acts online, and the production, distribution or possession of indecent images of children. Online child sexual abuse takes different forms and can lead to or be preceded by contact abuse. Financial gain can be a feature of online child sexual abuse and it can involve serious organised crime'[4].

In the UK, the terms 'child pornography', 'kiddie porn' or 'child porn' are widely considered to be unacceptable because they may be seen to legitimise or minimise the gravity of images that are not pornography. The widely held view is that these images are permanent records of children being sexually abused and as such should be referred to as 'child sexual abuse images' or 'indecent images of children'.

LEGISLATION

CHILD ABUSE IMAGES

The Protection of Children Act 1978 and subsequent amendments by the Criminal Justice Act 1988 and the Criminal Justice and Public Order Act 1994 made the taking, distribution, possession or publication of indecent images of children, by any means, illegal. The Criminal Justice and Court Service Act 2000 increased the maximum penalty for taking, taking and distributing images in recognition that real children were abused in order to produce the images.

Although we cannot be categorical that all contemporaneous prosecutions for child abuse image offences are for online rather than hard copy images, the rise in cautions and convictions is consistent with the growth and use of new technologies to access and circulate such images. In 1999, the Home Office estimated that there were 7,000 hard copy child abuse images in circulation in the UK: by 2012, at least 26 million images had been confiscated by just five of England and Wales's 43 police services[5]. The huge expansion in the trading of child abuse images, and other forms of virtual violence against children such as sexual grooming online, was directly linked to the expansion of information communication technologies and the wide scale use of web browsers.

Child abuse images proliferated because technological advances lowered the cost of production of images, dramatically increased their availability and reduced the likelihood of those producing and possessing them being detected[6]. The Internet provides accessibility, affordability and anonymity for offenders[7], enables paedophiles to communicate with each other and acts as a conduit to potential victims. By 2005 nearly one-third of all sexual convictions in England and Wales were for internet-related sexual offending[8].

UK law in relation to indecent images of children is fairly comprehensive, but there is one area of the UK law in relation to child abuse images that needs clarification. Internet service providers (ISPs) have no obligation to monitor content that is passing through their servers – their responsibility begins only once they have actual knowledge of the existence of unlawful material. Therefore clarification of the responsibility for the removal of images when they are in transit between ISPs, under the Regulation of Investigatory Powers Act 2000 (RIPA), is needed.

SELF-GENERATED IMAGES

Even when a sexual image of a child has been self-generated, so-called sexting, this is still an illegal image. UK police have taken the view that in the vast majority of cases it will not be in the best interests of any child to prosecute them for taking, possessing or distributing such images, and in particular recommend against the use of legislation that would attract sex offender registration[9].

However, it is vital that young people are made aware of the potential long-term effects of taking and sending sexual images of themselves. A four-week study by the Internet Watch Foundation (IWF) found 7,723 images and 5,076 videos online that they assessed as being self-generated content featuring young people. In 88% of them the content assessed had been harvested from its original upload location and reposted on a third-party 'parasite website' over which the young people depicted had no control regarding its removal or onward distribution[10]. Therefore, as well as potentially being used to humiliate, embarrass or otherwise bully a young person, self generated indecent images are considered by UK police as 'a high threat in terms of proliferation of images and the potential for persistent victimisation' as well as extortion.

SEXUAL GROOMING

The Sexual Offences Act 2003 in England and Wales predates the widespread use of the Internet and the huge growth in the number of offenders trading child abuse images and abusing children online. The current offence of grooming within that act requires that an offender communicated with a child on one occasion and subsequently arranged to meet the child. However, nowadays the ultimate goal for many offenders is not necessarily to meet a child; the Internet give offenders new ways to exert control and influence over children without ever having to touch them, and they may live hundreds of miles away from the child. The end goal may now be to persuade the child to abuse himself or herself via webcam, for example. In 2012–2013 the police in England and Wales recorded 373 cases of grooming[11].

The Sexual Offences (Northern Ireland) Order 2008 exactly mirrors the legislation in England and Wales. In Scotland, the Sexual Offences (Scotland) Act 2009, having been passed several years after the law governing England and Wales, was more able to take into account the emerging influence of the Internet on offender behaviour. As a result, that act recognised that sexual communication may not always end in a face-to-face meeting and instead made it an offence to send or direct sexual communication to a child for the purpose of obtaining sexual gratification or humiliating, distressing or alarming the child. The Serious Crimes Act 2014, and accompanying legislation in Northern Ireland, subsequently introduced a similar law in England, Wales and Northern Ireland, and outlawed the possession of paedophile manuals.

EUROPEAN LEGISLATION

At the European level, legislation to combat the sexual abuse and sexual exploitation of children and child abuse images (Directive 2011/93/EU) was hailed as a landmark piece of legislation and one that would significantly improve the position of many children within the EU. It established EU-wide law in relation to indecent images of children and online grooming, specified minimum penalties for a range of offences, made it mandatory for every member state to introduce measures to ensure the prompt removal of web pages containing indecent images of children and if that removal was not possible, enabled discretionary blocking of some sites that hosted these images. The UK had very little to do to meet these requirements, but for some countries, it was a significant change.

The Budapest Convention and the Lanzarote Convention together aim to provide a comprehensive legal framework for protecting children against sexual abuse and exploitation, including online. The Budapest Convention on Cybercrime[12] and the 2007 Lanzarote Convention on the Protection of Children against Sexual Exploitation and Sexual Abuse[13] are conventions of the

Council of Europe. The United Kingdom is a signatory to both, though it has ratified only the former. A 2014 Department of Culture Media and Sport Select Committee inquiry report[14] recommended that the government press for wider international adoption of the Budapest and Lanzarote conventions and ratify the Lanzarote Convention as soon as practicable.

REMOVAL OF CHILD ABUSE CONTENT

'In 1996 the Metropolitan Police notified the Internet Service Providers Association (ISPA) that some newsgroup content being carried by UK Internet service providers (ISPs) contained indecent images of children. The police believed this may have constituted a publication offence under the Protection of Children Act 1978 by the ISPs. Efforts were then undertaken to find a way to combat the hosting of such content in the UK whilst protecting the Internet industry from being held criminally liable for providing access to such content'[15].

Subsequent discussions among the government, police and industry resulted in an agreement about who would be responsible for rating, reporting and removing indecent images of children from the internet – and a key outcome was the formation of the Internet Watch Foundation (IWF).

The IWF was established in 1996 and became an independent charity and public hotline in 2005. They receive public reports about online indecent images of children and then work with the police and the UK Internet industry to advise the latter about which images should be removed. Hosting companies agree to take down material that the IWF identifies as illegal. This is a voluntary arrangement, removal by these companies is not mandated in law, but in the main the model is an effective one, and 65% of all web pages hosting illegal content in the UK are removed with two hours[16], compared to much longer take-down times in other countries[17]. The voluntary model has been least effective in relation to the behaviour of internet-hosting companies. In 2016 there were 16 companies offering UK hosting space that had been used to host child abuse content, 3 of whom were IWF members. Of the 23 takedown notices for child abuse content in the UK, 20 notices were issued to 13 companies who were not IWF members, and who in turn took longer to remove content[18].

Until 2014, the IWF's remit had been limited to responding to reports about images made by the public and working on those leads to remove illegal content. From 2014, their remit was extended to, for the first time, proactively seeking out child abuse images and videos online. This new approach was funded by the UK's leading ISPs[19]. As a result the number of reports confirmed as child sexual abuse URLs rose from 13,182 in 2013 to 68,092 in 2015. This number looks set to increase further as the IWF, as well as Canada's Cybertip reporting hotline, are starting to deploy targeted web crawlers that allow their searches to be semi-automated.[20] Less than 1% of the material identified by the IWF is hosted in the UK and so effective cross-border co-operation is needed if the problem is to be adequately addressed.

At the time, there was also discussion about whether it would be appropriate for the IWF to have a role in proactively seeking out child abuse images on peer-to-peer networks as well as on the open web. At the IWF's Annual General Meeting in 2013, the charity was asked about any related plans. Lord Ken MacDonald QC, the former director of public prosecutions, having been commissioned by the IWF to undertake an audit of their compliance with human rights legislation, recommended that the IWF abandon any plans to investigate and disrupt the distribution of child abuse content over peer-to-peer networks. He argued that the investigation of peer-to-peer networks involves a degree of intrusion that, although appropriate in the context of a criminal investigation, is not an appropriate role for a private, non-policing body such as the IWF[21].

THE IWF'S INTERNATIONAL WORK

The IWF works on an international level, not just to ensure the removal of child abuse images hosted in other countries but also to build capacity in developing countries to develop reporting and take-down functions there.

The IWF is a leading member of INHOPE, the International Association of Internet Hotlines, a network of 51 hotlines in 45 countries worldwide, committed to stamping out child sexual abuse from the internet. Similar to the IWF, INHOPE hotlines offer the public a way of anonymously reporting internet material including indecent images of children. If an image is reported to the IWF that is hosted abroad, INHOPE is informed, or if there is no INHOPE hotline, the country's police are notified. INHOPE hotlines investigate and if the image is illegal according to their country's legislation the information is passed to the relevant policing body and in many cases the ISP hosting the content[22]. In 2016 the IWF made 55,891 reports of illegal content to INHOPE members. It has been argued that greater standardisation of the notice and take-down processes used by different hotlines worldwide is needed, alongside a global standard[23].

The IWF has also developed portals, which other countries without reporting mechanisms can implement. They enable people to report suspected online child sexual abuse images and videos for assessment by IWF analysts and are a cost-effective solution for countries without their own hotline, perhaps because they have low internet penetration or a low GDP. Mauritius was the first country to adopt the portal in 2013. In 2017 there are 16 portals in countries including India, Uganda, Bermuda and the British Virgin Islands.

The IWF has also worked with the International Telecommunication Union to build the capacity of developing countries to deal with internet child sexual abuse and exploitation. Most recently this involved commissioning the IWF to develop a countrywide assessment tool and to use this to assess the Republic of Uganda's provision to deal with child abuse images, leading to the launch of the aforementioned reporting portal. They are also active members of the Commonwealth Cybercrime Initiative and have helped countries such as Kenya and Trinidad and Tobago assess their capacity and capability to remove illegal content.

PUBLIC PERCEPTION

Research from the IWF in 2013[24] found that the vast majority of people in Britain think that child sexual abuse content (91%) and computer-generated images or cartoons of child sexual abuse (85%) should be removed from the Internet.

Child sexual abuse content was the top online concern: more people were concerned (83%) about websites showing the sexual abuse of children than other types of illegal, illicit or harmful material, such as terrorist, suicide, hate and violent pornography websites.

The research estimated that 1.5 million adults have stumbled across child abuse images while browsing online. The equivalent of 500,000 people, 4% of men and 2% of women, report having actually come into contact with it or stumbled across it. However, in 2012 just 40,000 reports about images were made to the IWF. Their survey showed that about 40% of Britons would not know how to report child abuse images if they encountered them. Of men 16% said they would just ignore them. This points to the need to improve the public's knowledge, and in particular the knowledge and willingness of certain demographics, of how to report child abuse content online and the necessity of doing so, no matter what the circumstances, for example, if a user is embarrassed at having come across it whilst watching legal adult pornography.

MULTI-AGENCY APPROACHES

The UK government recognised early on that a multi-agency approach would be necessary to protect children from online abuse and that the inclusion of the Internet industry would be vital.

INTERNET CRIME FORUM

The Internet Crime Forum was a joint police, Department of Trade and Industry and Internet industry body that was established to develop the relationship among the Internet industry, government and law enforcement in order to tackle internet crime and improve confidence in Internet use. In 1999 it formed a sub-group to look at child safety issues and produced a report, 'ChatWise, Street Wise'[25]. This made several recommendations for protecting children on the internet, including improved supervision of chat rooms and better display of safety messages. The report led to the formation of the Home Office Taskforce on Online Child Protection.

HOME OFFICE TASKFORCE ON CHILD PROTECTION ON THE INTERNET

In 2001 the then–home secretary, Jack Straw, established a Taskforce on Child Protection on the Internet to consider what could be done to tackle the serious child protection issues that were emerging with the increasing popularity of the Internet and in particular the potential risk of paedophiles contacting children though chat rooms and other online communications[26]. It was formed in response to concerns about the possible risk to children after a number of serious cases in which children had been groomed via the Internet and was a collaboration among the Internet industry, government departments and the main opposition parties, law enforcement and children's charities. Their aim was to make the UK 'the best and safest place in the world for children to use the Internet'[27]. It produced a number of good practice guidance documents for industry, proposed a new law to combat grooming as part of the Sexual Offences Act 2003[28] and laid the groundwork for the establishment of the CEOP by advocating the need for 'a central "clearing house," of police, child protection and internet experts that would provide co-ordinated and effective responses to concerns from the public and industry involved in providing inter-net services in the UK about online child protection, whether seeking advice or reporting suspicions or crimes'[29].

BYRON REVIEW

The *Byron Review*[30] was ordered in 2007 by then–prime minister Gordon Brown and published in March the next year. It focussed on children's use of video games and the Internet, but illegal material such as child abuse images were outside the scope of its review[31].

Byron noted that the original focus of the Home Office Taskforce had been the development of a joined-up approach to illegal child protection issues, such as online grooming and child abuse images. Nevertheless she did not recom-mend separating child protection issues online from the rest of the govern-ment's strategy for child internet safety, arguing that there was an inevitable overlap between work to address illegal activity and work to address online activity that was potentially harmful and inappropriate, though not necessarily illegal. A key recommendation of her review was the transformation of the Home Office Taskforce into a UK Council for Children's Internet Safety with responsibility for leading all child safety online strategy across government[32].

Byron's recommendation was echoed by a report from the Culture, Media and Sport Select Committee a few months later[33], which had a clear expectation that much of the council's effort would focus on child protection[34].

UK COUNCIL FOR CHILD INTERNET SAFETY

The UK Council for Child Internet Safety (UKCCIS) was subsequently established in 2008 and is supported by more than 200 organisations from a range of sectors and ministers from the departments for Education; Culture, Media and Sport; Children and Families; and the Home Office chairs its executive board jointly. Board members include the Internet Watch Foundation, children's and parents' organisations, regulators such as Ofcom and the British Board of Film Classification, CEOP and major businesses such as BT, BSkyB, Tesco and TalkTalk. It drew on the best emerging research, convening an evidence group initially chaired by professor Sonia Livingstone from the London School of Economics and Political Science, author of the pioneering EU Kids Online study[35].

However, its work has not led on all aspects of the government's work in relation to child internet safety as Byron recommended. Instead its focus has been on tackling inappropriate as opposed to illegal content, with key outcomes being initiatives such as the introduction of parental controls by internet service providers and the delivery of public awareness and education campaigns for parents and children. Arguably, a multi-stakeholder group with an independent chair to provide strategic leadership on tackling illegal child abuse activity online is still needed, along with an action plan and annual review of the UK's strategy for dealing with internet child sexual abuse.

THE ROLE OF NGOS

In 1999 the Children's Charities' Coalition on Internet Safety (CHIS) was founded in order to give a specific and ongoing focus to the work of charities in relation to online child sexual abuse. Most of UK's major children's charities are members, though some charities have been refused membership because they are not considered independent enough of the internet industry.

Meanwhile, the European NGO Alliance for Child Safety Online (eNACSO) is a European Union–funded project currently chaired by Save the Children Italy. eNACSO has members drawn from 19 EU member states and has associate members drawn from countries outside the EU (see www.enacso.eu). In many ways eNACSO replicates at a European level what CHIS does at a UK level.

Broadly speaking, NGOs based in the UK have been most active in delivering education and awareness campaigns about staying safe online, including linking to international initiatives such as the EU-part funded annual Safer Internet Day.

POLICING RESPONSE

OPERATIONS CATHEDRAL AND ORE

Operation Cathedral was a police operation led by the UK policing agency, the National Crime Squad, in co-operation with 12 other police forces around the world and in response to intelligence originally gained from police in the United States. It broke up an international ring called The WØnderland [sic] Club, which traded child abuse images over the Internet. In a coordinated sting, 104 suspects across 12 countries were arrested on September 1, 1998. Seven UK-based men were convicted for their part in the ring. The operation was significant because never before had such large collections of images been discovered: over 750,000 images and over 1,800 hours of digitised videos were seized.

The following year, Operation Ore began, again in reaction to information received from US law enforcement agencies. It became the UK's biggest and most controversial operation into child abuse images online, and more than 7,000 people were investigated. It led to almost 1,500 convictions and an esti- mated 39 suicides[36]. The validity of the police procedures and veracity of credit card payment information was questioned, and although there have been cases of the police being sued for malicious arrest[37], in 2010 the Court of Appeal refused a potentially landmark challenge on the safety of the convictions.

The majority of offenders had no previous convictions, and so it has been argued that Operation Ore was significant in making the UK public recognise that vast numbers of those who looked at child abuse images were not stereotypical oddball outsiders but in many cases where outwardly respectable, ordinary-looking men with families, jobs and friends. It also helped to change the public perception of child abuse images from being 'just a photograph' to an understanding that they involved a child being exploited and abused.

In the wake of these early operations, there was also recognition by the UK government and policing agencies that more proactive strategies were needed to identify offenders. The need to tailor sex offender management strategies for offenders who used the internet to obtain or create indecent images was also recognised. At that stage the options available included prohibiting own- ership or access to computers[38], neither of which ever came to pass.

NATIONAL POLICING: CEOP

The scale of the particular problem of internet child sexual abuse was recog- nised by the UK government in 2006, with the establishment of the specialist policing agency, the CEOP, although it was admitted later, 'at that point it was not clear what the challenges in providing online protection would be, and how these issues would be addressed by law enforcement'[39]. In 2008–2009 CEOP received 5,686 reports of online grooming and child sexual abuse images; by 2015 this had risen to 22,606, of which 19,788 were from industry. From the start CEOP adopted a partnership approach, including partnerships with Visa, Microsoft and the NSPCC, who seconded six child protection staff members to work there from the outset. Soon they began to work internationally, and in 2015 supported over 30 countries to build their capacity and capability to combat child sexual exploitation and abuse.

A REVIEW OF THE PROTECTION OF CHILDREN FROM SEX OFFENDERS 2007

A year after the establishment of CEOP, a government policy document, *A Review of the Protection of Children from Sex Offenders*[40], acknowledged that solutions needed to keep pace with technological developments. Proposals included changing the law to require all registered sex offenders to notify the police of any email addresses and developing the capability to monitor the online activities of child sex offenders. Other plans included trialing the use of mandatory polygraph tests, reviewing the use of satellite tagging and improving the use of the Violent and Sex Offender Register.

However, in 2010, it was reported that plans to require notification of email addresses had been put on hold, linked to human rights concerns[41]. The practicality and likely efficacy of the proposal had also come under fire[42], the increased availability of free email accounts in the intervening years having rendered the proposal unworkable.

LOCAL POLICING

High Tech Crime Units have existed in most local forces for some years[43] but there remains a great deal of variation in the capacity and capability of local forces to deal with internet child sexual abuse. Some agencies have called for a greater focus on tackling child abuse images at a local level from police and crime commissioners and in police and crime plans[44]. In 2013 the Director of CEOP was unable to say 'exactly how much capacity is invested in this across those 42 forces, the extent to which it looks similar and the extent that it can be interoperable'[45].

In July 2015 Her Majesty's Inspectorate of Constabulary (HMIC) published the results of an inspection into how forces deal with online child sexual exploitation. It found that just 55% of the cases they looked at involved good or adequate investigations, and they concluded that 'forces need to better understand the nature and potential scale of this type of offending to ensure that more is done to protect children from harm, and bring perpetrators to justice'[46].

CEOP AND INTERNATIONAL POLICING

The G8

In 2002, the G8 developed a strategy for protecting children from sexual exploitation on the internet[47]. A key outcome was the development of the Virtual Global Taskforce, an international alliance of law enforcement agencies working together to prevent and deter online child abuse, and championed in the UK by CEOP. Established in 2003, its members are predominantly police forces from developed countries[48], causing some commentators to ask if we are 'witnessing the development of an elite club of a comparatively small number of national police forces from the industrialised economies . . . To the extent that hitherto, the elite "club" consisted of countries with higher levels of internet penetration and usage, and were the same countries where most of the perpetrators lived, perhaps its emergence was understandable, even desirable. However as usage levels in the rest of the world start to mirror those in the already industrialised economies, it is of utmost importance that the current divide is rapidly narrowed'[49].

Another outcome from the G8's strategy in which CEOP played a key role was the 2010 establishment of a 'most wanted' website for suspected child sex offenders across G8 countries[50], intended to engage the public's help in looking for offenders and gaining intelligence. The site (http://www.usmarshals.gov/investigations/g8/) was initiated under the UK presidency of the G8 in 2007 and taken forward by CEOP in co-operation with Interpol[51]. It built on the success of CEOP's existing 'most wanted' site.

Another part of the G8 strategy was the creation of an international child abuse image database[52]. Hosted by Interpol and funded by the European Commission, the International Child Sexual Exploitation Image Database was eventually launched in 2009 as the successor to the Interpol Child Abuse Image Database that had been in use since 2001[53]. A next-generation database was launched in 2016 and includes video analysis tools. The UK is not a partner in the development of this project, but it is essential that the UK's new national child abuse image database[54], to which all UK forces were connected by November 2015, is fully compatible with it.

EUROPEAN CYBERCRIME CENTRE

The European Cybercrime Centre (EC3) was established within Europol in January 2013 in order to strengthen the law enforcement response to cybercrime in the EU[55]. The EU has commenced the European Multidisciplinary Platform Against Crime Threats (EMPACT) to react to the serious and organised crime threat across Europe. One of its three focus areas is crime that causes serious harm to victims, such as child sexual exploitation. Within the 2014–2017 programme, support was provided for a number of large child sexual exploitation police operations affecting the EU. This includes providing coordination, analytic and operational support to investigations of child abuse material across the internet. Other operations will seek to address cases of sexual blackmail of children and transnational child sex offenders who travel beyond the EU. UK police from the NCA's CEOP Command are involved in the delivery of this three-year programme of work.

GLOBAL ALLIANCE AGAINST CHILD SEXUAL ABUSE ONLINE

In December 2012 the European Commission and US Attorney General launched The Global Alliance Against Child Sexual Abuse Online. The countries of the alliance (27 EU countries at the launch plus 21 others) aim for international co-operation to fight child sexual abuse online. Participating countries committed to four key policy targets: victim identification and treatment, identification and prosecution of offenders, increased awareness of the issue and reduction of the availability of child abuse images online[56].

INTERNATIONAL CERTIFICATE FOR THE PROTECTION OF CHILDREN

In 2012 CEOP launched the International Certificate for the Protection of Children (ICPC)[57]. The aim was to better protect children from convicted UK child sex offenders who are seeking employment abroad that would bring them into close contact with children. The process is a criminal records check against police and intelligence databases in the UK that would reveal any convictions or reasons as to why someone should not work with children, similar to the Disclosure and Barring Service check that is required for anyone working professionally with children in England and Wales. To date, 26,708 applications have been received from 1862 organisations in 88 countries. CEOP claim that the ICPC is proving to be a deterrent because the number of applicants with a criminal history is small[58].

This is a welcome and innovative step to protect children overseas from UK sex offenders. However when just 19 countries in the world have a sex offender register and only 7 of these inform other countries if a registered sex offender travels into their territory[59], a global sex offender register would represent a more coordinated approach.

OFFENDERS

IDENTIFICATION

The identification of child sex offenders has always been difficult because their activities take place behind closed doors and because of the power dynamics involved in any sexually abusive relationship. In a way, the internet, and the ability to trace the IP addresses of those accessing images on the open web, could be seen to have given us a means by which some offenders can start to be identified. Whilst the relationship between contact and non-contact offending is a highly contested area, an appropriately precautionary approach would dictate that anyone accessing child sexual abuse images might be a potential risk to children and so should be risk assessed. Offenders accessing images on Peer2Peer networks and the 'dark' or 'hidden' web are harder to identify.

Whilst police undoubtedly use covert intelligence-gathering techniques to identify offenders, they do not encourage its use by others, for fear of jeopardising ongoing policing operations or in case it made it more difficult to secure a conviction in court. In the UK, vigilante groups such as Letzgo Hunting have posed as children online, arranged to meet those who contacted them, filmed the encounter, posted it on social media and passed it to the police. A children's rights group in the Netherlands, Terres des Hommes, took this approach even further in 2013 when they created a computer-generated persona, a 10-year-old Filipino girl called 'Sweetie', to highlight the issue of what they called 'webcam child sex tourism'. During a 10-week operation, they said that over 20,000 predators approached Sweetie to ask for webcam sex performances. Researchers used social media to gather information as to the identity of 1,000 abusers from 71 countries and handed their details to Interpol.

PROSECUTION

In 2011, a total of 2,312 people were arrested in England and Wales for taking, possessing or distributing indecent child images[60]. As understanding about the scale of the threat grew, arrest and prosecution rates came under understandable criticism. A select committee inquiry commented that

> 'there is a clear need to ensure that the police have adequate resources to track down and arrest online paedophiles in sufficient numbers to act as a meaningful deterrent to others. If necessary, additional funding should be provided to recruit and train a sufficiently large number of police officers adequate to the task'[61]. UK police developed new strategies with a focus on targeted, proactive operations coordinated with the National Crime Agency and the numbers of offenders arrested, and crucially of victims identified, began to rise.

SENTENCING

In 2002 the Sentencing Advisory Panel produced guidelines on the sentencing of offences involving indecent images of children. The guidelines used a modified version of the 10-point scale developed by staff at the COPINE (Combating Paedophile Information Networks in Europe) project in Ireland, but they reduced that rating system to five stages.

In 2012 the Sentencing Council for England and Wales published new guidelines about sexual offences and took into account the increased use of technology in offending[62]. The sentencing guidelines for some crimes, such as for sexual activity with a child, were adapted to cover offending committed remotely such as via webcam, and judges had to take into account offenders lying about their age, grooming via social media or asking children to share indecent photos of themselves. Filming and photographing victims, known as 'recording the crime', were listed as a new aggravating factor and the encryption of imagery increased sentence length. For child sexual abuse image offences, judges were to determine the offence category based on a three-point classification of images: images involving penetration, images of non-penetrative sexual activity and other indecent images.

RISK ASSESSMENT

The ability to accurately risk assess offenders and understand patterns of offending in order to inform the treatment and management of offenders is a crucial area of developing sex offender research. An officer from Kent Police Service developed the Kent Internet Risk Assessment Tool (KIRAT), which measures the risk of those who have downloaded child abuse images then going on to contact offend. It is now widely used across forces in England and Wales. In 2012 the European Commission provided funding under the Fighting International Internet Paedophilia (FIIP) project to develop the tool further, specifically exploring cultural specificity across partner countries and, dependent on findings, producing a bespoke European KIRAT tool for each partner country or a European-wide tool[63].

TREATMENT

In 2006, a specially designed Internet Sex Offender Treatment Programme (the i-SOTP) was accredited for use in the community by the National Probation Service[64]. It is a group work programme aimed at those assessed as having low- or medium-level deviancy. It is not yet known how widely it is available, how many offenders have received the programme or what the recidivism rates are of those who have.

The Lucy Faithfull Foundation is a charity that works with people who have sexually harmed or fear they may harm a child, including those who commit offences on the internet. Since 2002 they have offered a support helpline, the Stop It Now! Helpline, and programme called 'Inform Plus,' a group work course for anyone who has been arrested, cautioned or convicted for internet offences involving indecent images of children. The organisation also runs the 'Inform' programme, a course for partners, relatives and friends of anyone who has been accessing indecent images of children online. It offers a safe space for these people to explore their questions and anxieties in a supportive environment.

Offender support programmes were subsequently developed in other countries, perhaps the most widely known being the launch of Project Dunkelfeld in Germany in 2005.

MANAGEMENT

In England and Wales local criminal justice agencies must work in partnership to make arrangements to assess and manage the risk posed by sexual and violent offenders in their area. These arrangements are known as MAPPA (multi-agency public protection arrangements). Offenders who are living in the community post-conviction may be subject to a range of measures designed to manage their activities and behaviour and prevent re-offending. In the case of internet child sex offenders, specific conditions may be attached in an attempt to manage their use of the internet and computers.

The management of online offenders by imposing conditions to prevent them owning computers or accessing the Internet[65] was viewed as unworkable. In the case of *Regina v. Smith*[66] the Court of Appeal judge commented:

> 'A blanket prohibition on computer use or Internet access is impermissible. It is disproportionate because it restricts the defendant in the use of what is nowadays an essential part of everyday living for a large proportion of the public, as well as a requirement of much employment.'

In 2012, the Court of Appeal court overturned the terms of a Sexual Offences Prevention Order (SOPO), which sought to prohibit the offender from owning or having in his home any device that could access the internet as excessive, saying that it was now unreasonable to stop anyone from having access to the internet in his or her home[67]. Commentators said that the ruling effectively renders access to the internet a human right and denial of access a breach of an offender's right to a private and family life under Article 8 of the European Convention on Human Rights, enshrined in British law as the Human Rights Act 1998[68].

Increasingly, innovative technology is being used as part of the package of measures designed to manage those convicted of child sexual abuse image offences. Software can remotely monitor the offender's use of known mobile phones and computers, and field forensic software can help police quickly ascertain if illegal material has been accessed while undertaking notification visits to the offender's home.

VICTIMS

A key issue in protecting children who have been sexually abused in order to produce indecent images of children is the difficulty in identifying them. Only a relatively small number of children have been successfully identified from these images and therefore protected. In 2009, for example, the INTERPOL Child Abuse Image Database contained more than 550,000 images; from this database, just 870 children were identified and rescued[69]. In 2011–2012, 427 children were subject to safeguarding or child protection as a result of CEOP activity[70].

Added to this, there is a relative lack of understanding and evidence about the impact of this type of abuse and how having the sexual abuse recorded and distributed online may exacerbate the victim's suffering. In the UK, the NSPCC and CEOP are attempting to address this gap and have commissioned research by the University of Birmingham to report on the impact of online abuse, due for publication in mid 2017.

A further obstacle is a lack of understanding and professional expertise of those working with children, in particular social workers. Confidence in their ability to deal with sexual abuse when there is an online aspect is low. A lack of training and information for child protection workers on this topic was identified over a decade ago[71] and the situation has not greatly improved since. In a survey conducted by the British Association of Social Workers for the NSPCC, 50% of the respondents said they didn't know how to recognise the signs of the online sexual abuse of children, and the majority felt they needed more support[72]. Research by the Marie Collins Foundation found that an underpinning issue was training.

'In the UK and internationally the response to the needs of children and their families is, at best, ad hoc. Professionals lack confidence in assisting children in their recovery and it is apparent that this is due to a lack of adequate training. Currently, many professionals are attempting to deal with cases for which they are not equipped'[73].

The statutory guidance covering England – *Working Together to Safeguard Children 2013*[74] – recognises that children may be abused via the Internet but gives practitioners no detail about how to identify or respond to this type of abuse.

As well as a lack of professional development and specialist training for professionals, there is a lack of therapeutic treatment that is specially tailored to the needs of victims whose abuse has included an online dimension.

Finally, there is emerging evidence from ChildLine that a small number of children are experiencing harm as a result of having stumbled across indecent images of children when using the internet. One child reported the following:

> 'I'm disgusted with myself because I've been looking at child abuse images for pleasure. I know it's bad so I'm really embarrassed that I do it but I can't help it. I've been sending some images around a group I'm part of which I'm now starting to regret. I'm worried the police will find out and I'll get in trouble. I've deleted a lot of the material because I feel so anxious and ashamed of myself. I can't talk to anyone about what I've done because I know what they'll think of me'. (Boy, 12–15)

It is too early to say whether or not this access is because of changing patterns in how child abuse images are shared on the open web, but in 2013 the IWF reported an increase in the number of child abuse images hosted on social networking sites and commented 'one image on a high traffic service (such as a social media site) could be seen by thousands of users'[75]. Education initiatives for children, parents and professional such as Thinkuknow (www.thinkuknow.com), Internet Matters (www.internetmatters.org) and Safer Internet Day (www.saferinternet.org) have so far not provided much information about child abuse images, but this will be an area to consider in the future if greater numbers of children begin to report exposure to them.

RECENT DEVELOPMENTS

CEOP played a key role in bringing the issue of internet child sexual abuse to the fore of the public consciousness. Their 2012 threat assessment, *A Picture of Abuse,* quoted a meta-analysis of research looking at prevalence rates of contact sexual offending within different child abuse image offender samples, which established a correlation of 55%[76]. Freedom of information requests by agitating charities[77] led commentators to estimate that the number of child abuse images in existence in the UK could be as many as 360 million[78]. In May 2013 the chief executive officer of CEOP admitted that the police did not have enough capacity to arrest all the people they know are downloading images[79] and the next month CEOP's annual threat assessment stated that there were an estimated 50,000 individuals involved in downloading and sharing child abuse images in the UK[80]. The stage was set for some high-profile government intervention.

In the words of the IWF, 2013 was 'a rollercoaster year' for the child protection online community. The murders of Tia Sharpe and April Jones, and subsequent convictions of Mark Bridger and Stuart Hazell, both of whom had downloaded extensive collections of child abuse images and videos from the internet, generated a wave of public attention that was to have global consequences.

In summer 2013 Prime Minister David Cameron gave a major policy speech[81] in which he set out a package of measures to tackle the problem of indecent images of children. The policy initiatives outlined recognised that this type of child abuse involves commercial companies in a way that no other form of child abuse does, and so the role of industry was emphasised, in particular the internet service providers and the search engines. The following initiatives were announced:

1. The use of 'splash' pages. Those attempting to access URLs that have already been blocked by the IWF because they contain child abuse images would instead receive a warning screen giving them a message to desist. The screen would direct them to Stop It Now, a charity that supports adults with an interest in child abuse images to change their behaviour. A six-month pilot, coordinated by the IWF and involving the UK's largest internet service providers and mobile operators, began in autumn 2013[82].
2. Ongoing work with search engines to deter would-be offenders (no details would be provided).
3. The creation of a National Database of Illegal Images in order to reduce duplication by police forces and to 'enable the industry to use digital hash tags from the database to proactively scan for, block and take down those images wherever they occur.'
4. The creation of a new UK-US taskforce intended to stimulate innovative solutions within the Internet industry in order to put an end to internet child sexual abuse.
5. A challenge to search engines. The government's starting point was that there are some search terms that are so offensive that anyone who searches for them should not be able to find any related material. Recognising that this was technically difficult, he issued a challenge to search engines to fix this problem, stating that 'the search engines are not doing enough to take responsibility. Indeed, in this specific area, they are effectively denying responsibility.' He refused to accept that no term should be blocked because of potential freedom-of-speech arguments and threatened that the government was prepared to use legislation to make this happen if necessary.

It was this last initiative that caused the most debate at the time. Detractors argued that sex offenders don't use search engines on the 'open' Internet[83] and that the bigger problem was offenders accessing images on peer-to-peer websites and the so-called dark or hidden internet. Rebuttals cited the number of reports received by the IWF about images on the open web (at that point 13,343 images reported in 2013) and research by that organisation and the Lucy Faithfull Foundation, which demonstrated that keyword searching via search engines is still a commonly used method for those seeking child sexual abuse images and videos online[84]. The possible deterrent effect was also cited, particularly in preventing initial queries from those 'curious' users searching for images for the first time. Some took a pragmatic approach and saw the eradication of child abuse images from the open internet as an important intermediate goal[85].

Later in 2013, a follow-up summit was held[86]. The government said that Google and Microsoft had initially argued that 'it was against the very principle of the Internet and search engines to block material even if there was no doubt that some of the search terms being used by paedophiles were abhorrent in a modern society,' but nevertheless they had put in place a series of ground-breaking measures, to be rolled out globally, providing only 'clean' results in response to dubious search terms. It was confirmed by the director general of the National Crime Agency that initial tests showed that the changes introduced by the search engines were working. Later research found that 'the blocking efforts by Google and Microsoft have resulted in a 67% drop in the past year in web-based searches for child sexual exploitation material'[87].

The measures agreed at the second summit included the following:

- The introduction of new algorithms that would block child abuse images, videos and pathways that lead to illegal content, covering 100,000 unique searches on Google worldwide; these search changes were to be rolled out in 159 languages.
- Microsoft (Bing and Yahoo! search engines) prevented all child abuse images, videos and pathways to them from being accessed via a blacklist of terms supplied by the National Crime Agency, and they were working on an expansion of this approach to block all child abuse content against a much wider list of search terms.
- Stopping auto-complete features from offering people child abuse–related search terms.
- A plan to tackle peer-to-peer networks featuring child abuse images.
- Google developed new technology to put a unique identification mark on illegal child abuse videos, enabling all copies to be removed from the web once a single copy is identified. This was a logical extension of the work Microsoft had already done on their Photo DNA product to create a way of identifying still child abuse images.
- Joint work among Google, Microsoft, the IWF and CEOP to tackle the problem of peer-to-peer networks, intended to establish a new reporting process to remove pathways to child sexual abuse images[88].
- The joint UK-US taskforce should include a specific, in-depth programme of work on how to tackle offenders using the 'hidden Internet' to view and share child abuse images.
- The UK would host an international summit to bring together all relevant stakeholders to agree to international follow-up to the agreements reached.

That summit would include a specific focus on protecting the victims of online child abuse and how to work internationally to prevent children being exploited online. That summit became known as WePROTECT 2014.

Alongside this industry-focussed activity, the government made it clear that they would not hesitate to legislate when appropriate and committed to giving 'CEOP and the police all the powers they need to keep pace with the changing nature of the Internet.' New legislation ranged from closing loopholes to emergency legislation.

Meanwhile there was cross-party agreement on the need for emergency legislation giving the security services access to people's phone and internet records. The Data Retention and Investigatory Powers Bill completed its passage through the House of Commons in just one day in July 2014, despite opposition from civil liberties campaigners. The government argued that the powers within the legislation were 'particularly important for targeting serious criminals, including drug dealers, paedophiles and fraudsters'[89]. The bill was later found to be unlawful by the High Court, who ruled that it was inconsistent with European Union Law. A subsequent Investigatory Powers Bill became law in December 2016 the government again arguing during its passage through Parliament that it was necessary in order to tackle child sexual exploitation[90].

The adequacy of police capacity to deal with internet child sexual abuse came into sharp focus in 2014. The report of an inquiry by the Department of Culture Media and Sport Select Committee[91] recommended that the government should examine whether adequate resources are being deployed to track down online paedophiles in sufficient numbers to act as a meaningful deterrent to others. If not, they recommended that additional funding should be provided to recruit and train a sufficiently large number of police officers adequate to the task.

Later in 2014, Operation Notarise[92], a six-month operation coordinated by the NCA and involving police forces across England, Wales, Scotland and Northern Ireland, led to the arrest of 660 suspected child sex offenders. Despite the success of the operation, the Shadow Home Secretary wrote to the Home Secretary[93] highlighting concerns that over 10,000 suspects had been identified by Operation Notarise but that the police lacked the capacity to pursue these suspects. NCA Deputy Director General Phil Gormley admitted, 'we are not going to simply arrest our way out of this problem'[94].

At the end of 2014 the UK government further cemented its reputation as being at the fore of tackling this issue when it hosted the global WePROTECT summit about online child sexual exploitation, at which key members from more than 50 countries and the world's leading technology and innovation companies convened. The summit sought commitments on: action to identify and protect victims, action to remove child sexual abuse material from the internet, strengthened co-operation across the world to track down perpetrators, and the building of global capacity. The UK government made the following commitments:

- A new joint team between the National Crime Agency (NCA) and the Government Communications Headquarters (GCHQ) deploying all the techniques and expertise used to track down terrorists to track down paedophiles on the 'darknet.'
- An extra £10 million to create further specialist online child sexual abuse teams within the NCA.
- The establishment of a single secure database of indecent images of children – the Child Abuse Image Database (CAID) – to help UK law enforcement improve and speed up investigations. This went live the same month, and a year later all forces in the UK were connected to it, and victims were being identified[95].
- A £50 million pledge over five years contributing to a newly established global child protection fund to be administered by UNICEF.
- A new UK law making it illegal for an adult to send a sexual communication to a child.

A further summit was held in Abu Dhabi a year later, bringing together governments, policing, NGOs, industry and civil society organisations to pledge global action to eliminate online child sexual exploitation. A range of commitments was made by key industry players including Google, Facebook, Yahoo, Microsoft.

It was also announced that the Global Alliance Against Child Sexual Abuse Online (led by the U.S. Department of Justice and the EU Commission), and the WePROTECT initiative (brought together by the UK) would be merged, marking 'a turning point in the international response to this crime.'[96] The vision of this new initiative is an ambitious one – more victims identified and safeguarded, more perpetrators apprehended, an end to online child sexual exploitation – that can only be delivered by a truly collaborative and global approach.

CONCLUSION

The UK's public policy response to internet child sexual abuse has been progressive, but in a very fast-moving area it is difficult to stay ahead of the challenges. Education of children and young people and their parents and carers will always be necessary, but it must be accompanied by innovative public policy responses, law enforcement tactics and technological innovations that are able to rise to the scale and complexity of the challenge. The dark web and live streaming capabilities pose a major challenge to law enforcement, and given that in 2014 the Minister for Policing, Criminal Justice and Victims said that the government did not have technological expertise necessary to tackle the problem[97], industry and technology leaders certainly have a key role to play. A global coalition of the willing has so far yielded impressive results through partnership and collaboration and the UK has positioned itself, through initiatives such as WePROTECT, as both willing and able to play a leadership role on the international stage. Capacity building to support child protection concerns will be crucial as 4G technology moves into so-far unconnected parts of the world; otherwise, the problem of internet child sexual abuse may well get worse before it gets better.

NOTES

1 Child Exploitation and Online Protection Centre. (2013). *Threat assessment of child sexual exploitation and abuse*. London, UK: Author. Retrieved August 28, 2013, from http://ceop.police.uk/Documents/ceopdocs/CEOP_TACSEA2013_240613%20FINAL.pdf

2 Department for Education. (2011). *Tackling child sexual exploitation: Action plan* [PDF]. London, UK: Author.

3 Barnardo's. (2012). *Cutting them free: How is the UK progressing in protecting its children from sexual exploitation* [PDF]. London, UK: Author.

4 https://www.nspcc.org.uk/globalassets/documents/research-reports/how-safe-children-2014-report.pdf

5 NSPCC. (2012). *Call for urgent action to stamp out trade of child abuse images, 15 October 2012*. Retrieved July 23, 2013, from https://www.facebook.com/nspcc/posts/374002519343712

6 Davidson, J., Quayle, E., Morgenbesser, L., & Brown, S. (2010). Editorial to a special edition about child sexual abuse and the internet: Offenders, victims and managing the risk. *Journal of Sexual Aggression, 16*(2).

7 Cooper, A. (1998). Sexuality and the internet: Surfing into the new millennium. *CyberPsychology and Behavior, 1*(2), 187–193.

8 Middleton, D., Mandeville-Norden, R., & Hayes, E. (2009). Does treatment work with internet sex offenders? Emerging findings from the Internet Sex Offender Treatment Programme (i-SOTP). *Journal of Sexual Aggression, 15*(1), 5–19.

9 ACPO. (2011). *ACPO CPAI lead's position on young people who post self-taken indecent images*. London, UK: CEOP. Retrieved from http://ceop.police.uk/Documents/ceopdocs/externaldocs/ACPO_Lead_position_on_Self_Taken_Images.pdf

10 http://www.iwf.org.uk/about-iwf/news/post/334-young-people-are-warned-they-may-lose-control-over-their-images-and-videos-once-they-are-uploaded-online

11 http://www.nspcc.org.uk/Inform/resourcesforprofessionals/sexualabuse/statistics_wda87833.html

12 http://conventions.coe.int/Treaty/Commun/Cher_cheSig.asp?NT=185&CM=8&DF=&CL=ENG

13 http://conventions.coe.int/Treaty/Commun/Cher_cheSig.asp?NT=201&CM=1&DF=&CL=ENG

14 https://www.publications.parliament.uk/pa/cm201314/cmselect/cmcumeds/729/729.pdf
15 https://www.iwf.org.uk/about-iwf/iwf-history
16 https://www.iwf.org.uk/what-we-do/who-we-are/annual-reports
17 For example, outside Europe and North America, after 10 days just 50% of child abuse image URLs have been removed. See p. 12 of the following: https://www.iwf.org.uk/report/2014-annual-report
18 https://www.iwf.org.uk/what-we-do/who-we-are/annual-reports
19 https://www.gov.uk/government/news/tackling-illegal-images-new-proactive-approach-to-seek-out-child-sexual-abuse-content
20 https://www.cybertip.ca/app/en/media_release_201701_project_arachnid and http://www.wired.co.uk/article/child-sexual-abuse-removed-internet-iwf
21 https://publicaffairs.linx.net/news/?p=10195
22 http://www.inhope.org/gns/who-we-are/at-a-glance.aspx
23 Wei, W. (2011). *Online child sexual abuse content: The development of a comprehensive, transferable international internet notice and takedown system.* The Nominet Trust and the Internet Watch Foundation. Retrieved from https://www.iwf.org.uk/resources/independent-report-on-international-notice-and-takedown-system
24 https://www.iwf.org.uk/news/new-study-reveals-child-sexual-abuse-content-as-top-online-concern-and-potentially-1-5m-adults
25 www.Internetcrimeforum.org.uk/chatwise_streetwise.html
26 Home Office Taskforce on Child Protection on the Internet. (2003). *Good practice models and guidance for industry on chat services, instant messaging and web-based services.* Retrieved July 29, 2014, from http://webarchive.nationalarchives.gov.uk/+/http://www.homeoffice.gov.uk/documents/ho_model.pdf?view=Binary
27 http://webarchive.nationalarchives.gov.uk/20100413151426/police.homeoffice.gov.uk/operational-policing/crime-disorder/child-protection-taskforce.html
28 Hansard, 28 Nov. 2002, Column 426W. Retrieved from http://www.publications.parliament.uk/pa/cm200203/cmhansrd/vo021128/text/21128w15.htm
29 Home Office press release from July 31, 2001. Retrieved July 29, 2014, from http://www.wired-gov.net/wg/wg-news-1.nsf/54e6de9e0c383719802572b9005141ed/ad7bd3b963f26f16802572ab004b451c?OpenDocument
30 Byron, T. (2008). *Safer children in a digital world.* Retrieved from http://dera.ioe.ac.uk/7332/1/Final%20Report%20Bookmarked.pdf
31 Ibid., p. 51.
32 Ibid., p. 70, paras 3.122 and 3.125.
33 http://www.parliament.the-stationery-office.co.uk/pa/cm200708/cmselect/cmcumeds/353/353.pdf
34 Byron, op cit., p. 66, recommendation 5.
35 EUKidsOnline.http://www.lse.ac.uk/media@lse/research/EUKidsOnline/Home.aspx
36 http://www.theguardian.com/uk/2009/jul/02/web-child-abuse-inquiry-challenge
37 http://www.bbc.co.uk/news/magazine-20237564
38 National Probation Service for England and Wales. (2004). *Sex offender strategy for the National Probation Service.* Retrieved August 25, 2013, from http://217.35.77.12/archive/england/papers/justice/pdfs/Sex%20Offender%20Strategy%20Sep%2004.pdf

39   Child Exploitation and Online Protection Centre. (2010). *The way forward*. London, UK: Home Office. Retrieved from https://www.gov.uk/government/uploads/system/uploads/attachment_data/file/228968/7785.pdf

40   Home Office. (2007). *Review of the protection of children from sex offenders*. London: Author. Retrieved July 25, 2013, from http://webarchive.nationalarchives.gov.uk/20100413151441/http://www.homeoffice.gov.uk/documents/CSOR/chid-sex-offender-review-1306072835.pdf?view=Binary

41   Beckford, M., & Stokes, P. (2010). Human rights laws stopped Home Office tracking sex offenders' emails. *Daily Telegraph* (March 10) [online]. Retrieved March 2013 from http://www.telegraph.co.uk/news/uknews/law-and-order/7406462/Human-rights-laws-stopped-Home-Office-tracking-sex-offenders-emails.html

42   Williams, C. (2009). Sex offender email monitoring plan mothballed. *The Register* (March 18). Retrieved August 9, 2013, from http://www.theregister.co.uk/2009/03/18/offender_email/

43   Association of Chief Police Officers. (2007). *Good practice guide for computer based electronic evidence*. London, UK: 7safe. Retrieved July 31, 2013, from http://www.7safe.com/electronic_evidence/ACPO_guidelines_computer_evidence.pdf

44   http://www.publications.parliament.uk/pa/cm201314/cmselect/cmcumeds/729/729we14.htm

45   http://www.publications.parliament.uk/pa/cm201314/cmselect/cmcumeds/729/729.pdf (page 70 of the full document).

46   https://www.justiceinspectorates.gov.uk/hmic/publications/online-and-on-the-edge-real-risks-in-a-virtual-world/

47   Hansard, 28 Nov. 2002, Column 426W. Retrieved from http://www.publications.parliament.uk/pa/cm200203/cmhansrd/vo021128/text/21128w15.htm

48   Retrieved July 30, 2014, from http://www.virtualglobaltaskforce.com/who-we-are/

49   Carr, J., & Hilton, Z (2010). Combatting child abuse images on the internet: International perspectives. In J. Davidson & P. Gottschalk (Eds.), *Internet child abuse: Current research and policy* (p. 63). Abingdon, Oxon, UK: Routledge.

50   http://www.ceop.police.uk/Media-Centre/Press-releases/2010/World-shrinks-for-missing-child-sex-offenders-as-CEOPs-Most-Wanted-goes-global/

51   See p. 31 of the following: http://ceop.police.uk/Documents/CEOP_AnnualReview_09-10.pdf

52   http://www.statewatch.org/news/2003/may/09g8.htm

53   http://www.interpol.int/Crime-areas/Crimes-against-children/Victim-identification

54   https://www.gov.uk/government/publications/child-abuse-image-database

55   https://www.europol.europa.eu/sites/default/files/publications/ec3_first_year_report.pdf

56   http://ec.europa.eu/dgs/home-affairs/what-we-do/policies/organized-crime-and-human-trafficking/global-alliance-against-child-abuse/index_en.htm

57   http://www.ceop.police.uk/ICPC/; http://www.ceop.police.uk/Media-Centre/Press-releases/2012/CEOP-launch-a-new-way-to-prevent-UK-child-sex-offenders-from-abusing-children-overseas-/; http://www.acro.police.uk/icpc/

58   E-mail correspondence with CEOP (June 2014).

59   Andy Baker, former Deputy Chief of CEOP, speaking at Ineqe conference, London, UK, June 30, 2014.

60   http://www.mirror.co.uk/news/uk-news/mirror-special-investigation-sickening-child-1379519
61   See p. 3 of the following: http://www.publications.parliament.uk/pa/cm201314/cmselect/cmcumeds/729/729.pdf
62   http://sentencingcouncil.judiciary.gov.uk/media/974.htm and http://sentencingcouncil.judiciary.gov.uk/docs/Final_Sexual_Offences_Definitive_Guideline_content_(web).pdf
63   http://www.kent.police.uk/advice/community_safety/initiatives/Fiip%20project/fiip_about_the_project.html
64   Middleton et al., op cit.
65   National Probation Service for England and Wales, op cit.
66   *Regina v. Smith* [July 19, 2011] EWCA Crim 1772 [online]. Retrieved July 25, 2013, from http://www.bailii.org/ew/cases/EWCA/Crim/2011/1772.html
67   *Regina v. Philip Michael Jackson* [November 9, 2012] EWCA Crim 2602 [online]. Retrieved July 25, 2013, from Lexis Nexis.
68   Beckford, M., & Stokes, P. (2010). Human rights laws stopped Home Office tracking sex offenders' emails. *Daily Telegraph* (March10) [online]. Retrieved March 26, 2013, from http://www.telegraph.co.uk/news/uknews/law-and-order/7406462/Human-rights-laws-stopped-Home-Office-tracking-sex-offenders-emails.html
69   Maalla, Najat M'jid. (2009, July 13). *Report of the Special Rapporteur on the sale of children, child prostitution and child pornography* (p. 15). A/HRC/12/23. New York, NY: United Nations. In March 2009 the database was replaced by the Interpol-managed International Child Sexual Exploitation Image Database.
70   CEOP Annual Review 2011–2012 and Centre Plan 2012–2013.
71   Renold, E., & Creighton, S., with Atkinson, C., & Carr, J. (2003). *Images of abuse: A review of the evidence on child pornography* (p. 61). London, UK: NSPCC.
72   https://www.basw.co.uk/news/article/?id=556
73   http://www.mariecollinsfoundation.org.uk/news/post/7-child-victims-of-online-abuse-let-down-by-lack-of-training
74   See p. 85 of the following: https://www.gov.uk/government/publications/working-together-to-safeguard-children
75   IWF 2013 annual report: https://www.iwf.org.uk/assets/media/annual-reports/annual_report_2013.pdf
76   Child Exploitation and Online Protection Centre. (2012). *A Picture of abuse*. London, UK: Author. Retrieved August 20, 2013, from http://ceop.police.uk/Documents/ceopdocs/CEOP%20IIOCTA%20Executive%20Summary.pdf
77   NSPCC. (2012). *Call for urgent action to stamp out trade of child abuse images* (Oct. 15). Retrieved July 23, 2013, from http://www.nspcc.org.uk/news-and-views/media-centre/press-releases/2012/12-10-15-urgent-action-child-abuse-images/urgent-action-child-abuse-images_wdn92344.html
78   http://www.huffingtonpost.co.uk/john-carr/child-pornography-the-unbelievable-truth-ab_b_1970969.html
79   Interview with ITV News (May 28, 2013).
80   Child Exploitation and Online Protection Centre. (2013). *Threat assessment of child sexual exploitation and abuse*. London, UK: Author. Retrieved August 28, 2013, from http://ceop.police.uk/Documents/ceopdocs/CEOP_TACSEA2013_240613%20FINAL.pdf
81   https://www.gov.uk/government/speeches/the-Internet-and-pornography-prime-minister-calls-for-action

82 See p. 7 of the following: https://www.iwf.org.uk/assets/media/annual-reports/annual_report_2013.pdf
83 http://www.bbc.co.uk/news/uk-24980765
84 See p. 20 of the following: https://www.iwf.org.uk/report/2013-annual-report
85 https://www.publications.parliament.uk/pa/cm201314/cmselect/cmcumeds/729/729.pdf
86 https://www.gov.uk/government/news/pm-hosts-Internet-safety-summit and https://www.gov.uk/government/news/Internet-safety-summit-at-downing-street-communique
87 Steel, C. M. S. (2015). Web-based child pornography: The global impact of deterrence efforts and its consumption on mobile platforms. *Child Abuse & Neglect* 44 (2015) 150–158.
88 http://www.nationalcrimeagency.gov.uk/news/259-summit-agrees-action-to-rid-internet-of-child-abuse
89 https://www.gov.uk/government/news/pm-and-deputy-pm-to-announce-emergency-security-legislation
90 https://www.gov.uk/government/uploads/system/uploads/attachment_data/file/473770/Draft_Investigatory_Powers_Bill.pdf
91 https://www.publications.parliament.uk/pa/cm201314/cmselect/cmcumeds/729/729.pdf
92 http://nationalcrimeagency.gov.uk/news/news-listings/411-uk-wide-operation-snares-660-paedophiles
93 http://press.labour.org.uk/post/92057150489/yvette-cooper-letter-to-theresa-may-on-tackling-child
94 Interview with BBC News. Retrieved July 16, 2014, from http://www.bbc.co.uk/news/uk-28326128
95 https://www.gov.uk/government/uploads/system/uploads/attachment_data/file/478006/4817_CAID_Booklet_v13_online4.pdf
96 http://www.weprotect.org/our-mission-and-strategy/
97 Damian Green keynote speech at the NSPCC, 'How Safe Are Our Children?' conference (April 2014).

12 The Role of Schools in Children's Online Safety

Martin Waller

We live in a world with constantly changing values, centralities and principalities. The ways in which we live and work within this new world are shifting even at the most fundamental and basic levels of our everyday life. Many of our old centralities are now defunct and we live in a world where the ability to access and transform information with speed and ease is central to everyday life (Millard, 2003). Within this new digital age we find that internet technologies and services are permeating into nearly every aspect of the way we operate in the world – not just in dramatic political uprisings of the so-called Arab Spring or Occupy Wall Street movements but also, perhaps more crucially, in more mundane ways that integrate into the daily practises of our everyday lives (Waller, 2013). Digital technologies have enabled us to individually and collectively organise our time through online calendars, email, shared documents and social networks. Within this context the use of such tools and services have become more than a matter of 'information technology' and are becoming the dominant means of entertainment, communication and expression in our society (Buckingham, 2002, p. 7). These new technologies have also brought with them new meaning-making systems, which are neither traditional nor regulated and do not always conform to traditional notions and architectures of communication. We live in a society in which the speed and wealth of information available through devices such as smartphones and tablets can be seen as revolutionary and overwhelming. The information age has brought with it an 'instant' and 'always-on' culture in which communication does not stop.

Many of these new internet technologies, which are changing the communicative landscape, include social elements that have created a shift and significant change in the way people communicate within the world. Services such as Facebook have changed the way that we share updates of our life and communicate with our friends. It is no longer necessary to write to a friend to enquire

Online Risk to Children: Impact, Protection and Prevention, First Edition.
Edited by Jon Brown.
© 2017 John Wiley & Sons, Ltd. Published 2017 by John Wiley & Sons, Ltd.

about his or her life because this information is easily accessible on his or her Facebook profile. Similarly services such as Instagram have changed the way in which we share information through photographs, and linked comments enable us to broadcast updates to a global audience. Such global audiences are not regulated and therefore there is a potential risk for using such services that allow creation of new audiences on a world-wide scale. Education therefore becomes central to providing children with the basis of the safe and appropriate use of such online systems. This chapter explores how online technologies have become implicated in children's literate lives and the resulting implications for education. I will outline ways in which schools can safely embrace such online networks, while providing children with a foundation of the safe use of such systems. Examples of classroom practice will also be explored to investigate how such networking systems can be used in a meaningful way to support children's learning.

ONLINE TECHNOLOGIES AND EDUCATION

Social media and technologies have fundamentally changed the communication landscape, and 'being literate' within these networks is crucial if our young people are going to succeed in our society. Such technologies have embedded within them a communication architecture that is negotiated and utilised by the user. They are therefore part of 'literacy' and what it means to be 'literate' in our society.

The literacy research community has long since recognised the importance of the social aspect of literacy (Barton, 2007). In this context, language and literacy need to be studied as they occur naturally in everyday life, which provides a powerful argument for using social technologies in the classroom. In the landmark 'A Pedagogy of Multiliteracies' (New London Group, 1996) researchers suggested that schooled literacy has traditionally meant teaching and learning to read and write in page-bound, official, standard forms of the national language, which results in a failure to recognise the diverse communicative practises that children are engaged with in the real world and in their own popular cultures. Such popular cultures have been traditionally ignored in schools on the grounds that they are somehow inherently illegitimate and anti-educational (Buckingham, 2002, p. 17). As Genishi and Hass Dyson (2009) state:

> 'There is a puzzling contrast – really an awesome disconnect – between the breathtaking diversity of school children and the uniformity, homogenization, and regimentation of classroom practices.' (p. 4)

Despite this 'awesome disconnect' there has been a reaffirmation of a standard written, national language, transmitted through a print-based pedagogy (Millard, 2003). However, being literate means seeing beyond the surface and being able to make meaning in more complex ways by drawing on life experiences, context and knowledge of the world through the meaning-making systems it offers. Merchant (2007) conveys a powerful argument to suggest that an educational system has the responsibility to provide young people with the tools and understanding necessary for interpreting the constructed nature of popular culture and to provide a critical view of new technologies. Such a view of literacy embeds online technologies as a meaning-making system and recognises the role it plays in communication and effectiveness in message transmission (O'Rouke, 2001). This view of technology rises out of the ways in which new industries, diversity and social mobility and progress all influence how we understand education (Kalantzis, Cope, & Fehring, 2002). The New London Group (1996) also suggests that 'literacy pedagogy now must account for the burgeoning variety of text forms associated with information and multimedia technologies' (p. 2). Teachers therefore need to develop pupils' understanding of how new meaning-making systems are deployed (Unsworth, 2001, p. 282). The need to engage with such technologies at a critical meaning-making level therefore becomes crucial, as O'Rouke (2001) suggests:

'A critical level of engagement also provides students with opportunities to develop their understanding about the way we construct and communicate information in our society, to learn how we might differ in other societies and to gain over such media themselves to the extent they can make informed decisions about its use.' (p. 2)

Such critical engagement is instrumental in equipping pupils with the skills necessary to communicate using online technologies but also understand the safe use of such systems. Despite this fact, many conservative educators view online technologies in a negative way and fail to let go of pre-existing assumptions about how the world works (boyd, 2007). Education needs to reflect the way in which online technologies are used in the real world to ensure that teaching and learning genuinely prepares pupils for the future so that they can think critically about the way in which these technologies can be used safety and appropriately.

THE BLURRING OF BOUNDARIES

Barton (2007) suggests that different literacies are associated with different domains of life such as home, school and work. Within such domains people act and communicate differently (Barton, 2007, p. 39). As Genishi and Hass Dyson (2009) attested, there is an 'awesome disconnect' between the diverse domains children move within and the schooled curriculum. If schools are to successfully build foundations for the safe use of online behaviours then realignment between home and school domains becomes crucial.

Children use multiple channels of communication where they articulate online networks with ease and at times without supervision or regulation. These practises are, as Millard (2003) suggests, implicated in popular culture through multiple representations as disparate cultures meet and co-mingle. Children learn habits of communicating linked to cultural, social and personal activities and the role of the school is to teach correct habits of communicating for different contexts – including online. Furthermore, the New London Group (1996) suggests that pedagogy take account of the cultural differences and the fluidity of movement between multimodal representations and literacy. The education system therefore has the responsibility to provide young people with the skills and understanding necessary for interpreting the constructed nature of popular culture (Merchant, 2007, p. 15). Schools also have the responsibility of teaching the safe use of online systems as part of their curricula. Ignoring such technologies and relegating them to 'home' use fails to recognise the way that technologies have changed our world and therefore have changed education. As Kress (2003) suggests:

'Even though they involve the new information and communication technologies, they constitute a revolution of a social and not just technological kind.' (p. 7)

Kress highlights the importance of a shift towards the social element of learning. In addition this highlights an important point for schools – the Internet is not just about technologies but also the social way in which we interact. Issues such as online bullying can easily arise if children are not taught the fact that the online world is still 'real' and that they are not completely anonymous.

Kress also highlights that within the new communicative landscape, mode and choice of mode are significant issues (Kress, 2003, p. 45). In this sense the need for 'writing' (be it in a multimodal way) for audience is critical – for the first time children can write for a real global audience but appropriate use must be discussed before this occurs. Interactive Web 2.0 systems are particularly effective at highlighting the affordances of different modes of meaning, as Davies and Merchant (2009) suggest:

'Web 2.0 spaces can exploit the affordances of different media from text, to still image, to moving image, to sound, and any combination of these.' (p. 4)

Web 2.0 places the focus on users and the created content from such users, either individually or collaboratively. In this sense the boundaries between offline and online are becoming blurred as children are able to create and remix information on the internet in ways that previous generations could not. However, schools must have a clear understanding of how these systems operate in order to ensure that children are safe online. Furthermore the use of such real-world communicative systems enables the opportunity to critically develop an understanding of the way in which information is constructed and communicated in our society, which will support users in making informed decisions about modal use in relation to audience and purpose (O'Rourke, 2001). Acknowledging the way in which multimodality occurs on the Internet enables children to have a greater understanding of the way information is created and shared in our society. Young people need to have an understanding that content on the Internet should be viewed with a critical eye and that not everything they read or view online can be trusted. This does not only apply to written text but also to images. Digital software enables users to easily manipulate photographs so that they do not necessarily reflect true reality. It is therefore important that children are able to see through this 'filter affect' to critically analyse online content.

In recent years, platforms such as online blogs, wikis and instant messengers have enabled international construction of discussion, debate and collaboration across cultures (Alexander, 2008). The widespread use of social networking systems (SNSs) such as Facebook and Instagram has enabled users to present themselves, articulate their social networks and establish connections with others within different contexts (Ellison, Steinfield, & Lampe, 2007). boyd and Ellison (2008) define SNS as follows:

'Web-based services that allow individuals to (1) construct a public profile or semi-public profile within a bounded system, (2) articulate a list of other users within whom they share a connection, and (3) view and traverse their list of connections and those made by others within the system.' (p. 221)

Users of such websites represent themselves digitally using text, images, video, links and quizzes to express how they see themselves (boyd, 2007, p. 2). Davies (2006) suggests that such online spaces can be seen as online digital 'cubby holes' – also linking to Wenger's notion of communities of practice (Wenger, 1998). Davies (2006) argues that blogs can disrupt the binaries of online and offline worlds (p. 60). Children need an understanding of the fact that the online and offline worlds are linked. Schools need to share with pupils the implications of acting inappropriately online and that such actions can have ramifications in the offline world. Schools need to support young people in understanding that postings online are documented for the world to see, as Pahl and Rowsell (2006) suggest:

'We leave traces of literate practices as we move through life, either on our email or in the form of notes, postcards and other communicative practices such as photographs.' (p. 5)

Such elements of a profile blur traditional notions of space where dualisms of offline and online identities are challenged (Davies, 2006, p. 62) but, more crucially, show that the online and offline worlds are inextricably linked to one another. Schools therefore need to teach young people that actions online can be made accountable in the offline world.

E-SAFETY AND MORAL PANICS

Online networking sites are now part and parcel of everyday life and are used by different individuals, cultures and social groups for different purposes. Some of the more negative uses are well documented in the media as well as the issue of the safety of school-aged users (boyd & Ellison, 2008; Rose, 2010). As Davies and Merchant (2009) suggest;

> 'Much of the moral panic around new media focuses on the idea that they distract the attention of children and young people from engaging with print literacy practices and are a causal factor in falling standards in literacy in schools.' (p. 111)

However, there is little evidence to suggest that children's reading of print has actually declined when using digital technologies (Buckingham, 2002, p. 8). boyd (2007) also suggests that a large proportion of adults panic and simply do not understand the shifts in terms of the changing communication landscape. This could suggest that some parents do not fully comprehend what their children are actually engaging with through online networks. The role of the school should therefore be to support parents in developing an understanding of such systems: how they are used and how they can ensure that their child is safe at home. Such an approach can address insecurities about a 'digital divide' in knowledge and understanding between parents and young people.

As with any activity or system, there are risks with online systems and services. However, the majority of these risks are primarily down to the user of the system. Technologies are not self-aware and they do not make mistakes. Social technologies can be used for overwhelmingly good things by users but also for negative and destructive purposes – as mentioned previously in this chapter, a critical understanding of such networks is therefore crucial for young people. It is clear that similar to the offline world there are dangers and risks that cannot be completely eliminated (Byron, 2008). boyd (2007) also suggests that if a teen is engaged in risky behaviour online then it is typically a sign that he or she is engaged in risky behaviour offline. She argues that the technology is too often blamed for what it reveals and suggests destroying the technology will not solve the underlying problems that are made visible through online spaces (boyd, 2007, p. 5).

A particular area of risk and concern for online communication is highlighted by Rose (2010), which is the tendency to 'over-share' too much information, such as location:

> 'Sharing location-based information just means there is another layer of personal information exposed which, in most cases, is not really necessary.' (p. 810)

Young people need to be aware that, if their profile is public, then they are broadcasting their location and life stories to a global, unfiltered, unmanaged and unknown audience. Schools could ask young people the question, "Do you need to share this information with the world?"

Location-based features and social networks continue to rise at a significant rate (Beaumont, 2010). Such services enable users to 'check in' at certain locations and gain experience points and badges as well as the title of 'mayor' if they check in most frequently at a particular venue. This essentially creates an online digital footprint of a user's offline activities and, as Rose (2010) suggests, is seen by many as unnecessary.

Davies and Merchant (2009) suggest that real-experiences of internet technologies within the education system are likely to be more effective than applying blocks, filters and other controls (p. 112). Embedding an internet technology into the everyday practises of a classroom enables pupils to have the opportunity to learn safe practises using online-mediated spaces within a real and meaningful context. Schools therefore need to take a proactive rather than reactive approach to e-safety, because ignoring online networks does not educate children to use them safely.

INTEGRATING ONLINE TECHNOLOGIES

Educators are always looking for inspirational ways to engage their pupils in learning. The use of digital technologies in schools has a long and varied history. What is clear is that using online technologies as an 'add-on' tool for learning and hoping for the best is not classed as best practise (Buckingham, 2002). Using technologies should always be about learning and integrating them in a relevant and meaningful way to educate pupils.

Marsh (2010) argues that using online networks in classrooms provides a context for reading through the construction of social networks where knowledge is co-constructed and distributed through social practises (p. 29). This has significant challenges for educators who are trying to provide real-world opportunities for children to engage in meaningful literacy practises. However, some educators are working with their children to experiment with online networks in their classrooms. In my previous work (Waller, 2010) I have written about how I have used Twitter with my Year 2 class as well as blogging (Waller, 2014). Such projects have enabled pupils to learn online safe practises in a relevant and meaningful way.

TWITTER IN THE PRIMARY CLASSROOM

Many classes across the globe now use Twitter to engage with real audiences. Teachers are always looking for ways to give writing an 'audience and purpose' and Twitter gives classrooms just that. I began using Twitter in my Year 2 class in 2008 and it was the first class Twitter feed of its kind (Waller, 2010). The aim of the project was to enable the children to engage with an audience for writing but also to teach young children safe online practises.

The motivation towards using a Twitter account addresses many areas such as the development of digital literacy skills, teaching e-safety principles, encouraging dis-engaged writers and evaluation and reflection of learning – a variety of learning areas where the technology added value. A single account was set up (@ClassroomTweets), which allowed children to 'tweet' and contribute towards the shared Twitter stream. All replies and communication were moderated and screened by the class teacher (Waller, 2010).

The Twitter account belonged to the class teacher and the children were allowed to type tweets – the class teacher then published them. Through this use of an authentic context, Marsh (2010) suggests the following:

'Reading in this context means not simply decoding, but involves the taking part in the construction of social networks in which knowledge is co-constructed and distributed.' (p. 29)

It was evident that children liked to share their work, experiences and interests with any audience (Waller, 2010). This online network enabled the children to share interests with a dynamic and global audience and engage in powerful writing, which is partly driven by the potency from the immediacy of publication (Davies, 2006, p. 60). The children were not fully aware of who their audience actually was but they created their own imagined audience (boyd, 2007). Such an audience is ambiguous (but still exists) and exchanges with members of the children's social network not only involved social participation but also, as Marsh (2010) suggests, resulted in the following:

'Reading is, in this example, a social practice that extends beyond the walls of the classroom and enables children to engage in forums in which inter-generational literacy is commonplace.' (p. 30)

In addition, when the children engaged in conversation with such users to exchange ideas, it mirrored the uses of technology they will encounter in leisure and employment in future years (Marsh, 2010, p. 30).

E-safety issues should always be at the forefront of an educational initiative when it involves the use of the Internet, and this was carefully considered before the use of Twitter in the classroom. The fact that Twitter is open and accessible to anybody with an Internet connection meant that the safety implications and rules needed to be discussed with the children (Waller, 2010). However, such issues were discussed in an open and contextually driven manner (Davies & Merchant, 2009), with the children realising why such precautions were needed when they started using the SNS. Three primary rules (Waller, 2010) were discussed with the children:

> '1. Children must not mention their name or any of their friends by name in tweets under any circumstances.
> 2. Children must not check for replies or messages (this prevents the possibility of them seeing any inappropriate material that may be viewable).
> 3. Children must not navigate away from our Twitter stream page and look at other people's profiles (in case of inappropriate content or language use).' (p. 15)

The rules were discussed in the context of real-world use and application and were always followed by the children because they understood the implications of not following them (Waller, 2010). Replies were always checked by adults before they were discussed with the children because there was always the possibility of inappropriate messages being sent given the open nature of Twitter (Waller, 2010). As a result children were not able to engage in 'private' discussion with any members of the social networking system. Throughout this project, Twitter enabled the children to engage with a real audience while learning e-safety principles at a very young age.

CLASS BLOGS

Blogs are online public writing environments in which postings (individual writing segments often containing hyperlinks to other online sources) are listed in reverse chronological order (Blood, 2002). They are classed as Web 2.0 systems (O'Reilly, 2005), which signals increased social interaction, networking and collaboration (Davies & Merchant, 2009). For many young people online self-expression and media consumption is a deeply engrained and engaging part of their lives (Ellison & Wu, 2008). Blogging is therefore a typical contemporary literacy practise that characterises social networking practises, which many children and young people engage in outside of school (Dowdall, 2006; Marsh, 2008).

An influx of class blogs have appeared in recent years, primarily because they support areas of the writing curriculum but also allow for tighter control than other more commercial and publicly accessible online services. Blogging systems can be customised and tailored to suit the needs of a school. In 2011, I completed a research project using a real class blog with a focus of developing writing and safe use of online social networks (Waller, 2014).

Class blogs can add a huge amount of value to children's learning, especially through the global aspect of blogs being accessible online. Visitors are able to comment on the posts that children publish. The extract shown in Figure 12.1 provides such an example.

The Royal Wedding of Will and Kate

The Royal family were so excited about the wedding that they wanted to look the best. The Queen had a blanket on her knees as soon as the driver opened the door the Queen dropped her blanked on the floor. After that Will and Harry arrived at Westminster Abbey. Kate arrived she smiled a lot she was so happy. Then the wedding started William did not want a ring that is what sum boys are like but Kates ring as very pretty. the end

This entry was posted on June 6, 2011, 9:14am and is filed under <u>Blog</u>. You can follow any response to this entry through <u>RSS 2.0</u>. You can leave a <u>response</u> or <u>trackback</u> from your own site.

COMMENTS (5)

#1 on June 6, 2011 – 1:14pm

Great to see you guys back on Twitter. I did not notice the Queen's blanket, so I have learnt something today. Thanks for the story.

#2 on June 6, 2011 - 1:55pm

What a brilliant report of such a great story. Well done all of you, keep up the good work.

#3 on June 6, 2011 - 4:01pm

I love how you reported on small details that even the newspapers and 'Hello Magazine' missed. Well done!

Figure 12.1   A representation of a blog post and comments written by one of the children.
Source: Waller (2014, p. 162).

The author of this published class blog in Figure 12.1 (who was seven years old) wrote a post about the royal wedding. The post then received an influx of comments from a global audience who encouraged the child. This was a huge motivating factor for the child who decided that they wanted to write more for their audience. Such an audience would not be possible without the use of the Internet and the enthusiasm and motivation for learning would not have occurred.

E-safety features were built into the blog to ensure that it was a safe and secure environment for the pupils. This included the fact that posts by the pupils needed to be moderated and controlled by the class teacher before publication. This was also the case for comments. In this sense the class teacher acted as the 'firewall' between the Internet and the pupils. The mediation of the teacher and the Internet is an essential protocol for schools to adopt, along with an appropriate e-safety and safeguarding policy, which should be adhered to by all staff members.

Children also needed to follow rules when using the classroom blog:

'1. Always use appropriate language and grammar in posts and comments.
2. Never write children's first and last names together. Children may only mention first names in blog posts and comments.
3. Children should not upload pictures of themselves, their friends or their family which would make them identifiable.
4. Everybody should be respectful of people's achievements and efforts when leaving comments.
5. If children are unhappy with anything that is written on the blog they must tell a member of the school staff immediately.' (Waller, 2014, p. 157)

Whenever introducing such rules for the use of online services, schools need to make clear to pupils why the rules are there and what they are protecting them from.

Other work based on class blogs has enabled children to engage with astronauts as well as Everest explorers through Skype Classroom. Such projects demonstrate the possibilities of using online technologies in the classroom, which create new opportunities and experiences for children that would not be available without the technologies. Digital technologies can afford exciting opportunities to our young people, but risk should be managed as with any new activity. Further information about these projects can be viewed at http://www.beyondnewhorizons.com.

IMPLICATIONS

Internet technologies have fundamentally changed areas of social participation and communication. The use of Twitter and class blogs in this chapter does not necessarily reflect the way that young people may choose to use such systems in the real world. The children do not create their own profiles, use their real names or engage in 'private' discussions in these school-based projects. However, through a managed and controlled environment the children are able to learn the competencies of such internet networks in a meaningful and relevant way. Furthermore, because good practise in relation to privacy and e-safety is embedded in the approach, the children learn such skills in context – rather than through the consequences of moral panics (Davies & Merchant, 2009). Schools therefore must take a proactive rather than reactive approach to e-safety. Digital technologies also provide children with an exciting opportunity to engage in new learning experiences. Such experiences reflect the way that meaning is made in the real world as opposed to the 'bubble' of a classroom (Waller, 2013).

CONCLUSION

It is clear that internet technologies have fundamentally changed the way we communicate in the world. It is also evident that such technologies will continue to feature in more areas of life, becoming even more closely interwoven with how we live and work in the world (Merchant, 2007, p. 126). The increasing convergence of media across multiple channels and networks presents a unique challenge to educators required to address such digital competencies and online safety (Buckingham, 2002, p. 12).

As Davies and Merchant (2009) suggest, embedding internet technologies in school involves a focussed look at how different kinds of services relate to educational objectives. However, moral panics over privacy concerns and online predators (Rose, 2010) create a dissonance between education and online technologies. Such factors have resulted in many schools choosing to embed closed systems where users cannot construct an audience or ignore such technologies completely. Projects that involved using Twitter in the primary classroom and blogging explored in this chapter show that meaningful engagement in the construction of social networks can support children in their learning development whilst also teaching important messages and skills in relation to e-safety.

It is very easy for schools to ignore internet technologies because of perceived risk. However, it is foolish and misguided to think that such meaning-making systems, which are becoming part and parcel of everyday life for many people, can be ignored in the education system without detriment. Schools need to work with their pupils and parents to develop a critical understanding of how these online networks operate and how they can safely use them. Getting the detail right is essential if educators are to help children develop a critical understanding of these online systems. Online tools and services are developing at a critical pace and are here to stay. It is time for schools to harness these online technologies in a safe and meaningful way, while ensure that young people are equipped with the tools and skills to be safe online in a world with constantly changing horizons.

REFERENCES

Alexander, B. (2008). Web 2.0 and emergent multiliteracies, *Theory into Practice, 47*(2), 150–160.

Barton, D. (2007). *Literacy: An introduction to the ecology of written language.* Oxford, UK: Blackwell.

Beaumont, C. (2010). Foursquare enjoys surge in popularity. *The Guardian* (Feb. 5). Retrieved August 29, 2010, from http://www.telegraph.co.uk/technology/social-media/7165699/Foursquare-enjoys-surge-of-popularity.html

Blood, R. (2002). *The weblog handbook: Practical advice on creating and maintaining your blog.* Cambridge, MA: Perseus Publishing.

boyd, d. (2007). Social network sites: Public, private, or what? *Knowledge Tree, 13*(May). Retrieved from http://kt.flexiblelearning.net.au/tkt2007/?page_id=28

boyd, d., & Ellison, N. (2008). Social network sites, definition, history, and scholarship. *Journal of Computer-Mediated Communication, 13,* 210–230.

Byron, T. (2008). *The Bryon review: Safer children in a digital world.* Nottingham, UK: DCSF Publications.

Buckingham, D. (2002). New media literacies: Informal learning, digital technologies and education. In D. Buckingham & A. McFarlane (Eds.), *A digitally driven curriculum?* London, UK: IPPR.

Davies, J. (2006). Escaping to the borderlands: An exploration of the internet as cultural space for teenaged wiccan girls. In K. Pahl & J. Rowsell (Eds.), *Travel notes from the new literacy studies: Instances of practice.* Clevedon, UK: Multilingual Matters.

Davies, J., & Merchant, G. (2009). *Web 2.0 for schools: Learning and social participation.* New York, NY: Peter Lang.

Dowdall, C. (2006). Dissonance between the digital created words of school and home. *Literacy, 40*(3), 153–163.

Ellison, N., Steinfield, C., & Lampe, C. (2007). The benefits of Facebook 'friends': Social capital and college students' use of online social network sites. *Journal of Computer-Mediated Communication, 12,* 1143–1168.

Ellison, N., & Wu, Y. (2008). Blogging in the classroom: A preliminary exploration of student attitudes and impact on comprehension. *Journal of Educational Multimedia and Hypermedia, 17*(1), 99–122. Retrieved from https://rhhstechcomm.wikispaces.com/file/view/Blogging.pdf

Genishi, C., & Hass Dyson, A. (2009). *Children, language, and literacy.* New York: Teachers College Press.

Kalantzis, M., Cope, B., & Fehring, H. (2002). *PEN: Multiliteracies; Teaching and learning in the new communications environment.* Marrickville, Australia: Primary English Teaching Association. Retrieved from http://www.eric.ed.gov/PDFS/ED465170.pdf

Kress, G. (2003). *Literacy in the new media age.* London, UK: Routledge.

Marsh, J. (2008). "Am I a couch potato?" Blogging as a critical literacy practice. In K. Cooper & R. E. White (Eds.), *Critical literacies in action: Social perspectives and teaching practices* (pp. 171–184). Rotterdam, The Netherlands: Sense Publishers.

Marsh, J. (2010). The ghosts of reading past, present and future. The materiality of reading in homes and schools. In K. Hall, U. Goswami, C. Harrison, S. Ellis, & J. Soler (Eds.), *Interdisciplinary perspectives on learning to read: Culture, cognition and pedagogy.* Oxon, UK: Routledge.

Merchant, G. (2007). Writing the future in the digital age. *Literacy, 41*(3), 118–128.

Millard, E. (2003). Towards a literacy of fusion: New times, new teaching and learning. *Reading, Literacy and Language, 37*(1), 3–8.

New London Group. (1996). A pedagogy of multiliteracies: Designing social futures. *Harvard Educational Review, 66*(1).

O'Reilly, T. (2005). What is Web 2.0? *O'Reilly: Spreading the knowledge of technology innovators blog*. Retrieved August 29, 2010, from http://oreilly.com/web2/archive/what-is-web-20.html

O'Rouke, M. (2001). Engaging students through ICT: A multiliteracies approach. *Teacher Learning Network Journal: Change, Growth and Innovation, 8*(3), 12–13.

Pahl, K., & Rowsell, J. (2006). *Literacy and education: Understanding new literacy studies in the classroom*. London, UK: Paul Chapman.

Rose, C. (2010). The security implications of ubiquitous social media. *Proceedings of the 2010 EABR & ETLC Conference*. Retrieved August 28, 2010, from http://www.cluteinstitute.com/proceedings/2010_Dublin_EABR_Articles/Article%20535.pdf

Unsworth, L. (2001). *Teaching multiliteracies across the curriculum: Changing contexts of text and image in classroom practice*. Buckingham, UK: Open University Press.

Waller, M. (2010). It's very very fun and ecsiting – using Twitter in the primary classroom. *English Four to Eleven* (Summer), 14–16.

Waller, M. (2013). More than tweets: Developing the 'new' and 'old' through online social networking. In G. Merchant, J. Gillien, J. Marsh, & J. Davies (Eds.), *Virtual literacies: Interactive spaces for children and young people* (pp. 126–141). London, UK: Routledge.

Waller, M. (2014). Social media, education and contentious literacies. In L. Unsworth & A. Thomas (Eds.), *English teaching & new literacies pedagogy: Interpreting and authoring digital multimedia narratives* (pp. 151–172). New York, NY: Peter Lang.

Wenger, E. (1998). *Communities of practice*. Cambridge, UK: Cambridge University Press.

Epilogue

Jon Brown

This collection of chapters has, amongst many other things, underlined the truly global nature of risk to children online. Although it is so important to recognise and appreciate the benefits of a digitally connected life it is also necessary to understand how children and young people can be groomed and abused online, the impact of this on them, how offenders operate to bring this about and how prevention and deterrence activity can play a key role in making children's lives safer online.

These closing comments provide something of a road map and future direction for the development and enhancement of children's safety online. In sketching out this route we should remind ourselves of the current context of children's lives online and of the speed of technological development. It is reasonable to assume that technological innovation and development will continue at a fast and probably accelerating rate for the foreseeable future. Internet use across the UK is nearing saturation in terms of connected households, but as connection speed and bandwidth increase overall, time connected will increase as will the range of what we all do online and in particular of how we communicate. There are digital differences in what children and young people do on line, mediated by education and sociology economic status, and these need to be explicitly recognised and addressed in policy and practice development; nevertheless, we will all stand to gain from this development and growth, and inevitably the nature and range of risks to children will multiply. The demand from those who want to view images of children being abused appears to be matching the growth of technological development, and the 2014 CEOP estimate of 50,000 people in the UK viewing child abuse imagery already seems to be a significant underestimate with some approximating that double this number might be more realistic.

The 'dark net or 'hidden internet,' which can be accessed through the use of software such as Tor (the Onion Router), has seen an increase in use in recent years; its origins lie in the libertarian foundations of the internet and its core

Online Risk to Children: Impact, Protection and Prevention, First Edition.
Edited by Jon Brown.
© 2017 John Wiley & Sons, Ltd. Published 2017 by John Wiley & Sons, Ltd.

principle of individual freedom of expression, and because of this it has quite predictably been adopted by those wishing to cover their tracks for a variety of reasons. Use of the dark net has been a key way in which offenders have shared and distributed child abuse imagery, and it undoubtedly has acted as an abuse facilitator and has been a significant contributory factor in the exponential rise in the number of child abuse images circulating online. We don't know and will not know conclusively whether technological development is contributing to a real-term increase in child sexual abuse and exploitation; however, an emerging law enforcement view is that this is the case.

It is often said but is nevertheless a truth that law enforcement, deterrence and prevention have lagged behind the activity of those who use the internet for illegal and abusive purposes, and those efforts will probably continue to do so. Industry expertise and knowledge can and should be used to greater effect to enhance this three-pronged attack on child abuse and exploitation online, but there needs to be an equal focus on and investment in primary prevention including work with children and young people in schools, advice and information for parents and better information and training for professionals as set out in Stephen Smallbone and Richard Wortley in Chapter 8. Target hardening through primary prevention work and through situational prevention offer the best prospect of reducing the incidence of abuse and exploitation online and offline, particularly if these efforts are delivered and coordinated internationally.

We have seen set out clearly by Ely Hanson in Chapter 6 the impact of online and abuse and exploitation of children and young people. These impacts are in the main familiar to those who have worked with victims of sexual abuse, but the way in which shame in particular plays a distinct role in affecting those groomed and abused online needs to be recognised and understood. It has implications for the delivery of help and therapeutic support and something that the NSPCC is examining. More broadly, the dearth of therapeutic support across the UK for children and young people (and adults) who have been sexually abused online or offline remains a national scandal, and the NSPCC has launched a campaign, It's Time, to lobby government to address this glaring gap in our health services. This lack of service provision is not matched by what we know about the causes, consequences and impacts of sexual abuse and exploitation; whilst we still have much to learn, the UK is leading the way in many respects in practice innovation, policy development and (with the US) research. Although in relation to research our knowledge development has to date been somewhat uneven; broadly we have learned more about offender behaviour than the impacts of abuse and exploitation, and this balance needs to be corrected.

The progress that has been made in a relatively short period of time in understanding how the abuse and exploitation of children online occurs, its impacts and how these can be treated and how the problem can be prevented should not be underestimated. However, there remains much to do, and a clear road map within a strategic framework that addresses the triad of prevention, deterrence and treatment is necessary to build on the progress made so far.

We need to build on the lead taken by the UK government in responding to the challenge and threat of child sexual abuse and exploitation online and establish a supra national global alliance, perhaps led by the UN, where the experience, knowledge and expertise of governments, industry, law enforcement, academia and NGOs can be brought together. We need global solutions to global threats that are not confined to political or geographical boundaries. The challenges in achieving this are, of course, significant; however, the points of join and consensus are greater than the differences in priority or philosophy.

The UK government's plans to establish a National Centre of Expertise for Child Sexual Abuse will be a major step forward in identifying and disseminating best practices in relation to the treatment and prevention of sexual abuse and should provide a much-needed focus, resource and catalyst in accelerating the development of thinking and practice in the UK.

Finally, at a practice and policy level we need a far greater focus on addressing the causes of the problem before children are harmed through much more primary prevention activity as described in this book. The emotional, psychological and indeed economic costs of abuse and exploitation are so significant that simply aiming to respond to the impact of its aftermath is practically and morally half-hearted and ultimately ineffective. Much online abuse and exploitation can be prevented with a converted effort locally, nationally and internationally, and we owe it to children across the world to ensure that they can reap the opportunities and benefits of a connected life without falling prey to risks that can and should be addressed.

Index

Page numbers in *italics* refer to figures, those in **bold** refer to tables.

Online Risk to Children: Impact, Protection and Prevention, First Edition.
Edited by Jon Brown.
© 2017 John Wiley & Sons, Ltd. Published 2017 by John Wiley & Sons, Ltd.